Wendy KG 1998 — Tualatin OR.

BEST REMEMBERED POEMS

EDITED AND ANNOTATED
BY

Martin Gardner

DOVER PUBLICATIONS, INC.
New York

ACKNOWLEDGMENTS

"Fire and Ice" and "Stopping by Woods on a Snowy Evening" from *The Poetry of Robert Frost*, edited by Edward Connery Lathem. Copyright 1923, © 1969. Copyright 1951 by Robert Frost. Reprinted by permission of Henry Holt and Company, Inc.

"The Little Toy Dog" and "The Hymn of the Battered Republic" are reprinted by permission of *Mad* magazine. "The Little Toy Dog" © 1976 by E. C. Publications, Inc. "The Hymn of the Battered Republic" © 1990 by E. C. Publications, Inc.

"Renascence," " 'Euclid Alone Has Looked on Beauty Bare' " and "First Fig" by Edna St. Vincent Millay. From *Collected Poems*, Harper & Row. Copyright 1912, 1922, 1923, 1940, 1950, 1951 by Edna St. Vincent Millay and Norma Millay Ellis. Reprinted by permission of Elizabeth Barnett, literary executor.

Published in Canada by General Publishing Company, Ltd., 30 Lesmill Road, Don Mills, Toronto, Ontario.

Published in the United Kingdom by Constable and Company, Ltd., 3 The Lanchesters, 162–164 Fulham Palace Road, London W6 9ER.

Best Remembered Poems is a new anthology, first published by Dover Publications, Inc., in 1992.

Manufactured in the United States of America
Dover Publications, Inc., 31 East 2nd Street, Mineola, N.Y. 11501

Library of Congress Cataloging-in-Publication Data

Best remembered poems / edited and annotated by Martin Gardner.
    p.   cm.
  Includes index.
  ISBN 0-486-27165-X (pbk.)
  1. English poetry. 2. American poetry. I. Gardner, Martin, 1914- .
PR1175.B457 1992
821.008—dc20

92-31321
CIP

CONTENTS

Contents

Contents

INTRODUCTION

"Best remembered," when applied to a poem, is a fuzzy expression. Poems highly regarded in one century may be forgotten in the next, and poems that "blush unseen" are often discovered generations later. Poems much studied by professors of literature may be unknown to everybody outside of academia. Poems everyone knows, such as "Casey at the Bat," are usually considered doggerel by the critics and unworthy of attention. Works that are well known in Canada or England may not be well known here in the U.S., and vice versa. Poems loved by the elderly may be unfamiliar to the middle-aged, and the young these days are generally too hooked on inane rock lyrics to read *any* poetry.

Even if a time, place and particular kind of reader are specified, how can one decide which poems are best known? William Harmon, who teaches English literature at the University of North Carolina, has examined what he considers our nation's most popular poems in a book titled *The Concise Columbia Book of Poetry: The Top 100 Poems* (Columbia University Press, 1990). Harmon selects as "top" those poems that have the most reprint listings in *The Columbia Granger's Index to Poetry*. This is one way to define "best remembered," but how accurately does it reflect public sentiment? Maybe it just reflects the taste of compilers, who have a notorious habit of cribbing from earlier collections.

One of the most successful of all anthologies—it is still in print— is *One Hundred and One Famous Poems*, first published in 1916. The compiler and original publisher, Roy J. Cook, wrote in his Preface: "A spirit of daring out of proportion to any hope of gain must at times possess a publisher." I recently glanced through this volume and was struck by the fact that about half its poems are now flyblown, and many are by authors whose names are as unfamiliar as the names in Samuel Johnson's *Lives of the Poets*. I will cite one typical example. Maltbie Davenport Babcock, a New York Presbyterian minister, authored a poem that begins:

> Be strong!
> We are not here to play, to dream, to drift;

We have hard work to do, and loads to lift;
Shun not the struggle—face it; 'tis God's gift.

Another long-selling anthology of popular verse is Hazel Felle-man's *Best Loved Poems of the American People* (1936). "Best loved" is far from the same as best remembered. Milton's *Paradise Lost*, for instance, is known to everybody, but few today have read it, and even fewer love it. One can recall poems assigned in high school or college without liking them or having glanced at them since. And just what does "best loved" mean? A poem intensely relished by a small group of readers, yet unknown to others? A poem moderately liked by everybody, but not passionately loved by anyone?

With all these dreary caveats in mind, and others I haven't mentioned, here are the poems that my intuition tells me are among the most well known at the moment among those in the United States who like poetry. I am not concerned with titles known to those who never read a book. (What poems would they call "best remembered," I wonder?) I have made no effort to conduct a survey. Indeed, I cannot imagine how any survey could with reasonable accuracy confirm or disconfirm my list. It goes without saying that no other anthologist would make the same selection. I myself might have made a different selection were I in a different mood.

Many well-known poems are not in this book because of their length. "Length," too, is a fuzzy term, but clearly a small book like this could not include Byron's *Don Juan* or *Childe Harold's Pilgrimage*, or even moderately long ballads such as Coleridge's "Ancient Mariner" or Keats's "The Eve of St. Agnes."

This book contains only one selection, "Abou Ben Adhem," that is a translation. I am among those who hold that poetry is untranslatable except for the plots of epics and long narrative verse. Like all so-called translations, I consider "Abou Ben Adhem" to be a fresh poem roughly based on the ideas in another. Nor is this collection the place (with a few exceptions, such as "Home, Sweet Home") for lyrics written to be set to music, even though many popular songs are poems in their own right and better known than most verse in this anthology.

The poems I have selected are not necessarily those I think are "best loved" either by critics or the general public. They certainly are not the poems best loved by me. Nor are they poems I consider the "greatest," whatever that may mean. They are, I repeat, poems I assume to be the best remembered, or at least among the best remembered, in the sense that they are the best known to ordinary

Americans who like poetry. Many poems I consider great, as well as poems not so great but which I personally cherish, are not here because they are not well known enough. Some poems I care not a rap about, and regard as doggerel, are here because they obviously are so well known. In some cases I may have cheated a bit by slipping in poems not so familiar now as they were in the recent past.

The selections are arranged alphabetically by author. My hope is that readers will enjoy rereading their favorites, and that here and there one may encounter a gem he or she has never seen before.

ELIZABETH AKERS ALLEN
(1832–1911)

ELIZABETH AKERS ALLEN was literary editor of the Portland, Maine, *Daily Advertiser*. "Rock Me to Sleep," her only poem of lasting popularity, first appeared in the Philadelphia *Saturday Evening Post* in 1860, under the pseudonym "Florence Percy." The poem was falsely claimed by Alexander Ball, a New Jersey harness maker and writer of doggerel, whose friends published an entire book defending his outrageous claim. The wild story is told by Mrs. Allen in her *Sunset Song and Other Verses* (1902) and by Burton E. Stevenson in *Famous Single Poems* (1923). No controversy over a poem's authorship was ever funnier or more bitter.

By 1923, thirty composers had set "Rock Me to Sleep" to music. It was sung in minstrel shows, issued as an illustrated gift book and printed on thousands of leaflets that were distributed to Civil War soldiers.

Rock Me to Sleep

Backward, turn backward, O Time, in your flight,
Make me a child again just for to-night!
Mother, come back from the echoless shore,
Take me again to your heart as of yore;
Kiss from my forehead the furrows of care,
Smooth the few silver threads out of my hair;
Over my slumbers your loving watch keep—
Rock me to sleep, mother—rock me to sleep!

Backward, flow backward, O tide of the years!
I am so weary of toil and of tears—
Toil without recompense, tears all in vain—
Take them and give me my childhood again!
I have grown weary of dust and decay,
Weary of flinging my soul-wealth away,
Weary of sowing for others to reap—
Rock me to sleep, mother—rock me to sleep!

Tired of the hollow, the base, the untrue,
Mother, O mother, my heart calls for you!
Many a summer the grass has grown green,
Blossomed and faded, our faces between;

Yet, with strong yearning and passionate pain,
Long I to-night for your presence again;
Come from the silence so long and so deep—
Rock me to sleep, mother—rock me to sleep!

Over my heart in the days that are flown,
No love like mother-love ever has shone;
No other worship abides and endures,
Faithful, unselfish, and patient, like yours;
None like a mother can charm away pain
From the sick soul and the world-weary brain;
Slumber's soft calms o'er my heavy lids creep—
Rock me to sleep, mother—rock me to sleep!

Come, let your brown hair, just lighted with gold,
Fall on your shoulders again as of old;
Let it drop over my forehead to-night,
Shading my faint eyes away from the light;
For with its sunny-edged shadows once more,
Haply will throng the sweet visions of yore;
Lovingly, softly, its bright billows sweep—
Rock me to sleep, mother—rock me to sleep!

Mother, dear mother, the years have been long
Since I last listened your lullaby song;
Sing, then, and unto my soul it shall seem
Womanhood's years have been only a dream.
Clasped to your heart in a loving embrace,
With your light lashes just sweeping my face,
Never hereafter to wake or to weep—
Rock me to sleep, mother—rock me to sleep!

MATTHEW ARNOLD
(1822–1888)

SON OF the headmaster of Rugby, and a graduate of Oxford, Arnold became a distinguished Victorian poet, essayist and critic of both literature and religion. His attacks on literal interpretation of the Bible made him one of England's pioneers in the "higher criticism" of Scripture. For ten years he was a professor of poetry at Oxford, and throughout his life held a variety of government posts related to education. "My poems," he wrote, represent, on the whole, the main movement of mind of the last quarter of a century, and thus they will probably have their day as people become conscious of what that movement of mind is, and interested in the literary productions which reflect it. It might fairly be urged that I have less poetical sentiment than Tennyson, and less intellectual vigor and abundance than Browning; yet, because I have perhaps more of a fusion of the two than either of them, I am likely enough to have my turn, as they have had theirs.

"Dover Beach," Arnold's best-known poem, is from his *New Poems* (1867). It was set to music by the American composer Samuel Barber.

Dover Beach

The sea is calm to-night,
The tide is full, the moon lies fair
Upon the Straits;—on the French coast, the light
Gleams, and is gone; the cliffs of England stand,
Glimmering and vast, out in the tranquil bay.
Come to the window, sweet is the night air!
Only, from the long line of spray
Where the ebb meets the moon-blanch'd sand,
Listen! you hear the grating roar
Of pebbles which the waves suck back, and fling,
At their return, up the high strand,
Begin, and cease, and then again begin,
With tremulous cadence slow, and bring
The eternal note of sadness in.

Sophocles long ago
Heard it on the Aegaean, and it brought
Into his mind the turbid ebb and flow
Of human misery; we
Find also in the sound a thought,
Hearing it by this distant northern sea.

The sea of faith
Was once, too, at the full, and round earth's shore
Lay like the folds of a bright girdle furl'd;
But now I only hear
Its melancholy, long, withdrawing roar,
Retreating to the breath
Of the night-wind down the vast edges drear
And naked shingles of the world.

Ah, love, let us be true
To one another! for the world, which seems
To lie before us like a land of dreams,
So various, so beautiful, so new,
Hath really neither joy, nor love, nor light,
Nor certitude, nor peace, nor help for pain;
And we are here as on a darkling plain
Swept with confused alarms of struggle and flight,
Where ignorant armies clash by night.

WILLIAM BLAKE
(1757–1827)

THE ARTIST, poet and mystic William Blake included his poem about the tiger in *Songs of Experience* (1794), where it was hand-lettered and accompanied by his drawing of a tiger prowling through a jungle. "Symmetry," in Blake's day, was a synonym for beauty. In *Portraits from Memory*, Bertrand Russell recalls meeting a Cambridge student friend who was quoting the poem "in the darkest part of a winding college staircase." Russell continues:

> I had never, till that moment, heard of Blake, and the poem affected me so much that I became dizzy and had to lean against the wall.

The Tyger

Tyger Tyger, burning bright,
In the forests of the night;
What immortal hand or eye,
Could frame thy fearful symmetry?

In what distant deeps or skies
Burnt the fire of thine eyes?
On what wings dare he aspire?
What the hand, dare sieze the fire?

And what shoulder, & what art,
Could twist the sinews of thy heart?
And when thy heart began to beat,
What dread hand? & what dread feet?

What the hammer? what the chain,
In what furnace was thy brain?
What the anvil? what dread grasp,
Dare its deadly terrors clasp!

When the stars threw down their spears
And water'd heaven with their tears:
Did he smile his work to see?
Did he who made the Lamb make thee?

Tyger Tyger burning bright,
In the forests of the night:
What immortal hand or eye,
Dare frame thy fearful symmetry?

FRANCIS WILLIAM BOURDILLON
(1852–1921)

EDUCATED AT Oxford, Bourdillon lived a quiet, happily married, uneventful life in England as a tutor. He was an ardent mountaineer and an authority on French literature, highly respected for his translation of *Aucassin et Nicolette*, a thirteenth-century French romance. Although he published many books of verse, only "The Night Has a Thousand Eyes," from *Among the Flowers and Other Poems* (1878), is remembered today.

The Night Has a Thousand Eyes

The night has a thousand eyes,
   And the day but one;
Yet the light of the bright world dies
   With the dying sun.

The mind has a thousand eyes,
   And the heart but one;
Yet the light of a whole life dies
   When love is done.

ROBERT BROWNING
(1812–1889)

FOR SOME reason—a decay of Protestant faith among critics?—Browning is much less studied now than fifty years ago when Browning clubs flourished all over the nation. He was such a distinguished poet in his day that he was buried in Westminster Abbey. The story of his romantic elopement with the poet Elizabeth Barrett Browning was the basis of Rudolf Besier's play *The Barretts of Wimpole Street* (1930), later made into a successful movie.

The song sung by the little silk-mill girl Pippa in *Pippa Passes* (1841) is surely Browning's most quoted, most memorized, lyric. It was set to music by Amy Beach, and recorded by several famous singers.

"Meeting at Night" (from *Dramatic Romances and Lyrics*, 1845) is one of Browning's best-loved love lyrics, happily free of the obscure lines that characterize his longer poems. Note how omitting the *n* of "in" gives line six a slushy sound, and how the *abccba* palindromic rhyme scheme suggests the slow movement of waves. Browning's short sequel, "Parting at Morning," has a similar palindromic rhyme scheme:

> Round the cape of a sudden came the sea,
> And the sun looked over the mountain's rim:
> And straight was a path of gold for him,
> And the need of a world of men for me.

Critics have worried about the meaning of this brief lyric's last two lines. Does "him" refer to the sun and its gold path on the water, or to the man who is returning to profitable work? Is "me" the man who speaks in "Meeting at Night" or is it the woman speaking about how a society of men needs *her?*

Pippa's Song

The year's at the spring
And day's at the morn;
Morning's at seven;
The hillside's dew-pearled;
The lark's on the wing;
The snail's on the thorn:
God's in his heaven—
All's right with the world!

Meeting at Night

The gray sea and the long black land;
And the yellow half-moon large and low;
And the startled little waves that leap
In fiery ringlets from their sleep,
As I gain the cove with pushing prow,
And quench its speed i' the slushy sand.

Then a mile of warm sea-scented beach;
Three fields to cross till a farm appears;
A tap at the pane, the quick sharp scratch
And blue spurt of a lighted match,
And a voice less loud, through its joys and fears,
Than the two hearts beating each to each!

WILLIAM CULLEN BRYANT
(1794–1878)

A SELF-EDUCATED journalist—he was chief editor of the New York *Evening Post* for half a century—Bryant was one of the nation's earliest and most revered nature writers. Most of "Thanatopsis," composed when he was only seventeen, first appeared in the *Daily Hampshire Gazette*, Northampton, Massachusetts, in 1811. Washington Irving edited Bryant's collected works, and Bryant himself edited the most famous of early anthologies, the mammoth *Family Library of Poetry and Song.*
   Bryant's calm, humorless aloofness was satirized by James Russell Lowell:

There is Bryant, as quiet, as cool, and as dignified,
As a smooth, silent iceberg that never is ignified . . .
He may rank (Griswold says so) first bard of your nation,
There's no doubt that he stands in supreme ice-olation;
Your topmost Parnassus he may set his heel on,
But no warm applauses come, peal following peal on—
He's too smooth and too polished to hang any zeal on.

Thanatopsis

To him who in the love of Nature holds
Communion with her visible forms, she speaks
A various language; for his gayer hours

She has a voice of gladness, and a smile
And eloquence of beauty, and she glides
Into his darker musings, with a mild
And healing sympathy, that steals away
Their sharpness, ere he is aware. When thoughts
Of the last bitter hour come like a blight
Over thy spirit, and sad images
Of the stern agony, and shroud, and pall,
And breathless darkness, and the narrow house,
Make thee to shudder and grow sick at heart;—
Go forth, under the open sky, and list
To Nature's teachings, while from all around—
Earth and her waters, and the depths of air—
Comes a still voice—Yet a few days, and thee
The all-beholding sun shall see no more
In all his course; nor yet in the cold ground,
Where thy pale form was laid with many tears,
Nor in the embrace of ocean, shall exist
Thy image. Earth, that nourish'd thee, shall claim
Thy growth, to be resolved to earth again,
And, lost each human trace, surrendering up
Thine individual being, shalt thou go
To mix for ever with the elements,
To be a brother to the insensible rock,
And to the sluggish clod, which the rude swain
Turns with his share, and treads upon. The oak
Shall send his roots abroad, and pierce thy mould.

    Yet not to thine eternal resting-place
Shalt thou retire alone, nor couldst thou wish
Couch more magnificent. Thou shalt lie down
With patriarchs of the infant world—with kings,
The powerful of the earth—the wise, the good,
Fair forms, and hoary seers of ages past,
All in one mighty sepulchre. The hills
Rock-ribb'd and ancient as the sun,—the vales
Stretching in pensive quietness between;
The venerable woods; rivers that move
In majesty, and the complaining brooks
That make the meadows green; and, pour'd round all,
Old Ocean's grey and melancholy waste,—
Are but the solemn decorations all

Of the great tomb of man. The golden sun,
The planets, all the infinite host of heaven,
Are shining on the sad abodes of death,
Through the still lapse of ages. All that tread
The globe are but a handful to the tribes
That slumber in its bosom.—Take the wings
Of morning, pierce the Barcan wilderness,
Or lose thyself in the continuous woods
Where rolls the Oregon and hears no sound
Save his own dashings—yet the dead are there:
And millions in those solitudes, since first
The flight of years began, have laid them down
In their last sleep—the dead reign there alone.
So shalt thou rest: and what if thou withdraw
In silence from the living, and no friend
Take note of thy departure? All that breathe
Will share thy destiny. The gay will laugh
When thou art gone, the solemn brood of care
Plod on, and each one as before will chase
His favourite phantom; yet all these shall leave
Their mirth and their employments, and shall come
And make their bed with thee. As the long train
Of ages glide away, the sons of men,
The youth in life's green spring, and he who goes
In the full strength of years, matron and maid,
The speechless babe, and the grey-headed man—
Shall one by one be gathered to thy side
By those who in their turn shall follow them.

    So live, that when thy summons comes to join
The innumerable caravan which moves
To that mysterious realm where each shall take
His chamber in the silent halls of death,
Thou go not, like the quarry-slave at night,
Scourged to his dungeon; but, sustain'd and soothed
By an unfaltering trust, approach thy grave,
Like one who wraps the drapery of his couch
About him, and lies down to pleasant dreams.

GELETT BURGESS
(1866–1951)

BURGESS WAS a prolific San Francisco author of humorous fiction and poetry, much of which he illustrated himself with amusing sketches. Collections of his verse about ill-mannered and unruly children, whom he called "Goops," are still in print. He loved to invent new words. Among the hundreds he coined for his dictionary *Burgess Unabridged* (1914) was "blurb." His *Are You a Bromide?* (1907) introduced the slang meaning of that chemical term.

"The Purple Cow," Burgess' most famous nonsense poem, first appeared in a magazine he edited, *The Lark*, in 1895. Endless parodies have been written, the best one by Burgess himself:

> O yes, I wrote the Purple Cow.
> I'm sorry now I wrote it.
> But I can tell you anyhow,
> I'll kill you if you quote it.

O. Henry produced this:

> I never beat a rotten egg,
> I never hope to beat one;
> But this you'll understand, I beg,
> I'd rather beat than eat one.

Another—this one anonymous:

> I've never seen a purple cow.
> My eyes with tears are full.
> I've never seen a purple cow,
> And I'm a purple bull.

The publicist Jim Moran, noted for his many practical jokes, once visited Burgess, bringing with him a cow painted purple.

The Purple Cow

I never saw a Purple Cow,
I never hope to see one;
But I can tell you, anyhow,
I'd rather see than be one.

ROBERT BURNS
(1759–1796)

ROBERT BURNS, Scotland's most famous poet and writer of song lyrics, never went to university, and received little formal schooling. He began life as a lowly farm laborer, an experience reflected in his poem "To a Mouse." "Tam o' Shanter," too long to include here, is the finest of all ballads featuring witches and warlocks. "'Is There for Honest Poverty,'" composed in 1795, has been called the greatest poem ever written in praise of democracy.

Burns died at the age of thirty-seven after a short life of intense creativity, drinking, womanizing and poverty. Like Kipling, his verse has been enormously popular with ordinary folk, even in nondemocratic nations like China. He once confessed:

> I am nae Poet, in a sense,
>> But just a Rhymer, like, by chance,
> An' hae to learning nae pretence,
>> Yet, what the matter?
> Whene'er my Muse does on me glance,
>> I jingle at her.

To a Mouse

On Turning Her Up in Her Nest with the Plough, November, 1785

I

Wee, sleekit, cowrin, tim'rous beastie,
O, what a panic's in thy breastie!
Thou need na start awa sae hasty
      Wi' bickering brattle![1]
I wad be laith to rin an' chase thee,
      Wi' murdering pattle![2]

II

I'm truly sorry man's dominion
Has broken Nature's social union,
An' justifies that ill opinion
      Which makes thee startle
At me, thy poor, earth-born companion
      An' fellow mortal!

III

I doubt na, whyles, but thou may thieve;
What then? poor beastie, thou maun live.
A daimen icker in a thrave[3]
        'S a sma' request;
I'll get a blessin wi' the lave,[4]
        An' never miss 't!

IV

Thy wee-bit housie, too, in ruin!
Its silly wa's the win's are strewin!
An' naething, now, to big[5] a new ane,
        O' foggage[6] green!
An' bleak December's win's ensuin,
        Baith snell[7] an' keen!

V

Thou saw the fields laid bare an' waste,
An' weary winter comin fast,
An' cozie here, beneath the blast,
        Thou thought to dwell,
Till crash! the cruel coulter past
        Out thro' thy cell.

VI

That wee bit heap o' leaves an' stibble,
Has cost thee monie a weary nibble!
Now thou's turned out, for a' thy trouble,
        But house or hald,[8]
To thole[9] the winter's sleety dribble,
        An' cranreuch[10] cauld!

VII

But Mousie, thou art no thy lane,[11]
In proving foresight may be vain:
The best-laid schemes o' mice an' men
        Gang aft agley,[12]
An' lea'e us nought but grief an' pain,
        For promis'd joy!

VIII

Still thou art blest, compared wi' me!
The present only toucheth thee:

But och! I backward cast my e'e,
        On prospects drear!
An' forward, tho' I canna see,
        I guess an' fear!

---

¹ *bickering brattle*] hurrying scamper.
² *pattle*] plough-staff.
³ *A daimen icker in a thrave*] an occasional ear of
corn in twenty-four sheaves.
⁴ *lave*] remainder.
⁵ *big*] build.
⁶ *foggage*] meadow grass.
⁷ *snell*] biting.
⁸ *But house or hald*] without house or property.
⁹ *thole*] endure, suffer.
¹⁰ *cranreuch*] hoar-frost.
¹¹ *no thy lane*] not alone.
¹² *agley*] awry.

'Is There for Honest Poverty'

I

Is there for honest poverty
    That hings his head, an' a' that?
The coward slave, we pass him by—
    We dare be poor for a' that!
For a' that, an' a' that,
    Our toils obscure, an' a' that,
The rank is but the guinea's stamp,
    The man's the gowd[1] for a' that.

II

What though on hamely fare we dine,
    Wear hoddin grey, an' a' that?
Gie fools their silks, and knaves their wine—
    A man's a man for a' that.
For a' that, an' a' that,
    Their tinsel show, an' a' that,
The honest man, tho' e'er sae poor,
    Is king o' men for a' that.

III

Ye see yon birkie[2] ca'd "a lord,"
    Wha struts, an' stares, an' a' that?

Tho' hundreds worship at his word,
He's but a cuif[3] for a' that.
For a' that, an' a' that,
His ribband, star, an' a' that,
The man o' independent mind,
He looks an' laughs at a' that.

IV

A prince can mak a belted knight,
A marquis, duke, an' a' that!
But an honest man's aboon his might—
Guid faith, he mauna fa'[4] that!
For a' that, an' a' that,
Their dignities, an' a' that,
The pith o' sense an' pride o' worth
Are higher rank than a' that.

V

Then let us pray that come it may
(As come it will for a' that)
That Sense and Worth o'er a' the earth
Shall bear the gree[5] an' a' that!
For a' that, an' a' that,
It's comin yet for a' that,
That man to man the world o'er
Shall brithers be for a' that.

---

[1] *gowd*] gold.
[2] *birkie*] conceited fellow.
[3] *cuif*] dolt, spiritless fellow.
[4] *mauna fa'*] must not claim.
[5] *bear the gree*] have the first place.

GEORGE GORDON, LORD BYRON
(1788–1824)

ONE OF England's greatest Romantic poets, Lord Byron (he inherited a barony) left England (which he despised as much as he did his mother) in his late twenties, never to return. Bisexual and startlingly handsome, his clubfoot did not deter him from swimming the Hellespont or from being pursued by beautiful women and good-looking boys. Politically radical, he died in Greece where he was training troops to fight for independence from Turkey.

"She Walks in Beauty" was inspired by seeing his cousin by marriage, Lady Wilmot Horton, in a ballroom. She was dressed in mourning, her gown adorned with silver spangles that glittered like stars. "The Destruction of Sennacherib" is based on the Old Testament accounts in II Chronicles 32 and II Kings 18 and 19.

A quatrain by one Bert Leston Taylor goes:

> Whene'er I quote, I seldom take
> From bards whom angel hosts environ,
> But usually from some damn rake,
> Like Byron.

She Walks in Beauty

She walks in beauty, like the night
  Of cloudless climes and starry skies;
And all that's best of dark and bright
  Meet in her aspect and her eyes:
Thus mellow'd to that tender light
  Which heaven to gaudy day denies.

One shade the more, one ray the less,
  Had half impair'd the nameless grace
Which waves in every raven tress,
  Or softly lightens o'er her face;
Where thoughts serenely sweet express
  How pure, how dear their dwelling-place.

And on that cheek, and o'er that brow,
  So soft, so calm, yet eloquent,
The smiles that win, the tints that glow,
  But tell of days in goodness spent,
A mind at peace with all below,
  A heart whose love is innocent!

The Destruction of Sennacherib

The Assyrian came down like the wolf on the fold,
And his cohorts were gleaming in purple and gold;

And the sheen of their spears was like stars on the sea,
When the blue wave rolls nightly on deep Galilee.

Like the leaves of the forest when Summer is green,
That host with their banners at sunset were seen:
Like the leaves of the forest when Autumn hath blown,
That host on the morrow lay wither'd and strown.

For the Angel of Death spread his wings on the blast,
And breathed in the face of the foe as he pass'd;
And the eyes of the sleepers wax'd deadly and chill,
And their hearts but once heaved, and for ever grew still!

And there lay the steed with his nostril all wide,
But through it there roll'd not the breath of his pride:
And the foam of his gasping lay white on the turf,
And cold as the spray of the rock-beating surf.

And there lay the rider distorted and pale,
With the dew on his brow and the rust on his mail;
And the tents were all silent, the banners alone,
The lances unlifted, the trumpet unblown.

And the widows of Ashur are loud in their wail,
And the idols are broke in the temple of Baal;
And the might of the Gentile, unsmote by the sword,
Hath melted like snow in the glance of the Lord!

BLISS CARMAN
(1861–1929)

A CANADIAN who lived in New York and died in New Canaan, Connecticut, this lifelong bachelor's bouncy rhymes are contained in some two dozen books, but only "A Vagabond Song," a poem about autumn, has made its way into anthologies.

Carman, in collaboration with Richard Hovey, wrote three series of *Songs from Vagabondia* (1894, 1896, 1900). In those days, "vagabond" was a term of praise for a person who today would be called a drifter.

Canada declared Carman Poet Laureate in 1928. A tribute to him by James Whitcomb Riley begins and ends with this stanza:

He is the morning's poet—
　　The bard of mount and moor,
The minstrel fine of dewy shine,
　　The dawning's troubadour.

A Vagabond Song

There is something in the autumn that is native to my blood—
Touch of manner, hint of mood;
And my heart is like a rhyme,
With the yellow and the purple and the crimson keeping time.

The scarlet of the maples can shake me like a cry
Of bugles going by.
And my lonely spirit thrills
To see the frosty asters like a smoke upon the hills.

There is something in October sets the gypsy blood astir;
We must rise and follow her,
When from every hill of flame
She calls and calls each vagabond by name.

LEWIS CARROLL
(1832–1898)

"LEWIS CARROLL" was the pseudonym used by Charles Lutwidge Dodgson, a shy, stammering Oxford University mathematician, when he wrote his two immortal fantasies about his child-friend Alice Liddell. In the first chapter of *Through the Looking-Glass* Alice picks up a book with reversed printing and reads "Jabberwocky" by holding it up to the mirror she has just passed through. " 'Somehow it seems to fill my head with ideas—only I don't exactly know what they are!' " Alice exclaims. " 'However, *somebody* killed *something:* that's clear.' " For commentary on the lines, see my *Annotated Alice* and *More Annotated Alice.*

Jabberwocky

'Twas brillig, and the slithy toves
　　Did gyre and gimble in the wabe;

All mimsy were the borogoves,
    And the mome raths outgrabe.

"Beware the Jabberwock, my son!
    The jaws that bite, the claws that catch!
Beware the Jubjub bird, and shun
    The frumious Bandersnatch!"

He took his vorpal sword in hand:
    Long time the manxome foe he sought—
So rested he by the Tumtum tree,
    And stood awhile in thought.

And, as in uffish thought he stood,
    The Jabberwock, with eyes of flame,
Came whiffling through the tulgey wood,
    And burbled as it came!

One, two! One, two! And through and through
    The vorpal blade went snicker-snack!
He left it dead, and with its head
    He went galumphing back.

"And hast thou slain the Jabberwock?
    Come to my arms, my beamish boy!
O frabjous day! Callooh, Callay!"
    He chortled in his joy.

'Twas brillig, and the slithy toves
    Did gyre and gimble in the wabe;
All mimsy were the borogoves,
And the mome raths outgrabe.

ARTHUR CHAPMAN
(1873–1935)

CHAPMAN BEGAN his journalism career as a reporter on the Chicago *Daily News*. He then moved to Denver where he wrote a daily column for the Denver *Republican*, became managing editor of the Denver *Times*, then settled in New York as a staff writer for the *Herald Tribune*. His son John became a noted drama critic on the New York *News*.

When a group of Western state governors convened in Buffalo in 1912 they were reported in the press as arguing over just where the West begins. This gave Chapman the idea for the poem "Out Where the West Begins," which appeared first in his own newspaper column. His 1917 book *Out Where the West Begins and Other Western Verses* opens with the title poem. The jacket of my copy, a ninth printing, has this to say:

> To-day it is perhaps the best-known bit of verse in America. It hangs framed in the office of the Secretary of the Interior at Washington. It has been quoted in Congress, and printed as campaign material for at least two Governors. It has crossed both the Atlantic and the Pacific, while throughout this country it may be found pinned on walls and pasted in scrapbooks innumerable.

I know the poem was set to music at least once because I own a copy of the sheet music by Estelle Philleo, published by Forster in Chicago (1917), and illustrated with sketches by Harold Bell Wright.

Out Where the West Begins

Out where the handclasp's a little stronger,
Out where the smile dwells a little longer,
   That's where the West begins;
Out where the sun is a little brighter,
Where the snows that fall are a trifle whiter,
Where the bonds of home are a wee bit tighter,
   That's where the West begins.

Out where the skies are a trifle bluer,
Out where friendship's a little truer,
   That's where the West begins;
Out where a fresher breeze is blowing,
Where there's laughter in every streamlet flowing,
Where there's more of reaping and less of sowing,
   That's where the West begins.

Out where the world is in the making,
Where fewer hearts in despair are aching,
   That's where the West begins;
Where there's more of singing and less of sighing,
Where there's more of giving and less of buying,
And a man makes friends without half trying—
   That's where the West begins.

SAMUEL TAYLOR COLERIDGE
(1772–1834)

ALTHOUGH WRITTEN in the summer of 1797, "Kubla Khan" was first published in a pamphlet of Coleridge's poems in 1816. It was preceded by a preamble in which Coleridge describes how he had fallen asleep in a chair after taking opium, having just read the following passage in a 1626 work:

> In Xamdu did Cublai Can build a stately Palace, encompassing sixteene miles of plaine ground with a wall, wherein are fertile Medowes, pleasant Springs, delightful Streames, and all sorts of beasts of chase and game, and in the middest thereof a sumptuous house of pleasure.

After three hours of vivid dreaming, Coleridge awoke and wrote down the beginning of a much longer poem that had formed in his mind.

> At this moment he was unfortunately called out by a person on business from Porlock, and detained by him above an hour, and on his return to his room, found, to his no small surprise and mortification, that though he still retained some vague and dim recollection of the general import of the vision, yet, with the exception of some eight or ten scattered lines and images, all the rest had passed away like the images on the surface of a stream into which a stone has been cast, but alas! without the after restoration of the latter!

"Xanadu" was the name given to the mansion in Orson Welles's movie *Citizen Kane*. "The Astrodome," a twenty-stanza parody by Tom Kach and Mary Sakami, ran in *Mad* magazine (December 1966). It begins:

> On Houston's soil did millionaires
> A garish Astrodome foresee:
> A palace where the baseball fan,
> 'Mid climate hideous to man,
>   Might loll more pleasantly.

Kubla Khan

In Xanadu did Kubla Khan
A stately pleasure-dome decree:
Where Alph, the sacred river, ran
Through caverns measureless to man
     Down to a sunless sea.
So twice five miles of fertile ground
With walls and towers were girdled round:

And there were gardens bright with sinuous rills,
Where blossomed many an incense-bearing tree;
And here were forests ancient as the hills,
Enfolding sunny spots of greenery.

But oh! that deep romantic chasm which slanted
Down the green hill athwart a cedarn cover!
A savage place! as holy and enchanted
As e'er beneath a waning moon was haunted
By woman wailing for her demon-lover!
And from this chasm, with ceaseless turmoil seething,
As if this earth in fast thick pants were breathing,
A mighty fountain momently was forced:
Amid whose swift half-intermitted burst
Huge fragments vaulted like rebounding hail,
Or chaffy grain beneath the thresher's flail:
And 'mid these dancing rocks at once and ever
It flung up momently the sacred river.
Five miles meandering with a mazy motion
Through wood and dale the sacred river ran,
Then reached the caverns measureless to man,
And sank in tumult to a lifeless ocean:
And 'mid this tumult Kubla heard from far
Ancestral voices prophesying war!
    The shadow of the dome of pleasure
    Floated midway on the waves;
    Where was heard the mingled measure
    From the fountain and the caves.
It was a miracle of rare device,
A sunny pleasure-dome with caves of ice!

    A damsel with a dulcimer
    In a vision once I saw:
    It was an Abyssinian maid,
    And on her dulcimer she played,
    Singing of Mount Abora.
    Could I revive within me
    Her symphony and song,
    To such a deep delight 'twould win me,
That with music loud and long,
I would build that dome in air,
That sunny dome! those caves of ice!
And all who heard should see them there,
And all should cry, Beware! Beware!

His flashing eyes, his floating hair!
Weave a circle round him thrice,
And close your eyes with holy dread,
For he on honey-dew hath fed,
And drunk the milk of Paradise.

STEPHEN CRANE
(1871–1900)

CRANE WAS born in Newark, New Jersey, the son of a conservative Methodist minister against whose faith Stephen early rebelled. His education consisted of half a year at Lafayette College and a semester at Syracuse University.

Maggie: A Girl of the Streets, Crane's first novel, was privately printed in 1893 under the pseudonym "Johnston Smith." It sold so miserably, and Crane was so poor, that he is said to have burned copies of the book to keep himself warm. However, his second novel, *The Red Badge of Courage* (1895), brought him instant fame. After working as a journalist and war correspondent for New York City newspapers, Crane settled in Surrey, England, with Cora Taylor, his common-law wife. She had been the madam of the Hotel de Dream, a classy whorehouse in Jacksonville, Florida.

Although best known for his Civil War novel and for his marvelous short stories, Crane also wrote two volumes of short, epigrammatic free verse: *The Black Riders and Other Lines* (1895) and *War Is Kind* (1899). "'A Man Said to the Universe,'" from *War Is Kind*, is the most often quoted of what were called his "prose poems." In his most acclaimed short story, "The Open Boat," Crane said the same thing this way: "A high cold star on a winter's night is the word he feels that she [the universe] says to him."

Crane died of tuberculosis when he was twenty-eight, in a German sanatorium. Cora returned to her former profession.

'A Man Said to the Universe'

A man said to the universe,
"Sir, I exist!"
"However," replied the universe,
"The fact has not created in me
A sense of obligation."

EMILY DICKINSON
(1830–1886)

ONE OF America's greatest poets, Emily Dickinson spent her entire life in Amherst, Massachusetts, as a timid, isolated, eccentric spinster—her shyness perhaps related to her being slightly walleyed. Her almost two thousand brief lyrics, or fragments of lyrics, were scribbled secretly and kept in a desk. Only a few were published in her lifetime, all anonymously and without her consent. To what extent she could call herself a Christian is obscure (she seldom went to church), but her verse is rich in Biblical allusions and haunted by death and the hope of immortality.

Emily's enigmatic life was the basis for a novel by Helen Hunt Jackson and a play by Susan Gaspell. "If I feel physically as if the top of my head were taken off," Emily once wrote, "I know that is poetry. . . . Is there any other way?" A poetic tribute to Emily by Ruth Brandes de Bedts ends with this stanza:

> What great travail was yours
>   To make your lines run straight
> Beneath the freight they bore
>   I dare not contemplate.

'I Never Saw a Moor'

I never saw a moor,
I never saw the sea;
Yet know I how the heather looks,
And what a wave must be.

I never spoke with God,
Nor visited in heaven;
Yet certain am I of the spot
As if the chart were given.

'If I Can Stop One Heart from Breaking'

If I can stop one heart from breaking,
I shall not live in vain;
If I can ease one life the aching,

Or cool one pain,
Or help one fainting robin
Unto his nest again,
I shall not live in vain.

'There Is No Frigate Like a Book'

There is no frigate like a book
  To take us lands away,
Nor any coursers like a page
  Of prancing poetry.
This traverse may the poorest take
  Without oppress of toll;
How frugal is the chariot
  That bears a human soul!

'Because I Could Not Stop for Death'

Because I could not stop for Death,
He kindly stopped for me;
The carriage held but just ourselves
And Immortality.

We slowly drove, he knew no haste,
And I had put away
My labor, and my leisure too,
For his civility.

We passed the school where children played,
Their lessons scarcely done;
We passed the fields of gazing grain,
We passed the setting sun.

We paused before a house that seemed
A swelling of the ground;
The roof was scarcely visible,
The cornice but a mound.

Since then 't is centuries; but each
Feels shorter than the day

I first surmised the horses' heads
Were toward eternity.

JOSEPH RODMAN DRAKE
(1795–1820)

ASIDE FROM the lyrics of our national anthem, Drake's "The American Flag" is the most famous of patriotic poems about the flag. It first appeared in the New York *Evening Post* in 1819. The only volume by Drake published during his lifetime was *The Croaker Papers* (1819), a collection of satirical poems by Drake and his friend Fitz-Greene Halleck that bore on its title page the pseudonym "Croaker and Company." Halleck is believed to have written the last stanza of "The American Flag."

Drake rated six pages in an 1881 *Cyclopedia of American Literature*, but only this poem of his is remembered today. Halleck wrote an elegy to Drake that opens:

> Green be the turf above thee,
> Friend of my better days!
> None knew thee but to love thee,
> Nor named thee but to praise.

The American Flag

When Freedom, from her mountain height,
   Unfurled her standard to the air,
She tore the azure robe of night,
   And set the stars of glory there;
She mingled with its gorgeous dyes
The milky baldric of the skies,
And striped its pure, celestial white
With streakings of the morning light;
Then, from his mansion in the sun,
She called her eagle bearer down,
And gave into his mighty hand,
The symbol of her chosen land.

Majestic monarch of the cloud!
   Who rear'st aloft thy regal form,
To hear the tempest-trumpings loud,

And see the lightning-lances driven,
  When strive the warriors of the storm,
And rolls the thunder-drum of heaven—
Child of the sun! to thee 'tis given
To guard the banner of the free,
To hover in the sulphur smoke,
To ward away the battle-stroke,
And bid its blendings shine afar,
Like rainbows on the cloud of war,
  The harbingers of victory!

Flag of the brave! thy folds shall fly
The sign of hope and triumph high,
When speaks the signal-trumpet tone,
And the long line comes gleaming on:
Ere yet the life-blood, warm and wet,
Has dimmed the glistening bayonet,
Each soldier eye shall brightly turn
Where thy sky-born glories burn,
And, as his springing steps advance,
Catch war and vengeance from the glance;
And when the cannon-mouthings loud
Heave in wild wreaths the battle-shroud,
And gory sabres rise and fall,
Like shoots of flame on midnight's pall;
  Then shall thy meteor-glances glow,
And cowering foes shall sink beneath
  Each gallant arm that strikes below
That lovely messenger of death.

Flag of the seas! on ocean wave
Thy stars shall glitter o'er the brave;
When death, careering on the gale,
Sweeps darkly round the bellied sail,
And frighted waves rush wildly back
Before the broadside's reeling rack,
Each dying wanderer of the sea
Shall look at once to heaven and thee,
And smile to see thy splendors fly
In triumph o'er his closing eye.

Flag of the free heart's hope and home,
  By angel hands to valor given;
The stars have lit the welkin dome,

And all thy hues were born in heaven.
Forever float that standard sheet!
  Where breathes the foe but falls before us,
With Freedom's soil beneath our feet,
  And Freedom's banner streaming o'er us?

RALPH WALDO EMERSON
(1803–1882)

EMERSON IS best known today as a writer of philosophical essays, but in his day he was also a popular poet. The latter half of his life was lived in Concord, Massachusetts, where on April 19, 1836, his "Concord Hymn" was distributed as a broadside at the completion of the Concord Battle Monument. The hymn was sung by those present, and its first stanza inscribed on the monument. The monument and the hymn commemorate the events of April 19, 1775, when the farmers of Concord fired on advancing British troops. The poem appears in Emerson's first collection of verse, *Poems* (1847).

Concord Hymn

*Sung at the Completion of the
Battle Monument, April 19, 1836*

By the rude bridge that arched the flood,
  Their flag to April's breeze unfurled,
Here once the embattled farmers stood,
  And fired the shot heard round the world.

The foe long since in silence slept;
  Alike the conqueror silent sleeps;
And Time the ruined bridge has swept
  Down the dark stream which seaward creeps.

On this green bank, by this soft stream,
  We set to-day a votive stone;
That memory may their deed redeem,
  When, like our sires, our sons are gone.

Spirit, that made those heroes dare
  To die, and leave their children free,

Bid Time and Nature gently spare
The shaft we raise to them and thee.

EUGENE FIELD
(1850–1895)

FIELD WORKED for newspapers here and there before he finally settled in Chicago as a columnist for the *Morning News*. His "Sharps and Flats" was one of the earliest columns in which a reporter could write about anything he liked. A statue of Field stands in Chicago's Lincoln Park.

"Little Boy Blue" is probably the best known of all poems on the death of a child, a common theme in the nineteenth century when such deaths were far more common than today. It first appeared in the first issue of a Chicago weekly literary journal called *America*, in 1888, and the following year in Field's *A Little Book of Western Verse*. The poem was not about the poet's own son, who died several years later. The name "Little Boy Blue," Field said, "came to me while I wanted a rhyme for the seventh line of the first stanza."

The penultimate line of the final stanza originally read: "That they never have seen our Little Boy Blue." Slason Thompson, *America*'s founder and editor, changed the line to its published form. Thompson had earlier edited a collection of newspaper verse, *The Humbler Poets*, and would later write a two-volume biography of his friend Field.

Field was fond of children, practical jokes and writing unprintable bawdy ballads in contrast to his sentimental verse. "Guess I'll go home now," he once told a friend, "and write some more mother rot."

A parody of "Little Boy Blue" by Frank Jacobs appeared in *Mad* magazine in 1976:

> The little toy dog is covered with dust;
> The Tinkertoys rot on the shelf;
> The little toy soldiers are gathering rust,
> And the teddy bear sits by himself.
>
> The little toy engine won't puff any more,
> And, golly, I feel like a boob—
> I've filled up his playroom with toys from the store,
> But my kid won't get up from the tube.

Little Boy Blue

The little toy dog is covered with dust,
    But sturdy and stanch he stands;
And the little toy soldier is red with rust,

And his musket molds in his hands.
Time was when the little toy dog was new
 And the soldier was passing fair,
And that was the time when our Little Boy Blue
 Kissed them and put them there.

"Now, don't you go till I come," he said,
 "And don't you make any noise!"
So toddling off to his trundle-bed
 He dreamed of the pretty toys.
And as he was dreaming, an angel song
 Awakened our Little Boy Blue,—
Oh, the years are many, the years are long,
 But the little toy friends are true.

Ay, faithful to Little Boy Blue they stand,
 Each in the same old place,
Awaiting the touch of a little hand,
 The smile of a little face.
And they wonder, as waiting these long years through,
 In the dust of that little chair,
What has become of our Little Boy Blue
 Since he kissed them and put them there.

Wynken, Blynken, and Nod

Dutch Lullaby

Wynken, Blynken, and Nod one night
 Sailed off in a wooden shoe,—
Sailed on a river of misty light
 Into a sea of dew.
"Where are you going, and what do you wish?"
 The old moon asked the three.
"We have come to fish for the herring-fish
 That live in this beautiful sea;
 Nets of silver and gold have we,"
 Said Wynken,
 Blynken,
 And Nod.

The old moon laughed and sung a song,
  As they rocked in the wooden shoe;
And the wind that sped them all night long
  Ruffled the waves of dew;
The little stars were the herring-fish
  That lived in the beautiful sea.
"Now cast your nets wherever you wish,
  But never afeard are we!"
So cried the stars to the fishermen three,
        Wynken,
        Blynken,
        And Nod.

All night long their nets they threw
  For the fish in the twinkling foam,
Then down from the sky came the wooden shoe,
  Bringing the fishermen home;
'T was all so pretty a sail, it seemed
  As if it could not be;
And some folk thought 't was a dream they'd dreamed
  Of sailing that beautiful sea;
But I shall name you the fishermen three:
        Wynken,
        Blynken,
        And Nod.

Wynken and Blynken are two little eyes,
  And Nod is a little head,
And the wooden shoe that sailed the skies
  Is a wee one's trundle-bed;
So shut your eyes while Mother sings
  Of wonderful sights that be,
And you shall see the beautiful things
  As you rock on the misty sea
  Where the old shoe rocked the fishermen three,—
        Wynken,
        Blynken,
        And Nod.

The Duel

The gingham dog and the calico cat
Side by side on the table sat;

'Twas half-past twelve, and (what do you think!)
Nor one nor t' other had slept a wink!
  The old Dutch clock and the Chinese plate
  Appeared to know as sure as fate
There was going to be a terrible spat.

    (I wasn't there; I simply state
    What was told to me by the Chinese plate!)

The gingham dog went "bow-wow-wow!"
And the calico cat replied "mee-ow!"
The air was littered, an hour or so,
With bits of gingham and calico,
  While the old Dutch clock in the chimney-place
  Up with its hands before its face,
For it always dreaded a family row!

    (Never mind: I'm only telling you
    What the old Dutch clock declares is true!)

The Chinese plate looked very blue,
And wailed, "Oh, dear! what shall we do!"
But the gingham dog and the calico cat
Wallowed this way and tumbled that,
  Employing every tooth and claw
  In the awfullest way you ever saw—
And, oh! how the gingham and calico flew!

    (Don't fancy I exaggerate—
    I got my news from the Chinese plate!)

Next morning where the two had sat
They found no trace of dog or cat;
And some folks think unto this day
That burglars stole that pair away!
  But the truth about the cat and pup
  Is this: they ate each other up!
Now what do you really think of that!

    (The old Dutch clock it told me so,
    And that is how I came to know.)

SAM WALTER FOSS
(1858–1911)

NEW HAMPSHIRE-BORN, and a graduate of Brown University, Foss began his
career as a journalist with several papers in Massachusetts. He was librarian
of the Somerville Public Library, Massachusetts, from 1898 until his death.
"The House by the Side of the Road," his only remembered poem, is from
Dreams in Homespun (1897), one of his five books of popular verse. Framed
printings of the poem may still hang on the walls of thousands of American
homes.

Of many parodies that have been written of this poem, I like best one by
Armand T. Ringer that begins:

> I'm a hermit soul that lives withdrawn
>   In the peace of my self-content,
> Far from the fumes of the cars and trucks
>   That pollute the firmament.
> There are souls that love to congest the paths
>   Where once the rabbits ran,
> But let me live far away from the road,
>   As far from the road as I can.

The House by the Side of the Road

> "He was a friend to man, and he lived
> In a house by the side of the road."—*Homer.*

There are hermit souls that live withdrawn
  In the place of their self-content;
There are souls like stars, that dwell apart,
  In a fellowless firmament;
There are pioneer souls that blaze their paths
  Where highways never ran—
But let me live by the side of the road
  And be a friend to man.

Let me live in a house by the side of the road,
  Where the race of men go by—
The men who are good and the men who are bad,
  As good and as bad as I.
I would not sit in the scorner's seat,
  Or hurl the cynic's ban—

Let me live in a house by the side of the road
  And be a friend to man.

I see from my house by the side of the road,
  By the side of the highway of life,
The men who press with the ardor of hope,
  The men who are faint with the strife.
But I turn not away from their smiles nor their tears,
  Both parts of an infinite plan—
Let me live in a house by the side of the road
  And be a friend to man.

I know there are brook-gladdened meadows ahead
  And mountains of wearisome height;
That the road passes on through the long afternoon
  And stretches away to the night.
But still I rejoice when the travelers rejoice,
  And weep with the strangers that moan,
Nor live in my house by the side of the road
  Like a man who dwells alone.

Let me live in my house by the side of the road—
  It's here the race of men go by.
They are good, they are bad, they are weak, they are
     strong,
  Wise, foolish—so am I;
Then why should I sit in the scorner's seat,
  Or hurl the cynic's ban?
Let me live in my house by the side of the road
  And be a friend to man.

ROBERT FROST
(1874–1963)

AFTER SEVERAL laboring jobs and a period of farming in New England, San Francisco-born Frost settled permanently on a farm in New Hampshire. Although he never graduated from college, he won twenty-five honorary degrees, and was the only poet to receive four Pulitzer Prizes. A mountain in Vermont is named after him.

    "Mending Wall" is from Frost's second book of verse, *North of Boston* (1914). "Fire and Ice" and "Stopping by Woods on a Snowy Evening" are from *New Hampshire* (1923).

Frost despised the poetry of Carl Sandburg, who is often considered his rival, even more than T. S. Eliot, Edmund Wilson and other critics disliked Frost's own work. Frost once called Sandburg "the most artificial and studied ruffian the world has had . . . the kind of writer who had everything to gain and nothing to lose by being translated." In recent years several biographies of Frost have portrayed him as a vain and even a cruel man who damaged the lives of many who were close to him.

Mending Wall

Something there is that doesn't love a wall,
That sends the frozen-ground-swell under it,
And spills the upper boulders in the sun;
And makes gaps even two can pass abreast.
The work of hunters is another thing:
I have come after them and made repair
Where they have left not one stone on a stone,
But they would have the rabbit out of hiding,
To please the yelping dogs. The gaps I mean,
No one has seen them made or heard them made,
But at spring mending-time we find them there.
I let my neighbour know beyond the hill;
And on a day we meet to walk the line
And set the wall between us once again.
We keep the wall between us as we go.
To each the boulders that have fallen to each.
And some are loaves and some so nearly balls
We have to use a spell to make them balance:
"Stay where you are until our backs are turned!"
We wear our fingers rough with handling them.
Oh, just another kind of out-door game,
One on a side. It comes to little more:
There where it is we do not need the wall:
He is all pine and I am apple orchard.
My apple trees will never get across
And eat the cones under his pines, I tell him.
He only says, "Good fences make good neighbours."
Spring is the mischief in me, and I wonder
If I could put a notion in his head:
"*Why* do they make good neighbours? Isn't it
Where there are cows? But here there are no cows.

Before I built a wall I'd ask to know
What I was walling in or walling out,
And to whom I was like to give offence.
Something there is that doesn't love a wall,
That wants it down." I could say "Elves" to him,
But it's not elves exactly, and I'd rather
He said it for himself. I see him there
Bringing a stone grasped firmly by the top
In each hand, like an old-stone savage armed.
He moves in darkness as it seems to me,
Not of woods only and the shade of trees.
He will not go behind his father's saying,
And he likes having thought of it so well
He says again, "Good fences make good neighbours."

Fire and Ice

Some say the world will end in fire,
Some say in ice.
From what I've tasted of desire
I hold with those who favor fire.
But if it had to perish twice,
I think I know enough of hate
To say that for destruction ice
Is also great
And would suffice.

Stopping by Woods on a Snowy Evening

Whose woods these are I think I know.
His house is in the village though;
He will not see me stopping here
To watch his woods fill up with snow.

My little horse must think it queer
To stop without a farmhouse near
Between the woods and frozen lake
The darkest evening of the year.

He gives his harness bells a shake
To ask if there is some mistake.
The only other sound's the sweep
Of easy wind and downy flake.

The woods are lovely, dark and deep.
But I have promises to keep,
And miles to go before I sleep,
And miles to go before I sleep.

THOMAS GRAY
(1716–1771)

BORN IN London, Gray was the only one of twelve children to survive childhood. In his final years he was a history professor at Cambridge, his alma mater, where he fell passionately in love with Charles Victor de Bonstetten, a handsome Swiss nobleman. Gray's most publicized romance—an on-again, off-again affair—was with the novelist Horace Walpole about whose cat Gray wrote an elegy.

Few of Gray's poems apart from "Elegy Written in a Country Churchyard" are read today, but at the time Adam Smith could write: "Gray joins to the sublimity of Milton the elegance and harmony of Pope." Originally titled "Stanza's Wrote In A Country Church-Yard," the "Elegy" was partly composed in 1742 but not published until almost ten years later when it appeared anonymously in the *Magazine of Magazines*. It was altered considerably as it went through many printings to become one of England and America's most popular poems.

The "Elegy's" scene is a church cemetery in Stoke Poges, a village in Buckinghamshire, where Gray himself was buried. The poem's "Thee" is Richard West, the best friend of Gray's youth, and who died prematurely. The Hampden mentioned in the fifteenth stanza is John Hampden, a rich country gentleman who refused to pay a ship-money tax imposed by Charles I.

Gray intended the following stanza to appear just before the poem's epitaph, but decided to remove it from the published version:

> There scattered oft, the earliest of the year,
> By hands unseen, are showers of violets found;
> The redbreast loves to build and warble there,
> And little footsteps lightly print the ground.

Elegy Written in a Country Churchyard

The Curfew tolls the knell of parting day,
  The lowing herd wind slowly o'er the lea,
The plowman homeward plods his weary way,
  And leaves the world to darkness and to me.

Now fades the glimmering landscape on the sight,
  And all the air a solemn stillness holds,
Save where the beetle wheels his droning flight,
  And drowsy tinklings lull the distant folds;

Save that from yonder ivy-mantled tow'r
  The moping owl does to the moon complain
Of such as, wand'ring near her secret bow'r,
  Molest her ancient solitary reign.

Beneath those rugged elms, that yew-tree's shade,
  Where heaves the turf in many a mould'ring heap,
Each in his narrow cell for ever laid,
  The rude Forefathers of the hamlet sleep.

The breezy call of incense-breathing Morn,
  The swallow twitt'ring from the straw-built shed,
The cock's shrill clarion, or the echoing horn,
  No more shall rouse them from their lowly bed.

For them no more the blazing hearth shall burn,
  Or busy housewife ply her evening care:
No children run to lisp their sire's return,
  Or climb his knees the envied kiss to share.

Oft did the harvest to their sickle yield,
  Their furrow oft the stubborn glebe has broke:
How jocund did they drive their team afield!
  How bow'd the woods beneath their sturdy stroke!

Let not Ambition mock their useful toil,
  Their homely joys, and destiny obscure;
Nor Grandeur hear with a disdainful smile
  The short and simple annals of the poor.

The boast of heraldry, the pomp of pow'r,
  And all that beauty, all that wealth e'er gave,
Awaits alike th' inevitable hour:
  The paths of glory lead but to the grave.

Nor you, ye Proud, impute to These the fault,
  If Memory o'er their Tomb no Trophies raise,
Where through the long-drawn aisle and fretted vault
  The pealing anthem swells the note of praise.

Can storied urn or animated bust
  Back to its mansion call the fleeting breath?
Can Honour's voice provoke the silent dust,
  Or Flatt'ry soothe the dull cold ear of death?

Perhaps in this neglected spot is laid
  Some heart once pregnant with celestial fire;
Hands, that the rod of empire might have sway'd,
  Or waked to ecstasy the living lyre.

But Knowledge to their eyes her ample page
  Rich with the spoils of time did ne'er unroll;
Chill Penury repress'd their noble rage,
  And froze the genial current of the soul.

Full many a gem of purest ray serene
  The dark unfathom'd caves of ocean bear:
Full many a flower is born to blush unseen,
  And waste its sweetness on the desert air.

Some village Hampden that with dauntless breast
  The little tyrant of his fields withstood,
Some mute inglorious Milton, here may rest,
  Some Cromwell guiltless of his country's blood.

Th' applause of list'ning senates to command,
  The threats of pain and ruin to despise,
To scatter plenty o'er a smiling land,
  And read their history in a nation's eyes,

Their lot forbade: nor circumscribed alone
  Their growing virtues, but their crimes confined;
Forbade to wade through slaughter to a throne,
  And shut the gates of mercy on mankind,

The struggling pangs of conscious truth to hide,
  To quench the blushes of ingenuous shame,
Or heap the shrine of Luxury and Pride
  With incense kindled at the Muse's flame.

Far from the madding crowd's ignoble strife
  Their sober wishes never learn'd to stray;

Along the cool sequester'd vale of life
    They kept the noiseless tenor of their way.

Yet ev'n these bones from insult to protect
    Some frail memorial still erected nigh,
With uncouth rhymes and shapeless sculpture deck'd,
    Implores the passing tribute of a sigh.

Their name, their years, spelt by th' unletter'd muse,
    The place of fame and elegy supply:
And many a holy text around she strews,
    That teach the rustic moralist to die.

For who, to dumb Forgetfulness a prey,
    This pleasing anxious being e'er resign'd,
Left the warm precincts of the cheerful day,
    Nor cast one longing ling'ring look behind?

On some fond breast the parting soul relies,
    Some pious drops the closing eye requires;
E'en from the tomb the voice of Nature cries,
    E'en in our Ashes live their wonted Fires.

For thee, who, mindful of th' unhonour'd dead,
    Dost in these lines their artless tale relate;
If chance, by lonely contemplation led,
    Some kindred spirit shall inquire thy fate,

Haply some hoary-headed Swain may say,
    'Oft have we seen him at the peep of dawn
Brushing with hasty steps the dews away
    To meet the sun upon the upland lawn.

'There at the foot of yonder nodding beech
    That wreathes its old fantastic roots so high,
His listless length at noontide would he stretch,
    And pore upon the brook that babbles by,

'Hard by yon wood, now smiling as in scorn,
    Mutt'ring his wayward fancies he would rove,
Now drooping, woeful wan, like one forlorn,
    Or crazed with care, or cross'd in hopeless love.

'One morn I miss'd him on the custom'd hill,
    Along the heath and near his fav'rite tree;
Another came, nor yet beside the rill,
    Nor up the lawn, nor at the wood was he;

'The next with dirges due in sad array
Slow through the church-way path we saw him borne.
Approach and read (for thou canst read) the lay
Graved on the stone beneath yon aged thorn.'

The Epitaph

*Here rests his head upon the lap of Earth
A Youth to Fortune and to Fame unknown.
Fair Science frown'd not on his humble birth,
And Melancholy mark'd him for her own.*

*Large was his bounty, and his soul sincere,
Heav'n did a recompense as largely send:
He gave to Mis'ry all he had, a tear,
He gain'd from Heav'n ('twas all he wish'd) a friend.*

*No farther seek his merits to disclose,
Or draw his frailties from their dread abode.
(There they alike in trembling hope repose,)
The bosom of his Father and his God.*

EDGAR GUEST
(1881–1959)

BORN IN Birmingham, England, Guest was brought to the United States as a boy, where at the age of twenty he began writing a daily poem for the Detroit *Free Press*. The syndication of these poems to newspapers throughout the country for more than half a century made Guest the most widely read and most prolific "bad poet" in the nation's history. His Christian Science faith may explain the happy quality of his sentimental doggerel.

"Home" is from the collection of verse *A Heap o' Livin'* (1916), and "It Couldn't Be Done" is from *A Path to Home* (1918). Norman Vincent Peale liked to preach sermons titled "How to Do Things That Can't Be Done." My father once said that the last line of the first two stanzas should be: "That couldn't be done, and sure enough he couldn't do it."

Home

It takes a heap o' livin' in a house t' make it home,
A heap o' sun an' shadder, an' ye sometimes have t' roam
Afore ye really 'preciate the things ye lef' behind,

An' hunger fer 'em somehow, with 'em allus on yer mind.
It don't make any differunce how rich ye get t' be,
How much yer chairs an' tables cost, how great yer luxury;
It ain't home t' ye, though it be the palace of a king,
Until somehow yer soul is sort o' wrapped round everything.

Home ain't a place that gold can buy or get up in a minute;
Afore it's home there's got t' be a heap o' livin' in it;
Within the walls there's got t' be some babies born, and then
Right there ye've got t' bring 'em up t' women good, an' men;
And gradjerly, as time goes on, ye find ye wouldn't part
With anything they ever used—they've grown into yer heart:
The old high chairs, the playthings, too, the little shoes they
    wore
Ye hoard; an' if ye could ye'd keep the thumbmarks on the door.

Ye've got t' weep t' make it home, ye've got t' sit an' sigh
An' watch beside a loved one's bed, an' know that Death is
    nigh;
An' in the stillness o' the night t' see Death's angel come,
An' close the eyes o' her that smiled, an' leave her sweet voice
    dumb.
Fer these are scenes that grip the heart, an' when yer tears
    are dried,
Ye find the home is dearer than it was, an' sanctified;
An' tuggin' at ye always are the pleasant memories
O' her that was an' is no more—ye can't escape from these.

Ye've got t' sing an' dance fer years, ye've got t' romp an' play,
An' learn t' love the things ye have by usin' 'em each day;
Even the roses 'round the porch must blossom year by year
Afore they 'come a part o' ye, suggestin' someone dear
Who used t' love 'em long ago, an' trained 'em jes' t' run
The way they do, so's they would get the early mornin' sun;
Ye've got t' love each brick an' stone from cellar up t' dome:
It takes a heap o' livin' in a house t' make it home.

It Couldn't Be Done

Somebody said that it couldn't be done,
    But he with a chuckle replied
That "maybe it couldn't," but he would be one

Who wouldn't say so till he'd tried.
So he buckled right in with the trace of a grin
    On his face. If he worried he hid it.
He started to sing as he tackled the thing
    That couldn't be done, and he did it.

Somebody scoffed: "Oh, you'll never do that;
    At least no one ever has done it";
But he took off his coat and he took off his hat,
    And the first thing we knew he'd begun it.
With a lift of his chin and a bit of a grin,
    Without any doubting or quiddit,
He started to sing as he tackled the thing
    That couldn't be done, and he did it.

There are thousands to tell you it cannot be done,
    There are thousands to prophesy failure;
There are thousands to point out to you one by one,
    The dangers that wait to assail you.
But just buckle in with a bit of a grin,
    Just take off your coat and go to it;
Just start in to sing as you tackle the thing
    That "cannot be done," and you'll do it.

SARAH JOSEPHA HALE
(1788–1879)

Mrs. Hale, distinguished editor of the Boston *Ladies' Magazine*, and later *Godey's Lady's Book*, also wrote novels, stories, poetry and plays. Today she is remembered only for the simple poem "Mary's Lamb." It first appeared in *Juvenile Miscellany* (September 1830), a children's magazine edited by Hale, and that same year in *Poems for Our Children*. The poem became famous after William McGuffey reprinted it anonymously in two of his readers. The poem's first stanza is perhaps the best-known bit of doggerel in English. Thomas Edison recited it in 1877 on the first phonograph record ever made.

Shortly before Mrs. Hale's death, a bitter controversy erupted. One Mary Elizabeth Sawyer, then in her seventies, claimed she was the original Mary. She had, she insisted, nursed back to health a nearly dead lamb that she had found on her father's farm in Sterling, Massachusetts. The lamb then began to follow her everywhere. One morning, as a prank, she let the lamb follow her into a classroom. This would have been about 1817, when Mary was eleven.

A twelve-year-old boy from Boston named John Roulstone, Jr., was visiting his uncle in Sterling at the time. Amused by the incident, Mary said, he wrote for her the poem's first three stanzas, which she memorized. Presumably Mrs. Hale later added the last three stanzas. Unfortunately, Roulstone died in 1822 while a freshman at Harvard, leaving no record of having penned the poem's first half.

A distressed Mrs. Hale stoutly denied Mary Sawyer's story. Today, critics consider Mrs. Hale the author of the entire poem, though at the time the controversy raged for years in newspapers and periodicals. The waters were muddied by Henry Ford. He bought Mary Sawyer's story, located the old schoolhouse she had attended, restored it, moved it to Sudbury and opened it as a tourist attraction. In 1928 Ford and his wife published a small book to sell to tourists, *The Story of Mary's Little Lamb*, which defends Mary Sawyer's dubious claim. The schoolhouse is still open to the public, and one can buy there a reprint of the book. For Mrs. Hale's side of the controversy see Chapter 17 of *The Lady of Godey's* (1931), a biography of Sarah Hale by Ruth Finley, and "The Tale behind Mary's Little Lamb" by Joseph Kastner, in *The New York Times Magazine* (April 13, 1980).

Hundreds of parodies of the poem's first stanza have been perpetrated, many early ones published in *Godey's Lady's Book*. Tiring of such whimsy, the editors ran their final parody in August 1872:

> Mary had a little lamb,
>   'Twas subject to the gout.
> At last she got disgusted,
>   And put it up the spout.

Here are three anonymous parodies of later vintage:

> Mary had a little lamb.
>   She put it on the shelf.
> And every time it wagged its tail
>   It spanked its little self.

> Mary had a little lamb,
>   With green peas on the side,
> And when her escort saw the check
>   The poor boob nearly died.

> Mary had a little watch.
>   She swallowed it one day.
> The doctor gave her castor oil
>   To pass the time away.

Currier & Ives published a handsome print of Mary and her lamb, and an early silent movie was based on the poem. Many illustrated editions have been published for children, including one in 1903 by William Wallace Denslow, who illustrated *The Wizard of Oz*.

Like all the verse in *Poems for Our Children*, "Mary's Lamb" was written at the request of the composer Lowell Mason, who set the poems to music. Mason was a popular composer of tunes, best known for his hymn "Joy to the World." A different tune for the poem appeared anonymously in 1832 in a book called *The Juvenile Lyre*. In 1867 the poem was published with the tune by which it is sung today, "Merrily We Roll Along."

Mary's Lamb

Mary had a little lamb,
  Its fleece was white as snow;
And everywhere that Mary went,
  The lamb was sure to go.

He followed her to school one day,
  Which was against the rule;
It made the children laugh and play
  To see a lamb at school.

And so the teacher turned him out,
  But still he lingered near,
And waited patiently about
  Till Mary did appear.

And then he ran to her, and laid
  His head upon her arm,
As if he said, "I'm not afraid—
  You'll keep me from all harm."

"What makes the lamb love Mary so?"
  The eager children cry.
"Oh, Mary loves the lamb, you know,"
  The teacher did reply.

"And you each gentle animal
  In confidence may bind,
And make them follow at your call,
  If you are only kind."

FELICIA DOROTHEA HEMANS
(1793–1835)

BORN IN Liverpool, Felicia Browne married a Captain Alfred Hemans, by whom she had five boys, but six years later she and the captain agreed to separate. Her first book of poems was published when she was fifteen, and her total output filled seven volumes. It is hard to believe that Lord Byron ranked her a greater poet than Keats, and that Wordsworth, in one of his poems, called her "that holy spirit, sweet as the spring." Shelley and Scott, too, admired her verse; indeed, she and Scott became good friends.

"Casabianca" (1829) celebrates an actual event. Louis de Casabianca commanded the *Orient*, a French ship, during the Battle of the Nile. His thirteen-year-old son remained on deck after the ship caught fire, to die when the ship's powder exploded. The poem inspired dozens of parodies. I recall the following one from my childhood:

> The boy stood on the burning deck.
> The flames 'round him did roar.
> He found a bar of Ivory Soap,
> And washed himself ashore.

The Breaking Waves Dashed High, a book edition of Mrs. Hemans' poem "The Landing of the Pilgrim Fathers in New England," illustrated by Miss L. B. Humphrey, was published in Boston by Lee and Shepard in 1883.

Casabianca

The boy stood on the burning deck,
  Whence all but he had fled;
The flame that lit the battle's wreck,
  Shone round him o'er the dead;
Yet beautiful and bright he stood
  As born to rule the storm!
A creature of heroic blood,
  A proud, though child-like form!

The flames roll'd on—he would not go
  Without his Father's word;
That Father, faint in death below,
  His voice no longer heard.
He call'd aloud. 'Say, father, say
  If yet my task is done!'
He knew not that the chieftain lay
  Unconscious of his son.

'Speak, father!' once again he cried,
  'If I may yet be gone!'
And but the booming shots replied,
  And fast the flames roll'd on.
Upon his brow he felt their breath,

And in his waving hair;
And look'd from that lone post of death
    In still, yet brave, despair;

And shouted but once more aloud,
    'My father! must I stay?'
While o'er him fast through sail and shroud,
    The wreathing fires made way.
They wrapt the ship in splendour wild,
    They caught the flag on high,
And stream'd above the gallant child
    Like banners in the sky.

There came a burst of thunder-sound—
    The boy—O! where was he?
—Ask of the winds that far around
    With fragments strewed the sea,
With mast, and helm, and pennon fair,
    That well had borne their part;
But the noblest thing which perish'd there
    Was that young faithful heart!

The Landing of the Pilgrim Fathers in New England

The breaking waves dashed high
    On a stern and rockbound coast,
And the woods against a stormy sky
    Their giant branches tossed.

And the heavy night hung dark
    The hills and waters o'er,
When a band of exiles moored their bark
    On the wild New England shore.

Not as the conqueror comes,
    They, the true-hearted, came;
Not with the roll of the stirring drums,
    And the trumpet that sings of fame.

Not as the flying come,
    In silence and in fear,—

They shook the depths of the desert gloom
  With their hymns of lofty cheer.

Amidst the storm they sang,
  And the stars heard, and the sea:
And the sounding aisles of the dim woods rang
  To the anthem of the free!

The ocean eagle soared
  From his nest by the white wave's foam:
And the rocking pines of the forest roared,—
  This was their welcome home!

There were men with hoary hair
  Amidst that pilgrim band:—
Why had *they* come to wither there,
  Away from their childhood's land?

There was woman's fearless eye,
  Lit by her deep love's truth;
There was manhood's brow serenely high,
  And the fiery heart of youth.

What sought they thus afar?
  Bright jewels of the mine?
The wealth of seas, the spoils of war?—
  They sought a faith's pure shrine!

Ay, call it holy ground,
  The soil where first they trod:
They have left unstained what there they found,—
  Freedom to worship God.

WILLIAM ERNEST HENLEY
(1849–1903)

HENLEY WAS born in Gloucester, England. Tuberculosis as a child forced the amputation of a foot. His other foot was saved, but only after twenty agonizing months in a hospital. He became an influential editor of several British literary periodicals, and a prolific writer of essays and poetry. He collaborated with his good friend Robert Louis Stevenson on four plays.

  G. K. Chesterton described Henley as "a sad, sensitive and tender-hearted pessimist, who endured pain that came from nowhere, and enjoyed pleasure that came from nowhere, with the exquisite appreciation of some timid child." The title of Henley's best-known poem, "Invictus" (1875), is Latin for "unconquerable." The poem is a favorite of secular humanists who see themselves and the human race as unconquerable masters of their fate in a mindless universe that cares not a fig for what happens to them.

Invictus

Out of the night that covers me,
   Black as the pit from pole to pole,
I thank whatever gods may be
   For my unconquerable soul.

In the fell clutch of circumstance
   I have not winced nor cried aloud.
Under the bludgeonings of chance
   My head is bloody, but unbow'd.

Beyond this place of wrath and tears
   Looms but the Horror of the shade,
And yet the menace of the years
   Finds and shall find me unafraid.

It matters not how strait the gate,
   How charged with punishments the scroll,
I am the master of my fate:
   I am the captain of my soul.

OLIVER WENDELL HOLMES
(1809–1894)

ONE OF the "Boston Brahmins," Holmes was both a distinguished physician and a world-renowned writer of essays, poetry, books on medical topics, a biography of Emerson and three novels about neurotics. His MD was obtained at Harvard where for thirty-five years he was a professor of anatomy and physiology, and for six years dean of the Medical School. His son, of the same name, was the noted Harvard law professor and U.S. Supreme Court justice.

"Old Ironsides," written when Holmes was twenty-one, was first published in the Boston *Daily Advertiser* (1830) to commemorate the warship *Constitution*, which had just been ordered dismantled. It was the public outcry aroused by this widely reprinted poem that saved the ship, which still floats today in the Charleston Navy yard where it is open to visitors.

"The Last Leaf" appeared in *The Amateur* (1831). It described Mayor Thomas Melville, grandfather of Herman, and one of the "Indians" who survived the Boston Tea Party. His old three-cornered hat is on display in Boston's Old State House. Readers were puzzled over the reference to the leaf being on the bough in the spring. Here is Holmes's explanation:

> His aspect among the crowds of a later generation reminded me of a withered leaf which has held to its stem through the storms of autumn and winter, and finds itself still clinging to its bough while the new growths of spring are bursting their buds and spreading their foliage all around it. I make this explanation for the benefit of those who have been puzzled by the lines,

"The last leaf upon the tree
In the spring."

Lincoln, who memorized the poem, called its final stanza "the most pathetic in the English language." The third line of the third stanza was originally "So forlorn." After critics complained of the poor rhyme, Holmes changed it to "Sad and wan," a line suggested by his friend Mrs. Charles Folsom. Holmes in his old age—he lived to be eighty-five—wrote about how he himself had become a "last leaf."

"The Deacon's Masterpiece" first appeared in the *Atlantic Monthly* (1858), a magazine Holmes named and helped edit. My mother, along with many others, took the poem to refer to the body's sudden breakdown in old age. But Holmes, an ardent Unitarian, may have intended it to be a parable about the breakdown of Protestant fundamentalism, especially in its then Calvinist mode. Alas, there is no sign yet of such a collapse.

Old Ironsides

Ay, tear her tattered ensign down!
Long has it waved on high,
And many an eye has danced to see
That banner in the sky;
Beneath it rung the battle-shout,
And burst the cannon's roar:
The meteor of the ocean air
Shall sweep the clouds no more!

Her deck, once red with heroes' blood,
Where knelt the vanquished foe,
When winds were hurrying o'er the flood,
And waves were white below,

No more shall feel the victor's tread,
  Or know the conquered knee:
The harpies of the shore shall pluck
  The eagle of the sea!

Oh, better that her shattered hulk
  Should sink beneath the wave!
Her thunders shook the mighty deep,
  And there should be her grave:
Nail to the mast her holy flag,
  Set every threadbare sail,
And give her to the god of storms,
  The lightning, and the gale!

The Last Leaf

I saw him once before,
As he passed by the door,
    And again
The pavement stones resound,
As he totters o'er the ground
    With his cane.

They say that in his prime,
Ere the pruning-knife of Time
    Cut him down,
Not a better man was found
By the Crier on his round
    Through the town.

But now he walks the streets,
And he looks at all he meets
    Sad and wan,
And he shakes his feeble head,
That it seems as if he said,
    "They are gone."

The mossy marbles rest
On the lips that he has prest
    In their bloom,
And the names he loved to hear

Have been carved for many a year
    On the tomb.

My grandmamma has said—
Poor old lady, she is dead
    Long ago—
That he had a Roman nose,
And his cheek was like a rose
    In the snow;

But now his nose is thin,
And it rests upon his chin
    Like a staff,
And a crook is in his back,
And a melancholy crack
    In his laugh.

I know it is a sin
For me to sit and grin
    At him here;
But the old three-cornered hat,
And the breeches, and all that,
    Are so queer!

And if I should live to be
The last leaf upon the tree
    In the spring,
Let them smile, as I do now,
At the old forsaken bough
    Where I cling.

The Deacon's Masterpiece; or, The Wonderful One-Hoss Shay

A Logical Story

Have you heard of the wonderful one-hoss shay,
That was built in such a logical way
It ran a hundred years to a day,
And then, of a sudden it—ah, but stay,
I'll tell you what happened without delay,
Scaring the parson into fits,

Frightening people out of their wits,—
Have you ever heard of that, I say?

Seventeen hundred and fifty-five.
Georgius Secundus was then alive,—
Snuffy old drone from the German hive.
That was the year when Lisbon-town
Saw the earth open and gulp her down,
And Braddock's army was done so brown,
Left without a scalp to its crown.
It was on the terrible Earthquake-day
That the Deacon finished the one-hoss shay.

Now in building of chaises, I tell you what,
There is always *somewhere* a weakest spot,—
In hub, tire, felloe, in spring or thill,
In panel, or crossbar, or floor, or sill,
In screw, bolt, thoroughbrace,—lurking still,
Find it somewhere you must and will,—
Above or below, or within or without,—
And that's the reason, beyond a doubt,
A chaise *breaks down*, but does n't *wear out*.

But the Deacon swore (as Deacons do,
With an "I dew vum," or an "I tell *yeou*")
He would build one shay to beat the taown
'n' the keounty 'n' all the kentry raoun';
It should be so built that it *couldn'* break daown:
—"Fur," said the Deacon, "'t's mighty plain
Thut the weakes' place mus' stan' the strain;
'n' the way t' fix it, uz I maintain,
          Is only jest
T' make that place uz strong uz the rest."

So the Deacon inquired of the village folk
Where he could find the strongest oak,
That could n't be split nor bent nor broke,—
That was for spokes and floor and sills;
He sent for lancewood to make the thills;
The crossbars were ash, from the straightest trees;
The panels of white-wood, that cuts like cheese,
But lasts like iron for things like these;
The hubs of logs from the "Settler's ellum,"—
Last of its timber,—they could n't sell 'em,
Never an axe had seen their chips,

And the wedges flew from between their lips,
Their blunt ends frizzled like celery-tips;
Step and prop-iron, bolt and screw,
Spring, tire, axle, and linchpin too,
Steel of the finest, bright and blue;
Thoroughbrace bison-skin, thick and wide;
Boot, top, dasher, from tough old hide
Found in the pit when the tanner died.
That was the way he "put her through."—
"There!" said the Deacon, "naow she'll dew!"

Do! I tell you, I rather guess
She was a wonder, and nothing less!
Colts grew horses, beards turned gray,
Deacon and deaconess dropped away.
Children and grandchildren—where were they?
But there stood the stout old one-hoss shay
As fresh as on Lisbon-earthquake day!

EIGHTEEN HUNDRED;—it came and found
The Deacon's masterpiece strong and sound
Eighteen hundred increased by ten;—
"Hahnsum kerridge" they called it then.
Eighteen hundred and twenty came;
Running as usual; much the same.
Thirty and forty at last arrive,
And then come fifty and FIFTY-FIVE.

Little of all we value here
Wakes on the morn of its hundredth year
Without both feeling and looking queer.
In fact, there's nothing that keeps its youth,
So far as I know, but a tree and truth.
(This is a moral that runs at large;
Take it. You're welcome. No extra charge.)

FIRST OF NOVEMBER,—the Earthquake-day.—
There are traces of age in the one-hoss shay,
A general flavor of mild decay,
But nothing local as one may say.
There could n't be,—for the Deacon's art
Had made it so like in every part
That there was n't a chance for one to start.
For the wheels were just as strong as the thills,
And the floor was just as strong as the sills,

And the panels just as strong as the floor,
And the whippletree neither less nor more,
And the back-crossbar as strong as the fore,
And spring and axle and hub *encore.*
And yet, *as a whole,* it is past a doubt
In another hour it will be *worn out!*

First of November, Fifty-five!
This morning the parson takes a drive.
Now, small boys, get out of the way!
Here comes the wonderful one-hoss shay,
Drawn by a rat-tailed, ewe-necked bay.
"Huddup!" said the parson.—Off went they.

The parson was working his Sunday's text,—
Had got to *fifthly,* and stopped perplexed
At what the—Moses—was coming next.
All at once the horse stood still,
Close by the meet'n'-house on the hill.
—First a shiver, and then a thrill,
Then something decidedly like a spill,—
And the parson was sitting upon a rock,
At half past nine by the meet'n'-house clock,—
Just the hour of the Earthquake shock!
—What do you think the parson found,
When he got up and stared around?
The poor old chaise in a heap or mound,
As if it had been to the mill and ground!
You see, of course, if you're not a dunce,
How it went to pieces all at once,—
All at once, and nothing first,—
Just as bubbles do when they burst.

End of the wonderful one-hoss shay.
Logic is logic. That's all I say.

THOMAS HOOD
(1799–1845)

HOOD EDITED several London magazines, including his own *Hood's Magazine,* and was an enormously popular author of both serious and comic verse. A lifelong sufferer of tuberculosis, Hood suggested that his epitaph be: "Here lies one who spat more blood and made more puns than any man living." Actually it reads: "He sang the song of the shirt."

"The Song of the Shirt" was first published anonymously in the Christmas issue of *Punch*, 1843. It and Elizabeth Barrett Browning's "The Cry of the Children" were England's two most influential verse protests against the sweatshops spawned by the Industrial Revolution. Various composers wrote music for Hood's song, which became so popular that drapers sold handkerchiefs with the words printed on them. The penultimate stanza of "The Song of the Shirt" was not in the poem's first publication.

"The Bridge of Sighs" is England's prize specimen of a poem, common in those days, about the death of a beautiful prostitute. (In the U.S. the most popular of such poems was John Watson's "Beautiful Snow," not included here because nobody now remembers it.) Hood took the name of his bridge from Venice's Bridge of Sighs, along which convicted criminals walked from the palace to the prison. The actual bridge that Hood had in mind is said to have been Waterloo Bridge over the Thames in London. It was a toll-free bridge often used by suicides.

The Song of the Shirt

With fingers weary and worn,
    With eyelids heavy and red,
A Woman sat, in unwomanly rags,
    Plying her needle and thread—
        Stitch! stitch! stitch!
In poverty, hunger, and dirt,
    And still with a voice of dolorous pitch
She sang the 'Song of the Shirt!'

'Work! work! work!
While the cock is crowing aloof!
    And work—work—work,
Till the stars shine through the roof!
It's O! to be a slave
    Along with the barbarous Turk,
Where woman has never a soul to save,
    If this is Christian work!

'Work—work—work
Till the brain begins to swim,
    Work—work—work
Till the eyes are heavy and dim!
Seam, and gusset, and band,
    Band, and gusset, and seam,

Till over the buttons I fall asleep,
    And sew them on in a dream!

'O, Men with Sisters dear!
    O, Men! with Mothers and Wives!
It is not linen you're wearing out,
    But human creatures' lives!
        Stitch—stitch—stitch,
    In poverty, hunger, and dirt,
Sewing at once, with a double thread,
    A Shroud as well as a Shirt.

'But why do I talk of Death?
    That Phantom of grisly bone,
I hardly fear his terrible shape,
    It seems so like my own—
    It seems so like my own,
        Because of the fasts I keep;
O God! that bread should be so dear,
    And flesh and blood so cheap!

'Work—work—work!
    My labour never flags;
And what are its wages? A bed of straw,
    A crust of bread—and rags.
That shatter'd roof,—and this naked floor—
    A table—a broken chair—
And a wall so blank, my shadow I thank
    For sometimes falling there!

'Work—work—work!
From weary chime to chime,
    Work—work—work
As prisoners work for crime!
    Band, and gusset, and seam,
    Seam, and gusset, and band,
Till the heart is sick, and the brain benumb'd,
    As well as the weary hand.

'Work—work—work,
In the dull December light,
    And work—work—work,
When the weather is warm and bright—
While underneath the eaves
    The brooding swallows cling,

As if to show me their sunny backs
    And twit me with the spring.

'O, but to breathe the breath
Of the cowslip and primrose sweet!—
    With the sky above my head,
And the grass beneath my feet;
For only one short hour
    To feel as I used to feel,
Before I knew the woes of want
    And the walk that costs a meal!

'O, but for one short hour!
    A respite however brief!
No blessed leisure for Love or Hope,
    But only time for Grief!
A little weeping would ease my heart,
    But in their briny bed
My tears must stop, for every drop
    Hinders needle and thread!

'Seam, and gusset, and band,
Band, and gusset, and seam,
    Work, work, work,
Like the Engine that works by Steam!
A mere machine of iron and wood
    That toils for Mammon's sake—
Without a brain to ponder and craze
    Or a heart to feel—and break!'

—With fingers weary and worn,
    With eyelids heavy and red,
A Woman sat, in unwomanly rags,
    Plying her needle and thread—
        Stitch! stitch! stitch!
    In poverty, hunger and dirt,
And still with a voice of dolorous pitch,—
Would that its tone could reach the Rich!—
    She sang this 'Song of the Shirt!'

The Bridge of Sighs

One more Unfortunate,
    Weary of breath,

Rashly importunate,
  Gone to her death!

Take her up tenderly,
  Lift her with care;
Fashion'd so slenderly,
  Young, and so fair!

Look at her garments
Clinging like cerements;
Whilst the wave constantly
  Drips from her clothing;
Take her up instantly,
  Loving, not loathing.

Touch her not scornfully;
Think of her mournfully,
  Gently and humanly;
Not of the stains of her,
All that remains of her
  Now is pure womanly.

Make no deep scrutiny
Into her mutiny
  Rash and undutiful:
Past all dishonour,
Death has left on her
  Only the beautiful.

Still, for all slips of hers,
  One of Eve's family—
Wipe those poor lips of hers
  Oozing so clammily.

Loop up her tresses
  Escaped from the comb,
Her fair auburn tresses;
Whilst wonderment guesses
  Where was her home?

Who was her father?
  Who was her mother?
Had she a sister?
  Had she a brother?
Or was there a dearer one

Still, and a nearer one
   Yet, than all other?

Alas! for the rarity
Of Christian charity
   Under the sun!
O, it was pitiful!
Near a whole city full,
   Home she had none.

Sisterly, brotherly,
Fatherly, motherly
   Feelings had changed:
Love, by harsh evidence,
Thrown from its eminence;
Even God's providence
   Seeming estranged.

Where the lamps quiver
So far in the river,
   With many a light
From window and casement,
From garret to basement,
She stood, with amazement,
   Houseless by night.

The bleak wind of March
   Made her tremble and shiver;
But not the dark arch,
Or the black flowing river:
Mad from life's history,
Glad to death's mystery,
   Swift to be hurl'd—
Anywhere, anywhere
   Out of the world!

In she plunged boldly—
No matter how coldly
   The rough river ran—
Over the brink of it,
Picture it—think of it,
   Dissolute Man!
Lave in it, drink of it,
   Then, if you can!

Take her up tenderly,
　　Lift her with care;
Fashion'd so slenderly,
　　Young, and so fair!

Ere her limbs frigidly
Stiffen too rigidly,
　　Decently, kindly,
Smooth and compose them;
And her eyes, close them,
　　Staring so blindly!

Dreadfully staring
　　Thro' muddy impurity,
As when with the daring
Last look of despairing
　　Fix'd on futurity.

Perishing gloomily,
Spurr'd by contumely,
Cold inhumanity,
Burning insanity,
　　Into her rest.—
Cross her hands humbly
As if praying dumbly,
　　Over her breast!

Owning her weakness,
　　Her evil behaviour,
And leaving, with meekness,
　　Her sins to her Saviour!

RICHARD HOVEY
(1864–1900)

WE MENTIONED earlier that Hovey collaborated with his friend Bliss Carman
on several collections of verse with "vagabondia" in the title. Born in Normal,
Illinois, and a Dartmouth graduate, Hovey was sixteen when his first book of
poetry was published. After abandoning plans to become an Episcopalian
minister, he tried his hand at newspaper reporting and acting. For a while he
lived abroad with Maurice Maeterlinck, the Belgian author whose works he

translated. In later years, after his marriage, he taught English literature at
Columbia University and its affiliate, Barnard College.

"The Sea Gypsy" is the only one of Hovey's poems remembered today.

The Sea Gypsy

I am fevered with the sunset,
I am fretful with the bay,
For the wander-thirst is on me
And my soul is in Cathay.

There's a schooner in the offing,
With her topsails shot with fire,
And my heart has gone aboard her
For the Islands of Desire.

I must forth again to-morrow!
With the sunset I must be
Hull down on the trail of rapture
In the wonder of the sea.

JULIA WARD HOWE
(1819–1910)

Mrs. Howe was one of America's most remarkable women: beautiful,
intelligent and tirelessly active as an abolitionist, suffragette and foe of
conservative Christianity. She wrote a biography of Margaret Fuller, a play
about a fallen woman, books on social reform and several volumes of verse.
With her physician husband she edited the Boston *Commonwealth*, an antislavery newspaper. The writer Laura Richards was her daughter. In 1987 the
Post Office honored her with a fourteen-cent stamp.

The "Battle Hymn of the Republic," one of the brightest gems of American
poetry, was first published anonymously in the *Atlantic Monthly* (February
1862). Mrs. Howe was paid four dollars for it. For some time she had wanted
to write lines that could be sung to the stirring tune of "John Brown's Body."
Here is how she described the poem's genesis:

> I awoke in the gray of the morning twilight; and as I lay waiting for
> the dawn, the long lines of the desired poem began to twine
> themselves in my mind. Having thought out all the stanzas, I said to
> myself, "I must get up and write these verses down, lest I fall asleep
> again and forget them." So, with a sudden effort, I sprang out of bed,

and found in the dimness an old stump of a pen which I remembered
to have used the day before. I scrawled the verses almost without
looking at the paper. . . . Having completed my writing I returned to
bed and fell asleep, saying to myself, "I like this better than most
things I have written."

The song was soon being belted out by marching regiments all over the
North. Fundamentalists who sing the song today imagine that the first stanza
refers literally to the Second Coming of Christ. But Julia was a nonordained
Unitarian minister for whom the Second Coming symbolized the world's
gradual progress toward peace and justice. She saw the Civil War as a great
battle in which God was trampling the serpent of slavery as a necessary step
in humanity's slow movement toward a better world. The poem is saturated
with Biblical phrases, all of which Mrs. Howe treats metaphorically.

The poem originally had a sixth stanza:

> He is coming like the glory of the morning on the wave,
> He is wisdom to the mighty, he is honor to the brave,
> So the world shall be his footstool, and the soul of wrong his slave,
>   Our God is marching on!

which Mrs. Howe wisely decided to omit. The song was a great favorite of
Lincoln's, who once wept when he heard it sung. It was sung at his funeral,
and also at the funerals of Herbert Hoover, Winston Churchill and Robert
Kennedy, and at Mrs. Howe's own funeral.

"The Hymn of the Battered Republic," a parody by our country's top writer
of comic verse, Frank Jacobs, appeared in *Mad* magazine (March 1991). Here
is the first of its six stanzas:

> Our eyes have seen the sorrow of a nation gone to pot,
> Where the loonies carry handguns and the passersby get shot,
> Where the farms are going under and the cities burn and rot—
>   The Glory Days are gone!
>
> Lordy, Lordy, how'd we do . . it?
> Now . . we have to suffer through . . it!
> Had . . our chance but really blew . . it!
>   The Glory Days are gone!

My footnotes to Julia's poem indicate where she made major changes before
she sent the poem to the *Atlantic Monthly*.

Battle Hymn of the Republic

Mine eyes have seen the glory of the coming of the Lord;
He is trampling out the vintage[1] where the grapes of wrath
    are stored!
He hath loosed the fateful lightning of his terrible swift sword;
    His truth is marching on.

I have seen Him in the watch-fires of a hundred circling
    camps;
They have builded Him an altar in the evening dews and
    damps;
I have read his righteous sentence by the dim and flaring
    lamps:
        His day is marching on.

I have read a fiery gospel writ in burnished rows of steel:
"As ye deal with my contemners, so with you my grace shall
    deal:
Let the Hero, born of woman, crush the serpent with his heel,
        Since God is marching on."

He has sounded forth the trumpet that shall never call retreat;
He is sifting out the hearts of men before his judgment-seat;[2]
Oh, be swift, my soul, to answer Him! be jubilant, my feet!
        Our God is marching on.

In the beauty[3] of the lilies Christ was born across the sea,
With a glory in his bosom that transfigures[4] you and me:
As he died to make men holy, let us die to make men free,
        While God is marching on.

---

[1] Originally "wine-press."
[2] Originally "He has waked the earth's dull sorrow with a high ecstatic beat."
[3] Originally "whiteness."
[4] Originally "shines out on."

LEIGH HUNT
(1784–1859)

HUNT WAS a London journalist—he edited a series of one-man periodicals—essayist, poet and political radical who crusaded for the abolition of slavery and child labor. An attack on the Prince Regent landed him and his brother in prison for two years. Hunt filled his cell with flowers, continued editing and was visited by Byron, Shelley and other poets. Dickens is said to have caricatured Hunt as Harold Skimpole in *Bleak House*.

"Abou Ben Adhem" (published in 1874) is a translation of a French poem based on an Islamic legend about how Allah, on the night of a certain feast day, checks in a golden book on the names of those who love him.

Hunt's other most familiar poem is the short lyric "Jenny Kiss'd Me." During a flu epidemic, Thomas Carlyle and his wife Jenny heard that Hunt

had been ill for weeks, and feared he might die. When Hunt recovered, he
called unexpectedly on the Carlyles. Mrs. Carlyle was so pleased to see him
that she jumped up and kissed him, and Hunt was so pleased that he wrote
his famous lyric for the *Monthly Chronicle*. Paul Dehn parodied the poem by
altering its last two lines to: "Say I've had a filthy cold / Since Jenny kiss'd
me."

Abou Ben Adhem

Abou Ben Adhem (may his tribe increase!)
Awoke one night from a deep dream of peace,
And saw, within the moonlight in his room,
Making it rich, and like a lily in bloom,
An angel writing in a book of gold:—
Exceeding peace had made Ben Adhem bold,
And to the presence in the room he said,
    'What writest thou?'—The vision rais'd its head,
And with a look made of all sweet accord,
Answer'd, 'The names of those who love the Lord.'
    'And is mine one?' asked Abou. 'Nay, not so,'
Replied the angel. Abou spoke more low,
But cheerly still; and said, 'I pray thee, then,
Write me as one that loves his fellow men.'
    The angel wrote, and vanish'd. The next night
It came again with a great wakening light,
And show'd the names whom love of God had blest,
And lo! Ben Adhem's name led all the rest.

Jenny Kiss'd Me

Jenny kiss'd me when we met,
    Jumping from the chair she sat in;
Time, you thief, who love to get
    Sweets into your list, put that in!
Say I'm weary, say I'm sad,
    Say that health and wealth have miss'd me,
Say I'm growing old, but add,
    Jenny kiss'd me.

JOHN KEATS
(1795–1821)

BORN IN London, the son of a livery-stable keeper, Keats died of consumption at the age of twenty-five in Rome, where he had gone to spend a winter in Shelley's villa. Keats had been introduced to Shelley by Leigh Hunt, and it was Shelley who helped Keats publish his first book of poetry in 1817.

Keats's life was not prolonged by the Italian doctor who bled him and kept him on a daily diet of one anchovy and one slice of bread. The poet requested that his tombstone bear the epitaph: "Here lies one whose name was writ in water." Shelley's "Adonais" was an elegy on the death of his friend. Never before or since has a poet accomplished so much in so short a time.

The three longer poems included here were all composed in 1819. Although Keats is now considered among the greatest of England's Romantic poets, his work was savagely attacked by many contemporary writers. Carlyle dismissed it as betraying a "weak-eyed maudlin sensibility." Byron, whose tastes in poetry were even more bizarre (or was it jealousy?), called Keats's verse "piss-a-bed poetry."

The sonnet on George Chapman's poor translation of Homer, written when Keats was twenty-one, was first printed in *The Examiner* (December 1, 1816) by its editor, Leigh Hunt, who had become the young poet's mentor. It was Balboa, not Cortez, who discovered the Pacific, but who cares? Cortez's "eagle eyes" were "wond'ring eyes" in the first version of the poem.

"La Belle Dame sans Merci" was first printed by Hunt in his magazine *The Indicator* (May 10, 1820). A second and superior version is the one given here. Asked why he had the knight kiss the eyelids of the lady four times, Keats replied in a letter:

> I was obliged to choose an even number that both eyes might have fair play. . . . Suppose I had said seven; there would have been three and a half a piece—a very awkward affair.

Robert Service proposed a rival theory:

> Them poets have their little tricks;
> I think John counted kisses four,
> Not two or three or five or six
>   *To rhyme with "sore."*

No one thought more highly of Keats than Service. His poem "Casino Calypso" tells of how, while visiting a famous gambling casino, he scorned the tables to read Keats in a corner of the kitchen:

> Your little book of limp green leather
> I sadly fear that I profane,
> Because we two are linked together
> In this rococo hall of gain;
> That I a piddling poetaster,
> A nuzzler of the muse's teats,

Should in this *milieu* con the Master—
Forgive me, Keats.

An enormous literature has debated the meaning of the last two lines of Keats's "Ode on a Grecian Urn." T. S. Eliot found them "meaningless" and "a serious blot on a beautiful poem." John Simon opened a movie review with: "One of the greatest problems of art—perhaps the greatest—is that truth is not beauty, beauty not truth. Nor is that all we need to know."

F. Scott Fitzgerald's *Tender Is the Night* takes its title, as do many other novels, from "Ode to a Nightingale." G. K. Chesterton called the last two lines of the penultimate stanza of the poem "the most potent piece of pure magic in English literature."

On First Looking into Chapman's Homer

Much have I travell'd in the realms of gold,
  And many goodly states and kingdoms seen;
  Round many western islands have I been
Which bards in fealty to Apollo hold.
Oft of one wide expanse had I been told
  That deep-brow'd Homer ruled as his demesne;
  Yet did I never breathe its pure serene
Till I heard Chapman speak out loud and bold:
Then felt I like some watcher of the skies
  When a new planet swims into his ken;
Or like stout Cortez when with eagle eyes
  He star'd at the Pacific—and all his men
Look'd at each other with a wild surmise—
  Silent, upon a peak in Darien.

La Belle Dame sans Merci

A Ballad

I

O, what can ail thee, knight-at-arms,
  Alone and palely loitering?
The sedge has wither'd from the lake,
  And no birds sing.

II

O, what can ail thee, knight-at-arms,
    So haggard and so woe-begone?
The squirrel's granary is full,
    And the harvest's done.

III

I see a lilly on thy brow,
    With anguish moist and fever dew;
And on thy cheeks a fading rose
    Fast withereth too.

IV

I met a lady in the meads,
    Full beautiful—a faery's child,
Her hair was long, her foot was light,
    And her eyes were wild.

V

I made a garland for her head,
    And bracelets too, and fragrant zone;
She look'd at me as she did love,
    And made sweet moan.

VI

I set her on my pacing steed,
    And nothing else saw all day long;
For sidelong would she bend, and sing
    A faery's song.

VII

She found me roots of relish sweet,
    And honey wild, and manna dew,
And sure in language strange she said—
    'I love thee true'.

VIII

She took me to her elfin grot,
    And there she wept and sigh'd full sore,
And there I shut her wild wild eyes
    With kisses four.

IX

And there she lulled me asleep
  And there I dream'd—Ah! woe betide!
The latest dream I ever dream'd
  On the cold hill side.

X

I saw pale kings and princes too,
  Pale warriors, death-pale were they all;
They cried—'La Belle Dame sans Merci
  Hath thee in thrall!'

XI

I saw their starved lips in the gloam,
  With horrid warning gaped wide,
And I awoke and found me here,
  On the cold hill's side.

XII

And this is why I sojourn here
  Alone and palely loitering,
Though the sedge has wither'd from the lake,
  And no birds sing.

Ode on a Grecian Urn

I

Thou still unravish'd bride of quietness,
  Thou foster-child of silence and slow time,
Sylvan historian, who canst thus express
  A flowery tale more sweetly than our rhyme:
What leaf-fring'd legend haunts about thy shape
  Of deities or mortals, or of both,
    In Tempe or the dales of Arcady?
  What men or gods are these? What maidens loth?
What mad pursuit? What struggle to escape?
    What pipes and timbrels? What wild ecstasy?

II

Heard melodies are sweet, but those unheard
    Are sweeter; therefore, ye soft pipes, play on;
Not to the sensual ear, but, more endear'd,
    Pipe to the spirit ditties of no tone:
Fair youth, beneath the trees, thou canst not leave
    Thy song, nor ever can those trees be bare;
        Bold Lover, never, never canst thou kiss,
Though winning near the goal—yet, do not grieve;
    She cannot fade, though thou hast not thy bliss,
        For ever wilt thou love, and she be fair!

III

Ah, happy, happy boughs! that cannot shed
    Your leaves, nor ever bid the Spring adieu;
And, happy melodist, unwearied,
    For ever piping songs for ever new;
More happy love! more happy, happy love!
    For ever warm and still to be enjoy'd,
        For ever panting, and for ever young;
All breathing human passion far above,
    That leaves a heart high-sorrowful and cloy'd,
        A burning forehead, and a parching tongue.

IV

Who are these coming to the sacrifice?
    To what green altar, O mysterious priest,
Lead'st thou that heifer lowing at the skies,
    And all her silken flanks with garlands drest?
What little town by river or sea shore,
    Or mountain-built with peaceful citadel,
        Is emptied of this folk, this pious morn?
And, little town, thy streets for evermore
    Will silent be; and not a soul to tell
        Why thou art desolate, can e'er return.

V

O Attic shape! Fair attitude! with brede
    Of marble men and maidens overwrought,
With forest branches and the trodden weed;
    Thou, silent form, dost tease us out of thought
As doth eternity: Cold Pastoral!

When old age shall this generation waste,
    Thou shalt remain, in midst of other woe
Than ours, a friend to man, to whom thou say'st,
    'Beauty is truth, truth beauty,'—that is all
        Ye know on earth, and all ye need to know.

Ode to a Nightingale

I

My heart aches, and a drowsy numbness pains
    My sense, as though of hemlock I had drunk,
Or emptied some dull opiate to the drains
    One minute past, and Lethe-wards had sunk:
'Tis not through envy of thy happy lot,
    But being too happy in thine happiness,—
        That thou, light-winged Dryad of the trees,
            In some melodious plot
        Of beechen green, and shadows numberless,
            Singest of summer in full-throated ease.

II

O, for a draught of vintage! that hath been
    Cool'd a long age in the deep-delved earth,
Tasting of Flora and the country green,
    Dance, and Provençal song, and sunburnt mirth!
O for a beaker full of the warm South,
    Full of the true, the blushful Hippocrene,
        With beaded bubbles winking at the brim,
            And purple-stained mouth;
        That I might drink, and leave the world unseen,
            And with thee fade away into the forest dim:

III

Fade far away, dissolve, and quite forget
    What thou among the leaves hast never known,
The weariness, the fever, and the fret
    Here, where men sit and hear each other groan;
Where palsy shakes a few, sad, last gray hairs,
    Where youth grows pale, and spectre-thin, and dies;
        Where but to think is to be full of sorrow

And leaden-eyed despairs,
  Where Beauty cannot keep her lustrous eyes,
    Or new Love pine at them beyond to-morrow.

IV

Away! away! for I will fly to thee,
  Not charioted by Bacchus and his pards,
But on the viewless wings of Poesy,
  Though the dull brain perplexes and retards:
Already with thee! tender is the night,
  And haply the Queen-Moon is on her throne,
    Cluster'd around by all her starry Fays;
      But here there is no light,
  Save what from heaven is with the breezes blown
    Through verdurous glooms and winding mossy ways.

V

I cannot see what flowers are at my feet,
  Nor what soft incense hangs upon the boughs,
But, in embalmed darkness, guess each sweet
  Wherewith the seasonable month endows
The grass, the thicket, and the fruit-tree wild;
  White hawthorn, and the pastoral eglantine;
    Fast fading violets cover'd up in leaves;
      And mid-May's eldest child,
  The coming musk-rose, full of dewy wine,
    The murmurous haunts of flies on summer eves.

VI

Darkling I listen; and, for many a time
  I have been half in love with easeful Death,
Call'd him soft names in many a mused rhyme,
  To take into the air my quiet breath;
Now more than ever seems it rich to die,
  To cease upon the midnight with no pain,
    While thou art pouring forth thy soul abroad
      In such an ecstasy!
  Still wouldst thou sing, and I have ears in vain—
    To thy high requiem become a sod.

VII

Thou wast not born for death, immortal Bird!
  No hungry generations tread thee down;

The voice I hear this passing night was heard
In ancient days by emperor and clown:
Perhaps the self-same song that found a path
Through the sad heart of Ruth, when, sick for home,
She stood in tears amid the alien corn;
The same that oft-times hath
Charm'd magic casements, opening on the foam
Of perilous seas, in faery lands forlorn.

VIII

Forlorn! the very word is like a bell
To toll me back from thee to my sole self!
Adieu! the fancy cannot cheat so well
As she is fam'd to do, deceiving elf.
Adieu! adieu! thy plaintive anthem fades
Past the near meadows, over the still stream,
Up the hill-side; and now 'tis buried deep
In the next valley-glades:
Was it a vision, or a waking dream?
Fled is that music:—Do I wake or sleep?

JOYCE KILMER
(1886–1918)

SERGEANT KILMER, born in New Brunswick, New Jersey, and a Columbia graduate, died under German gunfire on July 30, 1918, in the second Battle of the Marne. France awarded him a posthumous *Croix de Guerre*.

Kilmer's best-remembered poem, "Trees," first appeared in *Poetry* magazine (August 1913), when he was on the staff of *The New York Times Review of Books*. He received six dollars for the poem, later reprinted in his second book of verse, *Trees and Other Poems* (1914).

Critics continue to ridicule "Trees" for its mixed metaphors—how, for example, can a tree press its mouth to the earth and at the same time lift leafy arms to pray? Yet somehow the poem has a spare, crystalline quality. A convert to Roman Catholicism, Kilmer edited an anthology of Catholic verse and also a collection of poems by the Catholic writer Hilaire Belloc. Perhaps it is his poem's final reference to God that accounts for its continued popularity outside academia.

"Trees" was first set to music by Kilmer's mother, Annie, and later by Phyllis Fergus, Oscar Rasbach and others. There was a notable recording of the song by the opera star Madame Ernestine Schumann-Heink. A white oak on the Rutgers University campus (Kilmer attended Rutgers for several years) was said to have inspired the poem. In 1986, on the centennial of Kilmer's birth, a new white oak was planted to replace the old one that had died twenty-five years earlier.

Trees

I think that I shall never see
A poem lovely as a tree.

A tree whose hungry mouth is prest
Against the earth's sweet flowing breast;

A tree that looks at God all day,
And lifts her leafy arms to pray;

A tree that may in Summer wear
A nest of robins in her hair;

Upon whose bosom snow has lain;
Who intimately lives with rain.

Poems are made by fools like me,
But only God can make a tree.

RUDYARD KIPLING
(1865–1936)

NOVELIST, POET, short-story writer, antifeminist and militant Tory jingoist, Kipling was one of England's most widely read authors. Most critics, however, paid scant attention to his poetry until T. S. Eliot startled them by editing *A Choice of Kipling's Verse* (1941). Born in Bombay, India, Kipling was taken at the age of six to England where he lived most of his life although for several years he resided in Brattleboro, Vermont, on the estate of his American wife, Caroline Balestier. He accepted the Nobel Prize for Literature in 1907, but refused to be Poet Laureate after Tennyson's death in 1892. Henry James called Kipling "the most complete man of genius . . . I have ever known."

"Recessional," a hymn to be sung at the end of a church service, was written in 1897 to commemorate the 60th anniversary of Queen Victoria's reign. It was set to music by Reginald De Koven and others. "Mandalay" was beautifully set to music by the New York City composer and baritone Oley Speaks. Walter Damrosch wrote the tune for "Danny Deever." The first line of "Mandalay" contains a whopping mistake. Moulmein is on the west coast of Burma where it cannot look eastward to the sea. It looks westward to the Bay of Bengal. The dawn may come up from China, but not across any water. In his autobiographical *Something of Myself*, Kipling describes the song as "a sort of general mix-up of the singer's Far-Eastern memories against a background of the Bay of Bengal as seen at dawn from a troop-ship taking him there."

I suspect that more than any other poem, "If—" has been framed to hang on office walls to inspire businessmen. In recent years I have seen framed mottos that say: "If you can keep your head when all about you are losing theirs, then you don't understand the situation." "If—" has been parodied more often than any other Kipling poem. I have seen framed in antique stores an "If for Girls," by the American writer J. P. McEvoy, but I do not know when or where it was published. Frank Jacobs, in his *Mad for Better or Verse* (1968), has an amusing parody that begins:

> If you can change a tire on the thruway,
>   While stranded in the busy center lane;
> If you can find a foolproof, tried-and-true way
>   To housebreak an impossible Great Dane;

Every time England or America goes to war, some politician is sure to recite the refrain from "Tommy": "O it's Tommy this, an' Tommy that, an' 'Tommy, go away'; / But it's 'Thank you, Mister Atkins,' when the band begins to play."

Cary Grant played the soldier in a motion picture based on "Gunga Din," with a skin-dyed Sam Jaffe in the role of Din.

Recessional

God of our fathers, known of old,
  Lord of our far-flung battle-line,
Beneath whose awful Hand we hold
  Dominion over palm and pine—
Lord God of Hosts, be with us yet,
Lest we forget—lest we forget!

The tumult and the shouting dies;
  The Captains and the Kings depart:
Still stands Thine ancient sacrifice,
  An humble and a contrite heart.
Lord God of Hosts, be with us yet,
Lest we forget—lest we forget!

Far-called, our navies melt away;
  On dune and headland sinks the fire:
Lo, all our pomp of yesterday

Is one with Nineveh and Tyre!
Judge of the Nations, spare us yet,
Lest we forget—lest we forget!

If, drunk with sight of power, we loose
    Wild tongues that have not Thee in awe,
Such boastings as the Gentiles use,
    Or lesser breeds without the Law—
Lord God of Hosts, be with us yet,
Lest we forget—lest we forget!

For heathen heart that puts her trust
    In reeking tube and iron shard,
All valiant dust that builds on dust,
    And guarding, calls not Thee to guard,
For frantic boast and foolish word—
Thy mercy on Thy People, Lord!

                                        Amen.

Mandalay

By the old Moulmein Pagoda, lookin' eastward to the sea,
There's a Burma girl a-settin', and I know she thinks o' me;
For the wind is in the palm-trees, and the temple-bells they
    say:
'Come you back, you British soldier; come you back to
    Mandalay!'

    Come you back to Mandalay,
    Where the old Flotilla lay:
    Can't you 'ear their paddles chunkin' from Rangoon to
        Mandalay?
    On the road to Mandalay,
    Where the flyin'-fishes play,
    An' the dawn comes up like thunder outer China 'crost
        the Bay!

'Er petticoat was yaller an' 'er little cap was green,
An' 'er name was Supi-yaw-lat—jes' the same as Theebaw's[1]
    Queen,
An' I seed her first a-smokin' of a whackin' white cheroot,
An' a-wastin' Christian kisses on an 'eathen idol's foot:

Bloomin' idol made o' mud—
What they called the Great Gawd Budd—
Plucky lot she cared for idols when I kissed 'er where she
    stud!
On the road to Mandalay, etc.

When the mist was on the rice-fields an' the sun was droppin'
    slow,
She'd git 'er little banjo an' she'd sing '*Kulla-lo-lo!*'
With 'er arm upon my shoulder an' 'er cheek agin my cheek
We useter watch the steamers an' the *hathis*[2] pilin' teak.

Elephints a-pilin' teak
In the sludgy, squdgy creek,
Where the silence 'ung that 'eavy you was 'arf afraid to
    speak!
On the road to Mandalay, etc.

But that's all shove be'ind me—long ago an' fur away,
An' there ain't no 'busses runnin' from the Bank to Mandalay;
An' I'm learnin' 'ere in London what the ten-year soldier
    tells:
'If you've 'eard the East a-callin', you won't never 'eed naught
    else.'

No! you won't 'eed nothin' else
But them spicy garlic smells,
An' the sunshine an' the palm-trees an' the tinkly temple-
    bells;
On the road to Mandalay, etc.

I am sick o' wastin' leather on these gritty pavin'-stones,
An' the blasted Henglish drizzle wakes the fever in my bones;
Tho' I walks with fifty 'ousemaids outer Chelsea to the Strand,
An' they talks a lot o' lovin', but wot do they understand?

Beefy face an' grubby 'and—
Law! wot do they understand?
I've a neater, sweeter maiden in a cleaner, greener land!
On the road to Mandalay, etc.

Ship me somewheres east of Suez, where the best is like the
    worst,
Where there aren't no Ten Commandments an' a man can
    raise a thirst;

For the temple-bells are callin', and it's there that I would
  be—
By the old Moulmein Pagoda, looking lazy at the sea;

> On the road to Mandalay,
> Where the old Flotilla lay,
> With our sick beneath the awnings when we went to
>   Mandalay!
> Oh the road to Mandalay,
> Where the flyin'-fishes play,
> An' the dawn comes up like thunder outer China 'crost
>   the Bay!

---

[1] *Theebaw*] Thibau, a Burmese king from 1878 to 1885, conquered by the
British.
[2] *hathis*] elephants.

Danny Deever

'What are the bugles blown' for?' said Files-on-Parade.
'To turn you out, to turn you out,' the Colour-Sergeant said.
'What makes you look so white, so white?' said Files-on-
  Parade.
'I'm dreadin' what I've got to watch,' the Colour-Sergeant
  said.

> For they're hangin' Danny Deever, you can hear the
>   Dead March play,
> The regiment's in 'ollow square—they're hangin' him to-
>   day;
> They've taken of his buttons off an' cut his stripes away,
> An' they're hangin' Danny Deever in the mornin'.

'What makes the rear-rank breathe so 'ard?' said Files-on-
  Parade.
'It's bitter cold, it's bitter cold,' the Colour-Sergeant said.
'What makes that front-rank man fall down?' says Files-on-
  Parade.
'A touch o' sun, a touch o' sun,' the Colour-Sergeant said.

> They are hangin' Danny Deever, they are marchin' of
>   'im round,

They 'ave 'alted Danny Deever by 'is coffin on the
    ground;
An' 'e'll swing in 'arf a minute for a sneakin' shootin'
    hound—
O they're hangin' Danny Deever in the mornin'!

''Is cot was right-'and cot to mine,' said Files-on-Parade.
''E's sleepin' out an' far to-night,' the Colour-Sergeant said.
'I've drunk 'is beer a score o' times,' said Files-on-Parade.
''E's drinkin' bitter beer alone,' the Colour-Sergeant said.

They are hangin' Danny Deever, you must mark 'im to
    'is place,
For 'e shot a comrade sleepin'—you must look 'im in the
    face;
Nine 'undred of 'is county an' the regiment's disgrace,
While they're hangin' Danny Deever in the mornin'.

'What's that so black agin the sun?' said Files-on-Parade.
'It's Danny fightin' 'ard for life,' the Colour-Sergeant said.
'What's that that whimpers over'ead?' said Files-on-Parade.
'It's Danny's soul that's passin' now,' the Colour-Sergeant
    said.

For they're done with Danny Deever, you can 'ear the
    quick-step play,
The regiment's in column, an' they're marchin' us away;
Ho! the young recruits are shakin', an' they'll want their
    beer to-day,
After hangin' Danny Deever in the mornin'.

If—

If you can keep your head when all about you
    Are losing theirs and blaming it on you,
If you can trust yourself when all men doubt you,
    But make allowance for their doubting too;
If you can wait and not be tired of waiting,
    Or being lied about, don't deal in lies,
Or being hated don't give way to hating,
    And yet don't look too good, nor talk too wise:

If you can dream—and not make dreams your master;
    If you can think—and not make thoughts your aim,
If you can meet with Triumph and Disaster
    And treat those two impostors just the same;
If you can bear to hear the truth you've spoken
    Twisted by knaves to make a trap for fools,
Or watch the things you gave your life to, broken,
    And stoop and build 'em up with worn-out tools:

If you can make one heap of all your winnings
    And risk it on one turn of pitch-and-toss,
And lose, and start again at your beginnings
    And never breathe a word about your loss;
If you can force your heart and nerve and sinew
    To serve your turn long after they are gone,
And so hold on when there is nothing in you
    Except the Will which says to them: 'Hold on!'

If you can talk with crowds and keep your virtue,
    Or walk with Kings—nor lose the common touch,
If neither foes nor loving friends can hurt you,
    If all men count with you, but none too much;
If you can fill the unforgiving minute
    With sixty seconds' worth of distance run,
Yours is the Earth and everything that's in it,
    And—which is more—you'll be a Man, my son!

Tommy

I went into a public-'ouse to get a pint o' beer,
The publican 'e up an' sez, 'We serve no red-coats here.'
The girls be'ind the bar they laughed an' giggled fit to die,
I outs into the street again an' to myself sez I:

    O it's Tommy this, an' Tommy that, an' 'Tommy, go
        away';
    But it's 'Thank you, Mister Atkins,' when the band
        begins to play,
    The band begins to play, my boys, the band begins to
        play.
    O it's 'Thank you, Mister Atkins,' when the band begins
        to play.

I went into a theatre as sober as could be,
They gave a drunk civilian room, but 'adn't none for me;
They sent me to the gallery or round the music-'alls,
But when it comes to fightin', Lord! they'll shove me in the
    stalls!

> For it's Tommy this, an' Tommy that, an' 'Tommy, wait
>   outside';
> But it's 'Special train for Atkins' when the trooper's on
>   the tide,
> The troopship's on the tide, my boys, the troopship's on
>   the tide,
> O it's 'Special train for Atkins' when the trooper's on the
>   tide.

Yes, makin' mock o' uniforms that guard you while you sleep
Is cheaper than them uniforms, an' they're starvation cheap;
An' hustlin' drunken soldiers when they're goin' large a bit
Is five times better business than paradin' in full kit.

> Then it's Tommy this, an' Tommy that, an 'Tommy,
>   'ow's yer soul?'
> But it's 'Thin red line of 'eroes' when the drums begin to
>   roll,
> The drums begin to roll, my boys, the drums begin to
>   roll,
> O it's 'Thin red line of 'eroes' when the drums begin to
>   roll.

We aren't no thin red 'eroes, nor we aren't no blackguards
    too,
But single men in barricks, most remarkable like you;
An' if sometimes our conduck isn't all your fancy paints:
Why, single men in barricks don't grow into plaster saints;

> While it's Tommy this, an' Tommy that, an' 'Tommy,
>   fall be'ind,'
> But it's 'Please to walk in front, sir,' when there's trouble
>   in the wind,
> There's trouble in the wind, my boys, there's trouble in
>   the wind,
> O it's 'Please to walk in front, sir,' when there's trouble
>   in the wind.

You talk o' better food for us, an' schools, an' fires, an' all:
We'll wait for extra rations if you treat us rational.

Don't mess about the cook-room slops, but prove it to our face
The Widow's Uniform is not the soldier-man's disgrace.

> For it's Tommy this, an' Tommy that, an' 'Chuck him out, the brute!'
> But it's 'Saviour of 'is country,' when the guns begin to shoot;
> Yes it's Tommy this, an' Tommy that, an' anything you please;
> But Tommy ain't a bloomin' fool—you bet that Tommy sees!

Boots

We're foot—slog—slog—slog—sloggin' over Africa—
Foot—foot—foot—foot—sloggin' over Africa—
(Boots—boots—boots—boots—movin' up an' down again!)
    There's no discharge in the war!

Seven—six—eleven—five—nine-an'-twenty mile to-day—
Four—eleven—seventeen—thirty-two the day before—
(Boots—boots—boots—boots—movin' up an' down again!)
    There's no discharge in the war!

Don't—don't—don't—don't—look at what's in front of you.
(Boots—boots—boots—boots—movin' up an' down again);
Men—men—men—men—men go mad with watchin' em,
    An' there's no discharge in the war!

Try—try—try—try—to think o' something different—
Oh—my—God—keep—me from goin' lunatic!
(Boots—boots—boots—boots—movin' up an' down again!)
    There's no discharge in the war!

Count—count—count—count—the bullets in the bandoliers.
If—your—eyes—drop—they will get atop o' you!
(Boots—boots—boots—boots—movin' up an' down again)—
    There's no discharge in the war!

We—can—stick—out—'unger, thirst, an' weariness,
But—not—not—not—not the chronic sight of 'em—

Boots—boots—boots—boots—movin' up an' down again,
    An' there's no discharge in the war!

'Tain't—so—bad—by—day because o' company,
But night—brings—long—strings—o' forty thousand million
Boots—boots—boots—boots—movin' up an' down again.
    There's no discharge in the war!

I—'ave—marched—six—weeks in 'Ell an' certify
It—is—not—fire—devils, dark, or anything,
But boots—boots—boots—boots—movin' up an' down
   again,
    An' there's no discharge in the war!

Gunga Din

You may talk o' gin and beer
When you're quartered safe out 'ere,
An' you're sent to penny-fights an' Aldershot[1] it;
But when it comes to slaughter
You will do your work on water,
An' you'll lick the bloomin' boots of 'im that's got it.
Now in Injia's sunny clime,
Where I used to spend my time
A-servin' of 'Er Majesty the Queen,
Of all them blackfaced crew
The finest man I knew
Was our regimental bhisti,[2] Gunga Din.
       He was 'Din! Din! Din!
       You limping lump o' brick-dust, Gunga Din!
       Hi! slippery hitherao!
       Water, get it! Panee lao![3]
       You squidgy-nosed old idol, Gunga Din.'

The uniform 'e wore
Was nothin' much before,
An' rather less than 'arf o' that be'ind,
For a piece o' twisty rag
An' a goatskin water-bag
Was all the field-equipment 'e could find.
When the sweatin' troop-train lay
In a sidin' through the day,

Where the 'eat would make your bloomin' eyebrows crawl,
We shouted 'Harry By!'[4]
Till our throats were bricky-dry,
Then we wopped 'im 'cause 'e couldn't serve us all.
  It was 'Din! Din! Din!
  You 'eathen, where the mischief 'ave you been?
  You put some juldee[5] in it
  Or I'll marrow[6] you this minute
  If you don't fill up my helmet, Gunga Din!

  'E would dot an' carry one
  Till the longest day was done;
An' 'e didn't seem to know the use o' fear.
  If we charged or broke or cut,
  You could bet your bloomin' nut,
'E'd be waitin' fifty paces right flank rear.
  With 'is mussick[7] on 'is back,
  'E would skip with our attack,
An' watch us till the bugles made 'Retire,'
  An' for all 'is dirty 'ide
  'E was white, clear white, inside
When 'e went to tend the wounded under fire!
  It was 'Din! Din! Din!'
 With the bullets kickin' dust-spots on the green.
  When the cartridges ran out,
  You could hear the front-files shout,
'Hi! ammunition-mules an' Gunga Din!'

  I sha'n't forgit the night
  When I dropped be'ind the fight
With a bullet where my belt-plate should 'a' been.
  I was chokin' mad with thirst,
  An' the man that spied me first
Was our good old grinnin', gruntin' Gunga Din.
  'E lifted up my 'ead,
  An' he plugged me where I bled,
An' 'e guv me 'arf-a-pint o' water-green:
  It was crawlin' and it stunk,
  But of all the drinks I've drunk,
I'm gratefullest to one from Gunga Din.
  It was 'Din! Din! Din!'
 'Ere's a beggar with a bullet through 'is spleen;
  'E's chawin' up the ground,

An' 'e's kickin' all around:
For Gawd's sake git the water, Gunga Din!

'E carried me away
To where a dooli[8] lay,
An' a bullet come an' drilled the beggar clean.
'E put me safe inside,
An' just before 'e died:
'I 'ope you liked your drink,' sez Gunga Din.
So I'll meet 'im later on
At the place where 'e is gone—
Where it's always double drill and no canteen;
'E'll be squattin' on the coals,
Givin' drink to poor damned souls,
An' I'll get a swig in hell from Gunga Din!
Yes, Din! Din! Din!
You Lazarushian-leather[9] Gunga Din!
Though I've belted you and flayed you,
By the living Gawd that made you,
You're a better man than I am, Gunga Din!

---

[1] *Aldershot*] military camp near London.
[2] *bhisti*] water carrier.
[3] *Panee lao*] Bring water quickly.
[4] *Harry By*] enlisted man's equivalent for 'O brother.'
[5] *juldee*] be quick.
[6] *marrow*] hit.
[7] *mussick*] water skin.
[8] *dooli*] stretcher.
[9] *Lazarushian-leather*] humorous combination of Lazarus and Russian leather.

L'Envoi

(To 'The Seven Seas')

When Earth's last picture is painted, and the tubes are twisted
    and dried,
When the oldest colours have faded, and the youngest critic
    has died,
We shall rest, and, faith, we shall need it—lie down for an
    æon or two,
Till the Master of All Good Workmen shall set us to work
    anew!

And those that were good shall be happy: they shall sit in a
golden chair;
They shall splash at a ten-league canvas with brushes of
comets' hair;
They shall find real saints to draw from—Magdalene, Peter,
and Paul,
They shall work for an age at a sitting and never be tired at
all!

And only the Master shall praise us, and only the Master
shall blame;
And no one shall work for money, and no one shall work for
fame;
But each for the joy of the working, and each, in his separate
star,
Shall draw the Thing as he sees It for the God of Things as
They Are!

EDWARD LEAR
(1812–1888)

EDWARD LEAR and Lewis Carroll were England's two finest Victorian writers
of nonsense verse. Although both were friends of the Tennysons, for some
reason they never met or even mentioned each other. By profession Lear was
a skillful painter of landscapes, animals and birds. For a time he taught
drawing to Queen Victoria. He illustrated more than a hundred of Tennyson's
poems, and Tennyson's lyric "To E. L., on His Travels in Greece" (1853) was
a tribute to his friend.

Lear whimsically illustrated scores of his own limericks, all of them dull
because the last line, which should be a funny climax, merely modifies the first
line slightly, ending with the same word. But contemporaries such as Ruskin
thought them melodious and funny. G. K. Chesterton considered Lear's
nonlimerick verse superior to Carroll's. Carroll's nonsense verse, G. K. wrote,
"was merely mathematical and logical. Edward Lear's nonsense was emotional
and poetical. The long rolling lines of Lear have the feeling of fine poetry,"
such as:

> Far and few, far and few,
> Are the lands where the Jumblies live.

Lear suffered all his life from epileptic seizures and poor eyesight. He was a
homosexual whose greatest love was a young barrister with whom he made a
happy journey to Greece. It is believed that Lear's syphilis was contracted
from a male prostitute.

An unfinished sequel to "The Owl and the Pussy-Cat" was found in Lear's effects after his death. It begins:

> Our mother was the Pussy-Cat,
>   Our father was the Owl,
> And so we're partly little beasts
>   And partly little fowl. . . .
> We all believe that little mice,
> For food are singularly nice.

The Owl and the Pussy-Cat

The Owl and the Pussy-Cat went to sea
    In a beautiful pea-green boat.
They took some honey, and plenty of money,
    Wrapped up in a five-pound note.
The Owl looked up to the stars above,
    And sang to a small guitar,
"O lovely Pussy, O Pussy, my love,
    What a beautiful Pussy you are,
            You are,
            You are!
What a beautiful Pussy you are!"

Pussy said to the Owl, "You elegant fowl,
    How charmingly sweet you sing!
Oh! let us be married: too long we have tarried;
    But what shall we do for a ring?"
They sailed away, for a year and a day,
    To the land where the bong-tree grows;
And there in a wood a Piggy-wig stood,
    With a ring at the end of his nose,
            His nose,
            His nose,
    With a ring at the end of his nose.

"Dear Pig, are you willing to sell for one shilling
    Your ring?" Said the Piggy, "I will."
So they took it away, and were married next day
    By the Turkey who lives on the hill.
They dinèd on mince and slices of quince,
    Which they ate with a runcible spoon;

And hand in hand, on the edge of the sand
They danced by the light of the moon,
The moon,
The moon,
They danced by the light of the moon.

HENRY WADSWORTH LONGFELLOW
(1807–1882)

CRITICS TODAY look down on Longfellow's poetry as "too decorous, benign, and sweet" (as *The Oxford Companion to American Literature* has it), yet no native poet was ever more loved both here and abroad. In France, Baudelaire translated "The Song of Hiawatha," abandoning of course Longfellow's tom-tom beat. Longfellow himself did lots of translating, including Dante's entire *Divine Comedy*. A professor of modern languages at Harvard, Longfellow did much to introduce European literature to America. He is our only poet to have a marble bust in the Poet's Corner of Westminster Abbey.

It could be that Longfellow's serene but vague Christian faith is partly responsible for the shrugs of modern critics. It seems that for the most part only conservative Christian writers, such as Paul Elmer More, have praised his verse.

Poe was no Christian, but in his essay "The Poetic Principle" he has only good things to say about Longfellow's "The Day Is Done." Of the many parodies of this poem, one of the earliest (by Phoebe Cary) opens:

The day is done, and darkness
From the wing of night is loosed,
As a feather is wafted downward,
From a chicken going to roost.

"The Day Is Done" appeared as a proem to *The Waif*, a book of Longfellow's verse published in 1844. "A Psalm of Life," first published in *Knickerbocker* magazine (October 1838), also has had its share of parodies. "Tell me not in mournful wish-wash," wrote Ezra Pound, "Life's a sort of sugared dishwash."

"Paul Revere's Ride" was the first ballad in Longfellow's *Tales of a Wayside Inn* (1863). A silversmith and engraver, Revere was one of many couriers working for the rebels. Although the poem is historically inaccurate in details, Revere did make his ride on April 18, 1775; a ride that would be unremembered today had not Longfellow written about it.

"The Village Blacksmith" earned Longfellow fifteen dollars when it appeared in *Knickerbocker* (November 1840). It is perhaps the most popular poem ever written to extol the simple, honest laborer who toils patiently at his daily tasks. Does the moralizing of the last stanza offend you? It did Poe, for whom the poem expresses "the *beauty* of simple-mindedness as a genuine thesis; and this thesis is inimitably handled until the concluding stanza, where the spirit of legitimate poesy is aggrieved in the pointed antithetical deduction of a *moral* from what has gone before."

Longfellow wrote the poem about an actual smithy on Brattle Street in Cambridge, under a huge chestnut tree near where the poet lived. In spite of protests by Longfellow and others, the tree was deemed harmful to farmers driving under it, and in 1876 was cut down. Pieces of the tree were saved, and the children of Cambridge collected enough money to make from them a chair that was given to Longfellow on his seventy-second birthday. The poet thanked them with this quatrain:

> Only your love and rememberance could
>   Give life to this dead wood,
> And make these branches, leafless now so long,
>   Blossom again in song.

In Longfellow's day about a quarter of all trees in Eastern hardwood forests were chestnuts. Shortly after 1900 they were struck by a fungus blight that in a few decades wiped out millions. Today only a few are known to survive. Plant pathologists are trying to preserve the tree with another blight that may cancel the older one, but it is too early to know if this will succeed.

Willoughby Hunter Weiss, an opera singer, set "The Village Blacksmith" to music. Of numerous parodies, the funniest is Frank Jacobs' "The Village Hippie," reprinted from *Mad* in *Mad for Better or Verse* (1975). Here's the first stanza:

> Under his pad on 10th and B
> The Village Hippie stands;
> A turned-on acid-head is he
> With pale and shaking hands;
> And the flower jacket that he wears
> Hangs down in tattered strands!

"The Wreck of the Hesperus," which first ran in *The New World* (January 11, 1840), was based on an actual shipwreck in 1839 on a reef in Norman's Woe, near Gloucester. Twenty bodies were washed ashore, including that of a woman lashed to a mast.

Longfellow said he wrote "The Arrow and the Song" "at arrow speed. Literally an improvisation." It was set to music by Charles Beach Hawley, and later by Michael William Balfe. I forget who commented, after reading the first stanza, "You can lose a lot of arrows that way."

"Excelsior" is the most parodied of Longfellow's poems. Indeed, it is almost a parody of itself. For Longfellow, "Excelsior" meant "higher and higher," as the youth struggles upward only to die without gaining his objective. Longfellow wrote the poem in 1841, inspired by the New York State seal, which bore a shield with a rising sun and the motto *Excelsior*.

Oliver Wendell Holmes thought that "the repetition of the aspiring exclamation ... lifts every stanza a step higher," but Irvin Cobb thought the exclamation should be "Bonehead!" Harvard students used to sing a song, maybe still do, with each stanza ending in "Upidee!" and the lines laced with "la la's." Bret Harte wrote a parody in which each stanza ended with "Sapolio!"—the name of a soap. Longfellow's poem was set to music by, among others, Stephen Glover and John Blockley.

Today people are surprised when told that Longfellow penned the lines "There Was a Little Girl." The earliest known printing is in a souvenir for a French fair held in Boston on April 11, 1871—a publication called *The Balloon Post*. It was accompanied with music for three voices. Longfellow is said to have written the poem for his daughter Edith, whose gold hair is mentioned in "The Children's Hour."

The Day Is Done

The day is done, and the darkness
　　Falls from the wings of Night,
As a feather is wafted downward
　　From an eagle in his flight.

I see the lights of the village
　　Gleam through the rain and the mist,
And a feeling of sadness comes o'er me
　　That my soul cannot resist:

A feeling of sadness and longing,
　　That is not akin to pain,
And resembles sorrow only
　　As the mist resembles the rain.

Come, read to me some poem,
　　Some simple and heartfelt lay,
That shall soothe this restless feeling,
　　And banish the thoughts of day.

Not from the grand old masters,
　　Not from the bards sublime,
Whose distant footsteps echo
　　Through the corridors of Time.

For, like strains of martial music,
　　Their mighty thoughts suggest
Life's endless toil and endeavor;
　　And to-night I long for rest.

Read from some humbler poet,
　　Whose songs gushed from his heart,

As showers from the clouds of summer,
　　Or tears from the eyelids start;

Who, through long days of labor,
　　And nights devoid of ease,
Still heard in his soul the music
　　Of wonderful melodies.

Such songs have power to quiet
　　The restless pulse of care,
And come like the benediction
　　That follows after prayer.

Then read from the treasured volume
　　The poem of thy choice,
And lend to the rhyme of the poet
　　The beauty of thy voice.

And the night shall be filled with music,
　　And the cares, that infest the day,
Shall fold their tents, like the Arabs,
　　And as silently steal away.

A Psalm of Life

What the Heart of the Young Man
Said to the Psalmist

Tell me not, in mournful numbers,
　　Life is but an empty dream!—
For the soul is dead that slumbers,
　　And things are not what they seem.

Life is real! Life is earnest!
　　And the grave is not its goal;
Dust thou art, to dust returnest,
　　Was not spoken of the soul.

Not enjoyment, and not sorrow,
　　Is our destined end or way;
But to act, that each to-morrow
　　Find us farther than to-day.

Art is long, and Time is fleeting,
    And our hearts, though stout and brave,
Still, like muffled drums, are beating
    Funeral marches to the grave.

In the world's broad field of battle,
    In the bivouac of Life,
Be not like dumb, driven cattle!
    Be a hero in the strife!

Trust no Future, howe'er pleasant!
    Let the dead Past bury its dead!
Act,—act in the living Present!
    Heart within, and God o'erhead!

Lives of great men all remind us
    We can make our lives sublime,
And, departing, leave behind us
    Footprints on the sands of time;

Footprints,[1] that perhaps another,
    Sailing o'er life's solemn main,
A forlorn and shipwrecked brother,
    Seeing, shall take heart again.

Let us, then, be up and doing,
    With a heart for any fate;
Still achieving, still pursuing,
    Learn to labor and to wait.

---

[1] *Footprints*] "Footsteps," in earliest printings.

Paul Revere's Ride

Listen, my children, and you shall hear
Of the midnight ride of Paul Revere,
On the eighteenth of April, in Seventy-five;
Hardly a man is now alive
Who remembers that famous day and year.

He said to his friend, "If the British march
By land or sea from the town to-night,
Hang a lantern aloft in the belfry arch

Of the North Church tower as a signal light,—
One, if by land, and two, if by sea;
And I on the opposite shore will be,
Ready to ride and spread the alarm
Through every Middlesex village and farm,
For the country folk to be up and to arm."

Then he said, "Good night!" and with muffled oar
Silently rowed to the Charlestown shore,
Just as the moon rose over the bay,
Where swinging wide at her moorings lay
The Somerset, British man-of-war;
A phantom ship, with each mast and spar
Across the moon like a prison bar,
And a huge black hulk, that was magnified
By its own reflection in the tide.

Meanwhile, his friend, through alley and street,
Wanders and watches with eager ears,
Till in the silence around him he hears
The muster of men at the barrack door,
The sound of arms, and the tramp of feet,
And the measured tread of the grenadiers,
Marching down to their boats on the shore.

Then he climbed the tower of the Old North Church,
By the wooden stairs, with stealthy tread,
To the belfry-chamber overhead,
And startled the pigeons from their perch
On the sombre rafters, that round him made
Masses and moving shapes of shade,—
By the trembling ladder, steep and tall,
To the highest window in the wall,
Where he paused to listen and look down
A moment on the roofs of the town,
And the moonlight flowing over all.

Beneath, in the churchyard, lay the dead,
In their night-encampment on the hill,
Wrapped in silence so deep and still
That he could hear, like a sentinel's tread,
The watchful night-wind, as it went
Creeping along from tent to tent,
And seeming to whisper, "All is well!"
A moment only he feels the spell

Of the place and the hour, and the secret dread
Of the lonely belfry and the dead;
For suddenly all his thoughts are bent
On a shadowy something far away,
Where the river widens to meet the bay,—
A line of black that bends and floats
On the rising tide, like a bridge of boats.

Meanwhile, impatient to mount and ride,
Booted and spurred, with a heavy stride
On the opposite shore walked Paul Revere.
Now he patted his horse's side,
Now gazed at the landscape far and near,
Then, impetuous, stamped the earth,
And turned and tightened his saddle-girth;
But mostly he watched with eager search
The belfry-tower of the Old North Church,
As it rose above the graves on the hill,
Lonely and spectral and sombre and still.
And lo! as he looks, on the belfry's height
A glimmer, and then a gleam of light!
He springs to the saddle, the bridle he turns,
But lingers and gazes, till full on his sight
A second lamp in the belfry burns!

A hurry of hoofs in a village street,
A shape in the moonlight, a bulk in the dark,
And beneath, from the pebbles, in passing, a spark
Struck out by a steed flying fearless and fleet:
That was all! And yet, through the gloom and the light,
The fate of a nation was riding that night;
And the spark struck out by that steed, in his flight,
Kindled the land into flames with its heat.

He has left the village and mounted the steep,
And beneath him, tranquil and broad and deep,
Is the Mystic, meeting the ocean tides;
And under the alders that skirt its edge,
Now soft on the sand, now loud on the ledge,
Is heard the tramp of his steed as he rides.

It was twelve by the village clock,
When he crossed the bridge into Medford town.
He heard the crowing of the cock,
And the barking of the farmer's dog,

And felt the damp of the river fog,
That rises after the sun goes down.

It was one by the village clock,
When he galloped into Lexington.
He saw the gilded weathercock
Swim in the moonlight as he passed,
And the meeting-house windows, blank and bare,
Gaze at him with a spectral glare,
As if they already stood aghast
At the bloody work they would look upon.

It was two by the village clock,
When he came to the bridge in Concord town.
He heard the bleating of the flock,
And the twitter of birds among the trees,
And felt the breath of the morning breeze
Blowing over the meadows brown.
And one was safe and asleep in his bed
Who at the bridge would be first to fall,
Who that day would be lying dead,
Pierced by a British musket-ball.

You know the rest. In the books you have read,
How the British Regulars fired and fled,—
How the farmers gave them ball for ball,
From behind each fence and farm-yard wall,
Chasing the red-coats down the lane,
Then crossing the fields to emerge again
Under the trees at the turn of the road,
And only pausing to fire and load.

So through the night rode Paul Revere;
And so through the night went his cry of alarm
To every Middlesex village and farm,—
A cry of defiance and not of fear,
A voice in the darkness, a knock at the door,
And a word that shall echo forevermore!
For, borne on the night-wind of the Past,
Through all our history, to the last,
In the hour of darkness and peril and need,
The people will waken and listen to hear
The hurrying hoof-beats of that steed,
And the midnight message of Paul Revere.

The Village Blacksmith

Under a spreading chestnut-tree
   The village smithy stands;
The smith, a mighty man is he,
   With large and sinewy hands;
And the muscles of his brawny arms
   Are strong as iron bands.

His hair is crisp, and black, and long,
   His face is like the tan;
His brow is wet with honest sweat,
   He earns whate'er he can,
And looks the whole world in the face,
   For he owes not any man.

Week in, week out, from morn till night,
   You can hear his bellows blow;
You can hear him swing his heavy sledge,
   With measured beat and slow,
Like a sexton ringing the village bell,[1]
   When the evening sun is low.

And children coming home from school
   Look in at the open door;
They love to see the flaming forge,
   And hear the bellows roar,
And catch the burning sparks that fly
   Like chaff from a threshing-floor.

He goes on Sunday to the church,
   And sits among his boys;
He hears the parson pray and preach,
   He hears his daughter's voice,
Singing in the village choir,
   And it makes his heart rejoice.

It sounds to him like her mother's voice,
   Singing in Paradise!
He needs must think of her once more,
   How in the grave she lies;
And with his hard, rough hand he wipes
   A tear out of his eyes.[2]

Toiling,—rejoicing,—sorrowing,
   Onward through life he goes;

Each morning sees some task begin,
    Each evening sees it close;
Something attempted, something done,
    Has earned a night's repose.

Thanks, thanks to thee, my worthy friend,
    For the lesson thou hast taught!
Thus at the flaming forge of life
    Our fortunes must be wrought;
Thus on its sounding anvil shaped
    Each burning deed and thought.

---

[1] *the village bell*] "the old kirk chimes," in the first printing.
[2] *A tear . . . eyes*] "A tear from out his eyes," in the first printing.

The Wreck of the Hesperus

It was the schooner Hesperus,
    That sailed the wintry sea;
And the skipper had taken his little daughtèr,
    To bear him company.

Blue were her eyes as the fairy-flax,
    Her cheeks like the dawn of day,
And her bosom white as the hawthorn buds,
    That ope in the month of May.

The skipper he stood beside the helm,
    His pipe was in his mouth,
And he watched how the veering flaw did blow
    The smoke now West, now South.

Then up and spake an old Sailòr,
    Had sailed to the Spanish Main,
"I pray thee, put into yonder port,
    For I fear a hurricane.

"Last night, the moon had a golden ring,
    And to-night no moon we see!"
The skipper, he blew a whiff from his pipe,
    And a scornful laugh laughed he.

Colder and louder blew the wind,
 A gale from the Northeast,
The snow fell hissing in the brine,
 And the billows frothed like yeast.

Down came the storm, and smote amain
 The vessel in its strength;
She shuddered and paused, like a frighted steed,
 Then leaped her cable's length.

"Come hither! come hither! my little daughtèr,
 And do not tremble so;
For I can weather the roughest gale
 That ever wind did blow."

He wrapped her warm in his seaman's coat
 Against the stinging blast;
He cut a rope from a broken spar,
 And bound her to the mast.

"O father! I hear the church-bells ring,
 Oh say, what may it be?"
"'Tis a fog-bell on a rock-bound coast!"—
 And he steered for the open sea.

"O father! I hear the sound of guns,
 Oh say, what may it be?"
"Some ship in distress, that cannot live
 In such an angry sea!"

"O father! I see a gleaming light,
 Oh say, what may it be?"
But the father answered never a word,
 A frozen corpse was he.

Lashed to the helm, all stiff and stark,
 With his face turned to the skies,
The lantern gleamed through the gleaming snow
 On his fixed and glassy eyes.

Then the maiden clasped her hands and prayed
 That savèd she might be;
And she thought of Christ, who stilled the wave,
 On the Lake of Galilee.

And fast through the midnight dark and drear,
 Through the whistling sleet and snow,

Like a sheeted ghost, the vessel swept
    Tow'rds the reef of Norman's Woe.

And ever the fitful gusts between
    A sound came from the land;
It was the sound of the trampling surf
    On the rocks and the hard sea-sand.

The breakers were right beneath her bows,
    She drifted a dreary wreck,
And a whooping billow swept the crew
    Like icicles from her deck.

She struck where the white and fleecy waves
    Looked soft as carded wool,
But the cruel rocks, they gored her side
    Like the horns of an angry bull.

Her rattling shrouds, all sheathed in ice,
    With the masts went by the board;
Like a vessel of glass, she stove and sank,
    Ho! ho! the breakers roared!

At daybreak, on the bleak sea-beach,
    A fisherman stood aghast,
To see the form of a maiden fair,
    Lashed close to a drifting mast.

The salt sea was frozen on her breast,
    The salt tears in her eyes;
And he saw her hair, like the brown seaweed,
    On the billows fall and rise.

Such was the wreck of the Hesperus,
    In the midnight and the snow!
Christ save us all from a death like this,
    On the reef of Norman's Woe!

The Arrow and the Song

I shot an arrow into the air,
It fell to earth, I knew not where;
For, so swiftly it flew, the sight
Could not follow it in its flight.

I breathed a song into the air,
It fell to earth, I knew not where;
For who has sight so keen and strong,
That it can follow the flight of song?

Long, long afterward, in an oak
I found the arrow, still unbroke;
And the song, from beginning to end,
I found again in the heart of a friend.

The Children's Hour

Between the dark and the daylight,
  When the night is beginning to lower,
Comes a pause in the day's occupations,
  That is known as the Children's Hour.

I hear in the chamber above me
  The patter of little feet,
The sound of a door that is opened,
  And voices soft and sweet.

From my study I see in the lamplight,
  Descending the broad hall stair,
Grave Alice, and laughing Allegra,
  And Edith with golden hair.

A whisper, and then a silence:
  Yet I know by their merry eyes
They are plotting and planning together
  To take me by surprise.

A sudden rush from the stairway,
  A sudden raid from the hall!
By three doors left unguarded
  They enter my castle wall!

They climb up into my turret
  O'er the arms and back of my chair;
If I try to escape, they surround me;
  They seem to be everywhere.

They almost devour me with kisses,
  Their arms about me entwine,

Till I think of the Bishop of Bingen
   In his Mouse-Tower on the Rhine!

Do you think, O blue-eyed banditti,
   Because you have scaled the wall,
Such an old mustache as I am
   Is not a match for you all!

I have you fast in my fortress,
   And will not let you depart,
But put you down into the dungeon
   In the round-tower of my heart.

And there will I keep you forever,
   Yes, forever and a day,
Till the walls shall crumble to ruin,
   And moulder in dust away!

Excelsior

The shades of night were falling fast,
As through an Alpine village passed
A youth, who bore, 'mid snow and ice,
A banner with the strange device,
     Excelsior!

His brow was sad; his eye beneath,
Flashed like a falchion from its sheath,
And like a silver clarion rung
The accents of that unknown tongue,
     Excelsior!

In happy homes he saw the light
Of household fires gleam warm and bright;
Above, the spectral glaciers shone,
And from his lips escaped a groan,
     Excelsior!

"Try not the Pass!" the old man said;
"Dark lowers the tempest overhead,
The roaring torrent is deep and wide!"
And loud that clarion voice replied,
     Excelsior!

"Oh stay," the maiden said, "and rest
Thy weary head upon this breast!"
A tear stood in his bright blue eye,
But still he answered, with a sigh,
                Excelsior!

"Beware the pine-tree's withered branch!
Beware the awful avalanche!"
This was the peasant's last Good-night,
A voice replied, far up the height,
                Excelsior!

At break of day, as heavenward
The pious monks of Saint Bernard
Uttered the oft-repeated prayer,
A voice cried through the startled air,
                Excelsior!

A traveller, by the faithful hound,
Half-buried in the snow was found,
Still grasping in his hand of ice
That banner with the strange device,
                Excelsior!

There in the twilight cold and gray,
Lifeless, but beautiful, he lay,
And from the sky, serene and far,
A voice fell, like a falling star,
                Excelsior!

There Was a Little Girl

There was a little girl, she had a little curl
    Right in the middle of her forehead;
And when she was good, she was very, very good,
    And when she was bad, she was horrid.

JOHN McCRAE
(1872–1918)

LIEUTENANT-COLONEL John McCrae was a Canadian poet and physician who wrote *A Textbook of Pathology for Medical Students* (1914), and for a time was a professor of pathology at the University of Vermont. He served as a medical officer in both the Boer War and the First World War. In 1918 he died of pneumonia in a French hospital.

McCrae's poem "In Flanders Fields" was first published anonymously in *Punch* (December 8, 1915), and later in McCrae's posthumous *In Flanders Fields and Other Poems* (1919). Flanders is a region on the coast of Europe, across from the English Channel, partly in France and partly in Belgium. Thousands of Allied soldiers are buried there. The poem was enormously popular in the war years, and is surely one of the most memorable of all poems about the death of soldiers in modern wars. It inspired England's "Poppy Day" on which the Armistice is celebrated by selling artificial poppies on the streets to raise money for charitable causes involving servicemen and women.

Did McCrae intend "blow" in the first line of the poem to have the archaic meaning "bloom"? In a handwritten early version of his poem the word was "grow." Poppies, of course, suggest the sleep of the soldiers.

Dozens of rhymesters took up the challenge in the last stanza by writing sequels. The most anthologized is R. W. Lilliard's "America Answers," which has the same French rondeau form as McCrae's poem. It appeared in the New York *Evening Post* (1918), shortly after McCrae's death.

In Flanders Fields

In Flanders fields the poppies blow
Between the crosses, row on row,
    That mark our place; and in the sky
    The larks, still bravely singing, fly
Scarce heard amid the guns below.

We are the Dead. Short days ago
We lived, felt dawn, saw sunset glow,
    Loved and were loved, and now we lie
    In Flanders fields.

Take up our quarrel with the foe;
To you from failing hands we throw
    The torch; be yours to hold it high.

If ye break faith with us who die
We shall not sleep, though poppies grow
In Flanders fields.

EDWIN MARKHAM
(1852–1940)

MARKHAM WAS a teacher at a high school in Oakland, California, when the publication in 1899 of "The Man with the Hoe" (first in the San Francisco *Examiner*, then in a pamphlet titled *The Man with the Hoe and Other Poems*) made him famous. He moved East to settle in Port Richmond, Staten Island, where he wrote many volumes of verse, and books attacking the evils of unfettered capitalism.

"The Man with the Hoe" was inspired by Jean-François Millet's famous painting of a weary farmer leaning on his hoe. No more powerful verse has ever portrayed how farm labor can degrade human beings to the level of beasts. Markham wrote that when he first saw Millet's painting he stood before it for an hour "absorbing the majesty of its despair . . . the power and the terror of the thing growing upon my heart, the pity and sorrow of it eating into my soul." The British scientist Alfred Russel Wallace called Markham "the greatest poet of the social passion that has yet appeared in the world." It has been said that Whitman's poetry reflects social consciousness, whereas Markham is an early poet of social conscience.

The poet Presley, in Frank Norris' novel *The Octopus* (1910), was modeled on Markham. Presley writes a stirring poem about the oppression of California farmers, only to find it has no effect whatever on their exploitation by amiable business moguls who see nothing immoral in the consequences that flow from their greed.

The Man with the Hoe

Bowed by the weight of centuries he leans
Upon his hoe and gazes on the ground,
The emptiness of ages in his face,
And on his back the burden of the world.
Who made him dead to rapture and despair,
A thing that grieves not and that never hopes,
Stolid and stunned, a brother to the ox?
Who loosened and let down this brutal jaw?
Whose was the hand that slanted back this brow?

Whose breath blew out the light within this brain?
Is this the Thing the Lord God made and gave
To have dominion over sea and land;
To trace the stars and search the heavens for power;
To feel the passion of Eternity?
Is this the Dream He dreamed who shaped the suns
And marked their ways upon the ancient deep?
Down all the stretch of Hell to its last gulf
There is no shape more terrible than this—
More tongued with censure of the world's blind greed—
More filled with signs and portents for the soul—
More fraught with menace to the universe.

What gulfs between him and the seraphim!
Slave of the wheel of labor, what to him
Are Plato and the swing of Pleiades?
What the long reaches of the peaks of song,
The rift of dawn, the reddening of the rose?
Through this dread shape the suffering ages look;
Time's tragedy is in that aching stoop;
Through this dread shape humanity betrayed,
Plundered, profaned and disinherited,
Cries protest to the Judges of the World,
A protest that is also prophecy.

O masters, lords and rulers in all lands,
Is this the handiwork you give to God,
This monstrous thing distorted and soul-quenched?
How will you ever straighten up this shape;
Touch it again with immortality;
Give back the upward looking and the light;
Rebuild in it the music and the dream;
Make right the immemorial infamies,
Perfidious wrongs, immedicable woes?

O masters, lords and rulers in all lands,
How will the Future reckon with this Man?
How answer his brute question in that hour
When whirlwinds of rebellion shake the world?
How will it be with kingdoms and with kings—
With those who shaped him to the thing he is—
When this dumb Terror shall reply to God,
After the silence of the centuries?

JOHN MASEFIELD
(1878–1967)

AFTER A youth spent at sea, British-born John Masefield had a sequence of low-level jobs in America, including that of porter in a Greenwich Village saloon. He was never a bartender, as often reported. "What I really did," he told an interviewer, "was wash out cuspidors, sweep and scrub the floor, polish the foot-rails, wash glasses, and pacify any warring factions." He later settled in London where he became one of England's most prolific poets. He also wrote fifteen plays, twenty novels and many short stories and essays. He became Poet Laureate in 1930.

"Sea Fever" is the most anthologized of Masefield's maritime verse, with "Cargoes" running a close second. Both poems appear in his first book, *Salt-Water Ballads* (1902). The first line of "Sea Fever" originally began, "I must go down." Twenty years later Masefield changed it to "I must down," but after twenty more years he put "go" back. "Now, alas, I can't make up my mind," he said. The poem was set to music by John Ireland.

Sea Fever

I must go down to the seas again, to the lonely sea and the
  sky,
And all I ask is a tall ship and a star to steer her by,
And the wheel's kick and the wind's song and the white sail's
  shaking,
And a grey mist on the sea's face and a grey dawn breaking.

I must go down to the seas again, for the call of the running
  tide
Is a wild call and a clear call that may not be denied;
And all I ask is a windy day with the white clouds flying,
And the flung spray and the blown spume and the sea-gulls
  crying.

I must go down to the seas again to the vagrant gypsy life,
To the gull's way and the whale's way where the wind's like a
  whetted knife;
And all I ask is a merry yarn from a laughing fellow-rover,
And quiet sleep and a sweet dream when the long trick's over.

Cargoes

Quinquireme of Nineveh from distant Ophir
Rowing home to haven in sunny Palestine,
With a cargo of ivory,
And apes and peacocks,
Sandalwood, cedarwood, and sweet white wine.

Stately Spanish galleon coming from the Isthmus,
Dipping through the Tropics by the palm-green shores,
With a cargo of diamonds,
Emeralds, amethysts,
Topazes, and cinnamon, and gold moidores.

Dirty British coaster with a salt-caked smoke stack
Butting through the Channel in the mad March days,
With a cargo of Tyne coal,
Road-rail, pig-lead,
Firewood, iron-ware, and cheap tin trays.

HUGHES MEARNS
(1875–1965)

ALMOST EVERYONE supposes that "Antigonish," the quatrain about the man who wasn't there, is an old Mother Goose rhyme. Actually it was written by Hughes Mearns, a professor of education at New York University, and the author of numerous books of nonfiction as well as books of light verse.

The quatrain was originally written for the play *The Psyco-Ed*, which Mearns wrote in 1899 for an undergraduate English class at Harvard. The poem was first published in 1922 by Franklin P. Adams in his New York *World* column, "The Conning Tower."

What on earth does the title "Antigonish" mean? Mearns explained it two decades later. It seems that when he wrote the poem, papers were carrying stories about a haunted house in a village that was called either Antigona or Antigonia, but whenever reporters tried to investigate, the ghost was not there. Mearns also observed that the poem can be interpreted as describing the agony of wives whose husbands are never home.

It has been suggested that a quatrain about someone or something not there be called a "mearns." Here are five other examples of the form that Mearns himself later wrote:

As I was sitting in my chair
I *knew* the bottom wasn't there,
Nor legs, nor back, but *I just sat*
Ignoring little things like that.

As I was falling down the stair
I met a bump that wasn't there;
It might have put me on the shelf
Except I wasn't there myself.

As I was letting down my hair
I met a guy who didn't care;
He didn't care again today—
I *love* 'em when they get that way!

One night I met when stepping out
A gal who wasn't thereabout;
I said, "*Hel*-lo! And how are *you!*"
She didn't say; so I never knew.

As I was robbing Chelsea Bank
I met a non-existent Zanque;
He did not whiffle, wooze or wup—
That's *why* I had to shut him up.

Mearns's most influential book was *Creative Power* (1929), reporting on his classes with children at the Lincoln School of Teachers College, Columbia University. The book is mainly about techniques for teaching children to write poetry.

Mearns's first "mearns" was made into a hit song, "The Little Man Who Wasn't There," by Bernie Hannighen.

Antigonish

As I was going up the stair
I met a man who wasn't there!
He wasn't there again to-day!
I wish, I *wish* he'd stay away!

EDNA ST. VINCENT MILLAY
(1892–1950)

MAINE-BORN AND a graduate of Vassar, Edna St. Vincent Millay became the nation's most admired woman poet soon after "Renascence" was published, first in an anthology called *The Lyric Year*, when she was nineteen, and then in *Renascence and Other Poems* (1917). "This poem gives the central theme of Edna Millay's whole work," wrote Edmund Wilson in a moving essay on Millay in his *Shores of Light* (1952). He continues: "She is alone; she is afraid that the world will crush her; she must summon the strength to assert herself, to draw herself up to her full stature, to embrace the world with love; and the storm—which stands evidently for sexual love—comes to effect a liberation." Wilson believed her to be "one of the only poets writing in English in our time who have attained to anything like the stature of great literary figures."

Mathematicians consider her sonnet "'Euclid Alone Has Looked on Beauty Bare'" the finest poem ever written on the cold beauty of geometry, and of course almost anyone can recite the lines of "First Fig," the first poem in *A Few Figs from Thistles* (1920), having previously appeared in *Poetry* (June 1918).

Millay's early years were lived in Greenwich Village as a rebel bisexual bohemian. In the 1920s she was the idol of the "flaming youth" who loved being told one could enjoy sex without "meaningful relationships." Before she moved out of the Village with her Dutch husband, she lived at 75½ Bedford Street in a house so narrow you can stand in front of it and almost touch the sides.

Edmund Wilson, John Peale Bishop and Floyd Dell were among the many writers who fell in love with her. Wilson even proposed marriage. She is Rita Cavenagh in his novel *I Thought of Daisy*.

Edna became so obsessed with the winning of World War II that for five years she wrote almost nothing but war poems. The critics considered these poems worthless. She herself came to realize this, calling them "pious prostitution of poetry to propaganda." Her labors on such dismal verse may have contributed to her nervous breakdown in 1946. "There is nothing on this earth which can so much get on the nerves of a good poet," she wrote to Wilson, "as the writing of bad poetry. Anyway, finally I cracked up under it." From then on, all was downhill. She lived only a few more years, as a mentally depressed alcoholic.

Renascence

All I could see from where I stood
Was three long mountains and a wood;
I turned and looked another way,
And saw three islands in a bay.
So with my eyes I traced the line
Of the horizon, thin and fine,
Straight around till I was come
Back to where I'd started from;
And all I saw from where I stood
Was three long mountains and a wood.

Over these things I could not see;
These were the things that bounded me;
And I could touch them with my hand,
Almost, I thought, from where I stand.
And all at once things seemed so small
My breath came short, and scarce at all.
But, sure, the sky is big, I said;
Miles and miles above my head;
So here upon my back I'll lie
And look my fill into the sky.
And so I looked, and, after all,
The sky was not so very tall.
The sky, I said, must somewhere stop,
And—sure enough!—I see the top!
The sky, I thought, is not so grand;
I 'most could touch it with my hand!
And reaching up my hand to try,
I screamed to feel it touch the sky.
I screamed, and—lo!—Infinity
Came down and settled over me;
Forced back my scream into my chest,
Bent back my arm upon my breast,
And, pressing of the Undefined
The definition on my mind,
Held up before my eyes a glass
Through which my shrinking sight did pass
Until it seemed I must behold
Immensity made manifold;
Whispered to me a word whose sound
Deafened the air for worlds around,
And brought unmuffled to my ears
The gossiping of friendly spheres,
The creaking of the tented sky,
The ticking of Eternity.
I saw and heard, and knew at last
The How and Why of all things, past,
And present, and forevermore.
The Universe, cleft to the core,
Lay open to my probing sense
That, sick'ning, I would fain pluck thence
But could not,—nay! But needs must suck
At the great wound, and could not pluck
My lips away till I had drawn

All venom out.—Ah, fearful pawn!
For my omniscience paid I toll
In infinite remorse of soul.
All sin was of my sinning, all
Atoning mine, and mine the gall
Of all regret. Mine was the weight
Of every brooded wrong, the hate
That stood behind each envious thrust,
Mine every greed, mine every lust.
And all the while for every grief,
Each suffering, I craved relief
With individual desire,—
Craved all in vain! And felt fierce fire
About a thousand people crawl;
Perished with each,—then mourned for all!
A man was starving in Capri;
He moved his eyes and looked at me;
I felt his gaze, I heard his moan,
And knew his hunger as my own.
I saw at sea a great fog bank
Between two ships that struck and sank;
A thousand screams the heavens smote;
And every scream tore through my throat.
No hurt I did not feel, no death
That was not mine; mine each last breath
That, crying, met an answering cry
From the compassion that was I.
All suffering mine, and mine its rod;
Mine, pity like the pity of God.
Ah, awful weight! Infinity
Pressed down upon the finite Me!
My anguished spirit, like a bird,
Beating against my lips I heard;
Yet lay the weight so close about
There was no room for it without.
And so beneath the weight lay I
And suffered death, but could not die.

Long had I lain thus, craving death,
When quietly the earth beneath
Gave way, and inch by inch, so great
At last had grown the crushing weight,
Into the earth I sank till I

Full six feet under ground did lie,
And sank no more,—there is no weight
Can follow here, however great.
From off my breast I felt it roll,
And as it went my tortured soul
Burst forth and fled in such a gust
That all about me swirled the dust.

Deep in the earth I rested now;
Cool is its hand upon the brow
And soft its breast beneath the head
Of one who is so gladly dead.
And all at once, and over all
The pitying rain began to fall;
I lay and heard each pattering hoof
Upon my lowly, thatchèd roof,
And seemed to love the sound far more
Than ever I had done before.
For rain it hath a friendly sound
To one who's six feet underground;
And scarce the friendly voice or face:
A grave is such a quiet place.

The rain, I said, is kind to come
And speak to me in my new home.
I would I were alive again
To kiss the fingers of the rain,
To drink into my eyes the shine
Of every slanting silver line,
To catch the freshened, fragrant breeze
From drenched and dripping apple-trees.
For soon the shower will be done,
And then the broad face of the sun
Will laugh above the rain-soaked earth
Until the world with answering mirth
Shakes joyously, and each round drop
Rolls, twinkling, from its grass-blade top.
How can I bear it; buried here,
While overhead the sky grows clear
And blue again after the storm?
O, multi-colored, multiform,
Beloved beauty over me,
That I shall never, never see
Again! Spring-silver, autumn-gold,

That I shall never more behold!
Sleeping your myriad magics through,
Close-sepulchred away from you!
O God, I cried, give me new birth,
And put me back upon the earth!
Upset each cloud's gigantic gourd
And let the heavy rain, down-poured
In one big torrent, set me free,
Washing my grave away from me!

I ceased; and through the breathless hush
That answered me, the far-off rush
Of herald wings came whispering
Like music down the vibrant string
Of my ascending prayer, and—crash!
Before the wild wind's whistling lash
The startled storm-clouds reared on high
And plunged in terror down the sky,
And the big rain in one black wave
Fell from the sky and struck my grave.
I know not how such things can be;
I only know there came to me
A fragrance such as never clings
To aught save happy living things;
A sound as of some joyous elf
Singing sweet songs to please himself,
And, through and over everything,
A sense of glad awakening.
The grass, a-tiptoe at my ear,
Whispering to me I could hear;
I felt the rain's cool finger-tips
Brushed tenderly across my lips,
Laid gently on my sealèd sight,
And all at once the heavy night
Fell from my eyes and I could see,—
A drenched and dripping apple-tree,
A last long line of silver rain,
A sky grown clear and blue again.
And as I looked a quickening gust
Of wind blew up to me and thrust
Into my face a miracle
Of orchard-breath, and with the smell,—
I know not how such things can be!—

I breathed my soul back into me.
Ah! Up then from the ground sprang I
And hailed the earth with such a cry
As is not heard save from a man
Who has been dead, and lives again.
About the trees my arms I wound;
Like one gone mad I hugged the ground;
I raised my quivering arms on high;
I laughed and laughed into the sky,
Till at my throat a strangling sob
Caught fiercely, and a great heart-throb
Sent instant tears into my eyes;
O God, I cried, no dark disguise
Can e'er hereafter hide from me
Thy radiant identity!
Thou canst not move across the grass
But my quick eyes will see Thee pass,
Nor speak, however silently,
But my hushed voice will answer Thee.
I know the path that tells Thy way
Through the cool eve of every day;
God, I can push the grass apart
And lay my finger on Thy heart!

The world stands out on either side
No wider than the heart is wide;
Above the world is stretched the sky,—
No higher than the soul is high.
The heart can push the sea and land
Farther away on either hand;
The soul can split the sky in two,
And let the face of God shine through.
But East and West will pinch the heart
That can not keep them pushed apart;
And he whose soul is flat—the sky
Will cave in on him by and by.

'Euclid Alone Has Looked on Beauty Bare'

Euclid alone has looked on Beauty bare.
Let all who prate of Beauty hold their peace,

And lay them prone upon the earth and cease
To ponder on themselves, the while they stare
At nothing, intricately drawn nowhere
In shapes of shifting lineage; let geese
Gabble and hiss, but heroes seek release
From dusty bondage into luminous air.

O blinding hour, O holy, terrible day,
When first the shaft into his vision shone
Of light anatomized! Euclid alone
Has looked on Beauty bare. Fortunate they
Who, though once only and then but far away,
Have heard her massive sandal set on stone.

First Fig

My candle burns at both ends;
  It will not last the night;
But ah, my foes and oh, my friends—
  It gives a lovely light.

JOAQUIN MILLER
(1837–1913)

JOAQUIN MILLER's real name was Cincinnatus Hiner (or Heine) Miller. It is impossible to separate fact from fantasy in his autobiographical writings. He claimed to have lived a colorful frontier life on the West Coast as a lawyer, judge, newspaper editor, Indian fighter, gold miner, pony express rider and convicted horse thief.

No one paid attention to his poetry until he went to London where, after privately printing his first book of verse, he was lionized as the "Byron of Oregon." An incurable showman, he wore cowboy boots and a big sombrero, smoked two cigars at once, whooped when he entered a room, picked his teeth in public and liked to bite the ankles of young women. Such crude antics, he once said, "help sell the poems, and they tickle the Duchesses."

The poem that still keeps him in anthologies is "Columbus," from *Songs of the Soul* (1896), one of his many books of verse. He also wrote plays and novels, none of which are popular today.

Columbus

Behind him lay the gray Azores,
  Behind the Gates of Hercules;
Before him not the ghost of shores,
  Before him only shoreless seas.
The good mate said: "Now must we pray,
  For lo! the very stars are gone.
Brave Adm'r'l, speak; what shall I say?"
  "Why, say: 'Sail on! sail on! and on!'"

"My men grow mutinous day by day;
  My men grow ghastly wan and weak."
The stout mate thought of home; a spray
  Of salt wave washed his swarthy cheek.
"What shall I say, brave Adm'r'l, say,
  If we sight naught but seas at dawn?"
"Why, you shall say, at break of day:
  'Sail on! sail on! sail on! and on!'"

They sailed and sailed, as winds might blow,
  Until at last the blanched mate said:
"Why, now not even God would know
  Should I and all my men fall dead.
These very winds forget their way,
  For God from these dread seas is gone.
Now speak, brave Adm'r'l; speak and say"—
  He said: "Sail on! sail on! and on!"

They sailed. They sailed. Then spake the mate:
  "This mad sea shows his teeth to-night;
He curls his lip, he lies in wait,
  With lifted teeth, as if to bite:
Brave Adm'r'l, say but one good word;
  What shall we do when hope is gone?"
The words leapt like a leaping sword:
  "Sail on! sail on! sail on! and on!"

Then, pale and worn, he kept his deck,
  And peered through darkness. Ah, that night
Of all dark nights! And then a speck—
  A light! a light! a light! a light!
It grew, a starlit flag unfurled!

It grew to be Time's burst of dawn.
He gained a world; he gave that world
Its grandest lesson: "On! sail on!"

CLEMENT CLARKE MOORE
(1779–1863)

A PROFESSOR of Greek and Oriental literature at an Episcopalian theological seminary in the Chelsea district of Manhattan, Moore did his best to write classic poetry. None of it is of any interest today, but the ballad "A Visit from St. Nicholas," dashed off one winter to amuse his children, became immortal. It was published anonymously in the Troy *Sentinel*, New York (December 23, 1823). Many years passed before Moore could bring himself to admit he wrote it.

Moore's picture of Santa as a small elf derived in part from Washington Irving's portrayal of St. Nicholas in his humorous *History of New York*, including the pipe and the gesture of laying a finger alongside the nose. For more than you may care to know about the history of the ballad and its hundreds of sequels and parodies, see my *Annotated Night before Christmas* (1991).

A Visit from St. Nicholas

'Twas the night before Christmas, when all through the
      house
Not a creature was stirring, not even a mouse;
The stockings were hung by the chimney with care,
In hopes that St. Nicholas soon would be there;
The children were nestled all snug in their beds,
While visions of sugar-plums danced in their heads;
And mamma in her kerchief, and I in my cap,
Had just settled our brains for a long winter's nap,
When out on the lawn there arose such a clatter,
I sprang from the bed to see what was the matter.
Away to the window I flew like a flash,
Tore open the shutters, and threw up the sash.
The moon on the breast of the new-fallen snow
Gave a luster of mid-day to objects below,
When, what to my wondering eyes should appear,
But a miniature sleigh, and eight tiny reindeer,

With a little old driver, so lively and quick,
I knew in a moment it must be St. Nick.
More rapid than eagles his coursers they came,
And he whistled, and shouted, and called them by name;
"Now, *Dasher!*, now *Dancer!* now, *Prancer* and *Vixen!*
On, *Comet!* on, *Cupid!*, on, *Dunder* and *Blitzen!*
To the top of the porch! To the top of the wall!
Now, dash away! Dash away! Dash away all!"
As dry leaves that before the wild hurricane fly,
When they meet with an obstacle, mount to the sky;
So up to the housetop the coursers they flew,
With the sleigh full of toys, and St. Nicholas, too.
And then in a twinkling, I heard on the roof
The prancing and pawing of each little hoof.
As I drew in my head, and was turning around,
Down the chimney St. Nicholas came with a bound.
He was dressed all in fur, from his head to his foot,
And his clothes were all tarnished with ashes and soot;
A bundle of toys he had flung on his back,
And he looked like a peddler just opening his pack.
His eyes—how they twinkled!—his dimples how merry!
His cheeks were like roses, his nose like a cherry!
His droll little mouth was drawn up like a bow,
And the beard of his chin was as white as the snow;
The stump of a pipe he held tight in his teeth,
And the smoke it encircled his head like a wreath;
He had a broad face and a round little belly,
That shook when he laughed like a bowlful of jelly.
He was chubby and plump, a right jolly old elf,
And I laughed when I saw him, in spite of myself;
A wink of his eye and a twist of his head,
Soon gave me to know I had nothing to dread;
He spoke not a word, but went straight to his work,
And filled all the stockings; then turned with a jerk,
And laying his finger aside of his nose,
And giving a nod, up the chimney he rose;
He sprang to his sleigh, to his team gave a whistle,
And away they all flew like the down of a thistle;
But I heard him exclaim, ere he drove out of sight,
"Happy Christmas to all, and to all a good night!"

GEORGE POPE MORRIS
(1802–1864)

BORN IN Philadelphia, Morris became one of New York City's top journalists, as well as a popular writer of songs, poetry, stories, plays and operas. At the age of twenty-one he founded the weekly New York *Mirror* and *Ladies' Literary Gazette* in association with Samuel Woodworth, who wrote "The Old Oaken Bucket."

"Woodman, Spare That Tree!" initially ran in the New York *Mirror* under the title "The Oak" (January 17, 1837). The same title was on the sheet music by singer Henry Russell, issued the same year, as well as above the poem when it went into Morris' *The Deserted Bride and Other Poems* (1838). It changed to "Woodman, Spare That Tree!" in the book's enlarged 1853 edition.

Morris wrote the poem as lyrics for his friend Russell to sing. In his autobiography, *Cheer, Brothers, Cheer*, Russell prints a letter from Morris explaining what inspired him to write the poem. Morris was riding with a friend who asked him to turn down a road so he could see a large oak tree, of which the friend had fond memories, in front of his former home. Standing by the tree, sharpening an axe, was the cottage's present owner. The tree, he explained, was too close to the house and, besides, he needed it for firewood. In great agitation, the friend paid the man ten dollars to let the oak stand.

James Joyce, in *Ulysses*, writes of an organ playing 'a new and striking arrangement of "Woodman, Spare That Tree!"' and in *Finnegans Wake* is the exclamation "Spare, woodmann, spare!"

Of many parodies, one of the earliest, by John Love, Jr., is titled "Barber, Spare Those Hairs," and more recently Ogden Nash's parody that begins, "Pray, butcher, spare your tender calf."

Woodman, Spare That Tree!

Woodman, spare that tree!
Touch not a single bough!
In youth it sheltered me,
And I'll protect it now.

'Twas my forefather's hand
That placed it near his cot;
There, woodman, let it stand,
Thy ax shall harm it not!

That old familiar tree,
Whose glory and renown

Are spread o'er land and sea,
And wouldst thou hew it down?

Woodman, forbear thy stroke!
Cut not its earth-bound ties!
Oh! spare that aged oak,
Now towering to the skies.

When but an idle boy
I sought its grateful shade;
In all their gushing joy
Here too my sisters played.

My mother kissed me here
My father pressed my hand—
Forgive this foolish tear,
But let that old oak stand!

My heart-strings round thee cling,
Close as thy bark, old friend!
Here shall the wild-bird sing,
And still thy branches bend.

Old tree, the storm still brave!
And, woodman, leave the spot!
While I've a hand to save,
Thy ax shall harm it not.

ALFRED NOYES
(1880–1958)

ONCE A much admired British poet, Noyes is now so out of fashion that he is not even listed in early editions of *The Oxford Companion to English Literature*, and in the most recent edition his entry is only an inch long. Is it because his poetry is too melodious, too easy to understand, and because us older folk had to read "The Highwayman" in grade school? One of these days his verse will be "rediscovered," especially by scientists, who seem unaware that he wrote a trilogy, *The Torch-Bearers* (1922–1930), devoted entirely to poetry in praise of great scientists.

Educated at Oxford, Noyes also wrote essays, plays, novels and short stories. For nine years he was a professor of English at Princeton University. A convert to Roman Catholicism, he roundly drubbed Joyce's *Ulysses* for its sex scenes, calling it a novel that "would make a Hottentot sick." Ironically, he himself got into hot water with the Vatican for writing a book that praised Voltaire.

He failed to check with the Holy Office, which then had all of Voltaire's work on its *Index*. Noyes withdrew his book on Voltaire so that he might add a preface justifying why he wrote it.

The Highwayman

Part One

The wind was a torrent of darkness among the gusty trees.
The moon was a ghostly galleon tossed upon cloudy seas.
The road was a ribbon of moonlight over the purple moor,
And the highwayman came riding—
      Riding—riding—
The highwayman came riding, up to the old inn-door.

He'd a French cocked-hat on his forehead, a bunch of lace at
    his chin,
A coat of the claret velvet, and breeches of brown doe-skin.
They fitted with never a wrinkle. His boots were up to the
    thigh.
And he rode with a jewelled twinkle,
      His pistol butts a-twinkle,
His rapier hilt a-twinkle, under the jewelled sky.

Over the cobbles he clattered and clashed in the dark inn-
    yard.
He tapped with his whip on the shutters, but all was locked
    and barred.
He whistled a tune to the window, and who should be waiting
    there
But the landlord's black-eyed daughter,
      Bess, the landlord's daughter,
Plaiting a dark red love-knot into her long black hair.

And dark in the dark old inn-yard a stable-wicket creaked
Where Tim the ostler listened. His face was white and peaked.
His eyes were hollows of madness, his hair like mouldy hay,
But he loved the landlord's daughter,
      The landlord's red-lipped daughter,
Dumb as a dog he listened, and he heard the robber say—

"One kiss, my bonny sweetheart, I'm after a prize tonight,
But I shall be back with the yellow gold before the morning
    light;

Yet, if they press me sharply, and harry me through the day,
Then look for me by moonlight,
    Watch for me by moonlight,
I'll come to thee by moonlight, though hell should bar the
    way."

He rose upright in the stirrups. He scarce could reach her
    hand,
But she loosened her hair in the casement. His face burnt like
    a brand
As the black cascade of perfume came tumbling over his
    breast;
And he kissed its waves in the moonlight,
    (O, sweet black waves in the moonlight!)
Then he tugged at his rein in the moonlight, and galloped
    away to the west.

Part Two

He did not come in the dawning. He did not come at noon;
And out of the tawny sunset, before the rise of the moon,
When the road was a gypsy's ribbon, looping the purple moor,
A red-coat troop came marching—
    Marching—marching—
King George's men came marching, up to the old inn-door.

They said no word to the landlord. They drank his ale instead.
But they gagged his daughter, and bound her, to the foot of
    her narrow bed.
Two of them knelt at her casement, with muskets at their side!
There was death at every window;
    And hell at one dark window;
For Bess could see, through her casement, the road that *he*
    would ride.

They had tied her up to attention, with many a sniggering
    jest.
They had bound a musket beside her, with the muzzle beneath
    her breast!
"Now, keep good watch!" and they kissed her. She heard the
    doomed man say—
Look for me by moonlight;
    Watch for me by moonlight;
I'll come to thee by moonlight, though hell should bar the way!

She twisted her hands behind her; but all the knots held good!
She writhed her hands till her fingers were wet with sweat or
    blood!
They stretched and strained in the darkness, and the hours
    crawled by like years,
Till, now, on the stroke of midnight,
            Cold, on the stroke of midnight,
The tip of one finger touched it! The trigger at least was hers!

The tip of one finger touched it. She strove no more for the
    rest.
Up, she stood up to attention, with the muzzle between her
    breast.
She would not risk their hearing; she would not strive again;
For the road lay bare in the moonlight;
            Blank and bare in the moonlight;
And the blood of her veins, in the moonlight, throbbed to her
    love's refrain.

Tlot-tlot; tlot-tlot! Had they heard it? The horsehoofs ringing
    clear;
Tlot-tlot, tlot-tlot, in the distance? Were they deaf that they did
    not hear?
Down the ribbon of moonlight, over the brow of the hill,
The highwayman came riding—
            Riding—riding—
The red-coats looked to their priming! She stood up, straight
    and still.

Tlot-tlot, in the frosty silence! *Tlot-tlot,* in the echoing night!
Nearer he came and nearer. Her face was like a light.
Her eyes grew wide for a moment; she drew one last deep
    breath,
Then her finger moved in the moonlight,
            Her musket shattered the moonlight,
Shattered her breast in the moonlight and warned him—with
    her death.

He turned. He spurred to the west; he did not know who
    stood
Bowed, with her head o'er the musket, drenched with her own
    blood!
Not till the dawn he heard it, and his face grew grey to hear
How Bess, the landlord's daughter,
            The landlord's black-eyed daughter,

Had watched for her love in the moonlight, and died in the
 darkness there.

Back, he spurred like a madman, shouting a curse to the sky,
With the white road smoking behind him and his rapier
 brandished high.
Blood-red were his spurs in the golden noon; wine-red was his
 velvet coat;
When they shot him down on the highway,
        Down like a dog on the highway,
And he lay in his blood on the highway, with a bunch of lace
 at his throat.

.   .   .   .

And still of a winter's night, they say, when the wind is in the trees,
When the moon is a ghostly galleon tossed upon cloudy seas,
When the road is a ribbon of moonlight over the purple moor,
A highwayman comes riding—
        Riding—riding—
A highwayman comes riding, up to the old inn-door.

Over the cobbles he clatters and clangs in the dark inn-yard.
He taps with his whip on the shutters, but all is locked and barred.
He whistles a tune to the window, and who should be waiting there
But the landlord's black-eyed daughter,
        Bess, the landlord's daughter,
Plaiting a dark red love-knot into her long black hair.

The Barrel-Organ

There's a barrel-organ carolling across a golden street
    In the City as the sun sinks low;
With a silvery cry of linnets in its dull mechanic beat,
    As it dies into the sunset-glow;
And it pulses through the pleasures of the City and the pain
    That surround the singing organ like a large eternal light;
And they've given it a glory and a part to play again
    In the Symphony that rules the day and night.

And now it's marching onward through the realms of old
        romance,
    And trolling out a fond familiar tune,

And now it's roaring cannon down to fight the King of France,
  And now it's prattling softly to the moon,
And all around the organ there's a sea without a shore
  Of human joys and wonders and regrets,
To remember and to recompense the music evermore
  For what the cold machinery forgets. . . .

Yes; as the music changes,
  Like a prismatic glass,
It takes the light and ranges
  Through all the moods that pass;
Dissects the common carnival
  Of passions and regrets,
And gives the world a glimpse of all
  The colours it forgets.

And there *La Traviata* sighs
  Another sadder song;
And there *Il Trovatore* cries
  A tale of deeper wrong;
And bolder knights to battle go
  With sword and shield and lance,
Then ever here on earth below
  Have whirled into—*a dance!*—

Go down to Kew in lilac-time, in lilac-time, in lilac-time.
  Go down to Kew in lilac-time (it isn't far from London!),
And you shall wander hand in hand with love in summer's
  wonderland.
  Go down to Kew in lilac-time (it isn't far from London!).

The cherry-trees are seas of bloom and soft perfume and sweet
  perfume,
  The cherry-trees are seas of bloom (and oh, so near to
  London!),
And there they say when dawn is high and all the world's a
  blaze of sky,
  The cuckoo, though he's very shy, will sing a song for
  London.

The Dorian nightingale is rare, and yet they say you'll hear
  him there
  At Kew, at Kew in lilac-time (and oh, so near to London!),
The linnet and the throstle, too, and after dark the long halloo
  And golden-eyed *tu-whit*, *tu-whoo*, of owls that ogle London.

For Noah hardly knew a bird of any kind that isn't heard
  At Kew, at Kew in lilac-time (and oh, so near to London!),
And when the rose begins to pout and all the chestnut spires
    are out
  You'll hear the rest without a doubt, all chorussing for
  London:

Come down to Kew in lilac-time, in lilac-time, in lilac-time;
  Come down to Kew in lilac-time (it isn't far from London!),
And you shall wander hand in hand with love in summer's wonderland;
  Come down to Kew in lilac-time (it isn't far from London!).

And then the troubadour begins to thrill the golden street,
  In the City as the sun sinks low;
And in all the gaudy busses there are scores of weary feet
Marking time, sweet time, with a dull mechanic beat,
And a thousand hearts are plunging to a love they'll never
  meet,
Through the meadows of the sunset, through the poppies and
  the wheat,
  In the land where the dead dreams go.

        So it's Jeremiah, Jeremiah,
          What have you to say
        When you meet the garland girls
          Tripping on their way?

        All around my gala hat
          I wear a wreath of roses.
        (A long and lonely year it is
          I've waited for the May!).
        If any one should ask you,
          The reason why I wear it is—
        My own love, my true love, is
          coming home to-day.

And it's buy a bunch of violets for the lady,
  (*It's lilac-time in London! It's lilac-time in London!*)
Buy a bunch of violets for the lady
  While the sky burns blue above.
On the other side the street you'll find it shady,
  (*It's lilac-time in London! It's lilac-time in London!*)
But buy a bunch of violets for the lady,
  And tell her she's your own true love.

There's a barrel-organ carolling across a golden street
  In the City as the sun sinks glittering and slow;
And the music's not immortal; but the world has made it
    sweet,
And enriched it with the harmonies that make a song
    complete,
In the deeper heavens of music where the night and morning
    meet,
  As it dies into the sunset-glow;
And it pulses through the pleasures of the City and the pain
That surround the singing organ like a large eternal light,
  And they've given it a glory and a part to play again
In the Symphony that rules the day and night.

          And there, as the music changes,
            The song runs round again.
          Once more it turns and ranges
            Through all its joy and pain,
          Dissects the common carnival
            Of passions and regrets;
          And the wheeling world remembers all
            The wheeling song forgets.

          Once more *La Traviata* sighs
            Another sadder song.
          Once more *Il Trovatore* cries
            A tale of deeper wrong.
          Once more the knights to battle go
            With sword and shield and lance,
          Till once, once more, the shattered foe
            Has whirled into—*a dance!*

Come down to Kew in lilac-time, in lilac-time, in lilac-time.
  Come down to Kew in lilac-time (it isn't far from London!)
And you shall wander hand in hand with love in summer's wonderland.
  Come down to Kew in lilac-time (it isn't far from London!).

JOHN HOWARD PAYNE
(1791–1852)

ALTHOUGH BORN in New York, Payne spent most of his life moving here and
there to escape creditors. No one remembers him now, but in his day he was a

well-known actor and dramatist. In London he fell passionately in love with Shelley's widow, Mary, who had written *Frankenstein* when she was nineteen, and was then playing the field with beautiful men and women. Apparently Mary did not reciprocate. Payne died in Tunis while serving there as the American consul.

"Home, Sweet Home," his only claim to fame, was written in Paris in 1822. It was set to music by the British composer Sir Henry Bishop, and first sung in a performance of Payne's play *Clari, or, The Maid of Milan* (1823). It was one of Jenny Lind's favorite encores, always bringing down the house, and it provided Judy Garland's final remark in the 1939 film version of *The Wizard of Oz*.

In *The Life and Writings of John Howard Payne* (1875) we learn of two additional stanzas that Payne added to the sheet music:

> To *us*, in despite of the absence of years,
> How sweet the remembrance of *home* still appears!
> From allurements abroad, which but flatter the eye,
> The unsatisfied heart turns, and says with a sigh,
> > Home, home, sweet, sweet home!
> > There's no place like home!
> > There's no place like home!

> *Your* exile is blest with all fate can bestow;
> But *mine* has been checkered with many a woe!
> Yet, tho' different our fortunes, our thoughts are the same,
> And both, as we think of Columbia, exclaim,
> > Home, home, sweet, sweet home!
> > There's no place like home!
> > There's no place like home!

Michael Turner, in his *Parlour Song Book* (1973), quotes the following passage from Payne's diary:

> How often have I been in the heart of Paris, Berlin, London or some other city, and have heard persons singing or hand-organs playing 'Home! Sweet Home!', without having a shilling to buy myself the next meal, or a place to lay my head. The world has literally sung my song until every heart is familiar with its melody, yet I have been a wanderer from my boyhood.

It is one of the few songs, Turner adds, that has been celebrated in another song. Julian Jordan's "The Song That Reach'd My Heart," popular a hundred years ago, has this stanza:

> She sang a song, a song of home,
> A song that reach'd my heart.
> Home, home, sweet, sweet home.
> She sang the song of 'Home, Sweet Home',
> The Song that reach'd my heart.

Payne's childhood home in East Hampton, Long Island, has been preserved as a museum.

Home, Sweet Home

'Mid pleasures and palaces though we may roam,
Be it ever so humble, there's no place like home;
A charm from the sky seems to hallow us there,
Which, seek through the world, is ne'er met with elsewhere.
   Home, home, sweet, sweet home!
There's no place like home, oh, there's no place like home!

An exile from home, splendor dazzles in vain;
Oh, give me my lowly thatched cottage again!
The birds singing gayly, that came at my call—
Give me them—and the peace of mind, dearer than all!
   Home, home, sweet, sweet home!
There's no place like home, oh, there's no place like home!

I gaze on the moon as I tread the drear wild,
And feel that my mother now thinks of her child,
As she looks on that moon from our own cottage door
Thro' the woodbine, whose fragrance shall cheer me no more.
   Home, home, sweet, sweet home!
There's no place like home, oh, there's no place like home!

How sweet 'tis to sit 'neath a fond father's smile,
And the caress of a mother to soothe and beguile!
Let others delight 'mid new pleasure to roam,
But give me, oh, give me, the pleasures of home,
   Home, home, sweet, sweet home!
There's no place like home, oh, there's no place like home!

To thee I'll return, overburdened with care;
The heart's dearest solace will smile on me there;
No more from that cottage again will I roam;
Be it ever so humble, there's no place like home.
   Home, home, sweet, sweet home!
There's no place like home, oh, there's no place like home!

EDGAR ALLAN POE
(1809–1849)

POE WAS born in Boston, orphaned at the age of two, and expelled from West
Point. He was an influential magazine editor, critic, poet and pioneer author

of horror tales, science fiction and detective mysteries until poverty, alcohol and mental illness did him in at the age of forty.

Poe's verse has always been admired by some and pilloried by others. Emerson called him "the jingle man," and Lowell wrote in his *Fable for Critics:*

> Here comes Poe with his Raven, like Barnaby Rudge,
> Three fifths of him genius, and two fifths sheer fudge.

On the other hand, W. B. Yeats considered him a "great lyric poet," and Elizabeth Barrett Browning praised "The Raven" in the following portion of a letter that Poe greatly prized:

> Your *Raven* has produced a sensation, a "fit horror," here in England. Some of my friends are taken by the fear of it and some by the music. I hear of persons haunted by the "Nevermore," and one acquaintance of mine who has the misfortune of possessing a "bust of Pallas" never can bear to look at it in the twilight. I think you will like to be told that our great poet, Mr. Browning . . . was struck much by the rhythm of that poem.

Poe at first intended his mysterious bird to be an owl. The poem went through endless revisions to be published eventually in the New York *Mirror* (January 29, 1845). In his essay "The Philosophy of Composition" Poe gives a curious, detailed account of why he wrote the poem and how he constructed it.

"Annabel Lee" was published two days after Poe's death in the New York *Tribune* (October 9, 1849). No one is sure who Annabel was intended to represent, but most Poe experts think he had in mind his cousin Virginia Clemm, whom he married when he was twenty-six, she thirteen, and who died of tuberculosis eleven years later. She turns up as Annabel Leigh, Humbert Humbert's first love, in Nabokov's *Lolita.*

"To Helen," written in Poe's middle teens when he was at West Point, is said to commemorate the death of Mrs. Jane Stannard, the mother of a schoolmate. Poe idolized her. The lyric was first published in *Poems* (1831), where the last two lines of the middle stanza read:

> To the beauty of fair Greece,
> And the grandeur of old Rome.

Critics have debated the identity of the "weary, way-worn wanderer." Most believe it to be Ulysses, and that Poe substituted the inaccurate "Nicéan" for "Phaeacian" because it sounded better.

"The Bells," after many revisions, finally appeared posthumously in John Sartain's *Union Magazine* (November 1849). Here is the beginning of an early anonymous parody:

> Hear the fluter with his flute,
> Silver flute!
> Oh, what a world of wailing is awakened by its toot!
> How it demi-semi quavers
> On the maddened air of night!
> And defieth all endeavors
> To escape the sound or sight

Of the flute, flute, flute,
With its tootle, tootle, toot—
With reiterated tootings of exasperating toots,
The long protracted tootelings of agonizing toots
Of the flute, flute, flute, flute,
Flute, flute, flute,
And the wheezings and the spittings of its toots.

You'll find the rest of it in Slason Thompson's *The Humbler Poets* (1885). "The Bells" also inspired the title of Daniel Hoffman's biography *Poe Poe Poe Poe Poe Poe Poe* (1972).

The Raven

Once upon a midnight dreary, while I pondered, weak and
    weary,
Over many a quaint and curious volume of forgotten lore—
While I nodded, nearly napping, suddenly there came a
    tapping,
As of some one gently rapping, rapping at my chamber door.
"'Tis some visitor," I muttered, "tapping at my chamber
    door—
        Only this and nothing more."

Ah, distinctly I remember it was in the bleak December;
And each separate dying ember wrought its ghost upon the
    floor.
Eagerly I wished the morrow;—vainly I had sought to borrow
From my books surcease of sorrow—sorrow for the lost
    Lenore—
For the rare and radiant maiden whom the angels name
    Lenore—
        Nameless *here* for evermore.

And the silken, sad, uncertain rustling of each purple curtain
Thrilled me—filled me with fantastic terrors never felt before;
So that now, to still the beating of my heart, I stood repeating
"'Tis some visitor entreating entrance at my chamber door—
Some late visitor entreating entrance at my chamber door;—
        This it is and nothing more."

Presently my soul grew stronger; hesitating then no longer,
"Sir," said I, "or Madam, truly your forgiveness I implore;
But the fact is I was napping, and so gently you came rapping,

And so faintly you came tapping, tapping at my chamber
 door,
That I scarce was sure I heard you"—here I opened wide the
 door;—
  Darkness there and nothing more.

Deep into that darkness peering, long I stood there wondering,
 fearing,
Doubtful, dreaming dreams no mortal ever dared to dream
 before;
But the silence was unbroken, and the stillness gave no token,
And the only word there spoken was the whispered word,
 "Lenore!"
This I whispered, and an echo murmured back the word
 "Lenore!"
  Merely this and nothing more.

Back into the chamber turning, all my soul within me burning,
Soon again I heard a tapping somewhat louder than before.
"Surely," said I, "surely that is something at my window
 lattice;
Let me see, then, what thereat is, and this mystery explore—
Let my heart be still a moment and this mystery explore;—
  'Tis the wind and nothing more!"

Open here I flung the shutter, when, with many a flirt and
 flutter,
In there stepped a stately Raven of the saintly days of yore.
Not the least obeisance made he; not a minute stopped or
 stayed he;
But, with mien of lord or lady, perched above my chamber
 door—
Perched upon a bust of Pallas just above my chamber door—
  Perched, and sat, and nothing more.

Then this ebony bird beguiling my sad fancy into smiling,
By the grave and stern decorum of the countenance it wore,
"Though thy crest be shorn and shaven, thou," I said, "art
 sure no craven,
Ghastly grim and ancient Raven wandering from the Nightly
 shore—
Tell me what thy lordly name is on the Night's Plutonian
 shore!"
  Quoth the Raven, "Nevermore."

Much I marvelled this ungainly fowl to hear discourse so
    plainly,
Though its answer little meaning—little relevancy bore;
For we cannot help agreeing that no living human being
Ever yet was blessed with seeing bird above his chamber
    door—
Bird or beast upon the sculptured bust above his chamber
    door,
        With such name as "Nevermore."

But the Raven, sitting lonely on the placid bust, spoke only
That one word, as if his soul in that one word he did outpour.
Nothing farther then he uttered—not a feather then he
    fluttered—
Till I scarcely more than muttered "Other friends have flown
    before—
On the morrow *he* will leave me, as my hopes have flown
    before."
        Then the bird said "Nevermore."

Startled at the stillness broken by reply so aptly spoken,
"Doubtless," said I, "what it utters is its only stock and store
Caught from some unhappy master whom unmerciful Disaster
Followed fast and followed faster till his songs one burden
    bore—
Till the dirges of his Hope that melancholy burden bore
        Of 'Never—nevermore.'"

But the Raven still beguiling all my fancy into smiling,
Straight I wheeled a cushioned seat in front of bird, and bust
    and door;
Then, upon the velvet sinking, I betook myself to linking
Fancy unto fancy, thinking what this ominous bird of yore—
What this grim, ungainly, ghastly, gaunt, and ominous bird
    of yore
        Meant in croaking "Nevermore."

This I sat engaged in guessing, but no syllable expressing
To the fowl whose fiery eyes now burned into my bosom's
    core;
This and more I sat divining, with my head at ease reclining
On the cushion's velvet lining that the lamp-light gloated o'er,
But whose velvet violet lining with the lamp-light gloating
    o'er,
        She shall press, ah, nevermore!

Then, methought, the air grew denser, perfumed from an
  unseen censer
Swung by Seraphim whose foot-falls tinkled on the tufted
  floor.
"Wretch," I cried, "thy God hath lent thee—by these angels
  he hath sent thee
Respite—respite and nepenthe from thy memories of Lenore;
Quaff, oh quaff this kind nepenthe and forget this lost
  Lenore!"
  Quoth the Raven, "Nevermore."

"Prophet!" said I, "thing of evil!—prophet still, if bird or
  devil!—
Whether Tempter sent, or whether tempest tossed thee here
  ashore,
Desolate yet all undaunted, on this desert land enchanted—
On this home by Horror haunted—tell me truly, I implore—
Is there—*is* there balm in Gilead?—tell me—tell me, I
  implore!"
  Quoth the Raven "Nevermore."

"Prophet!" said I, "thing of evil—prophet still, if bird or
  devil!
By that Heaven that bends above us—by that God we both
  adore—
Tell this soul with sorrow laden if, within the distant Aidenn,
It shall clasp a sainted maiden whom the angels name
  Lenore—
Clasp a rare and radiant maiden whom the angels name
  Lenore."
  Quote the Raven "Nevermore."

"Be that word our sign of parting, bird or fiend!" I shrieked,
  upstarting—
"Get thee back into the tempest and the Night's Plutonian
  shore!
Leave no black plume as a token of that lie thy soul hath
  spoken!
Leave my loneliness unbroken!—quit the bust above my door!
Take thy beak from out my heart, and take thy form from off
  my door!"
  Quoth the Raven "Nevermore."

And the Raven, never flitting, still is sitting, *still* is sitting
On the pallid bust of Pallas just above my chamber door;

And his eyes have all the seeming of a demon's that is
    dreaming,
And the lamp-light o'er him streaming throws his shadow on
    the floor;
And my soul from out that shadow that lies floating on the
    floor
        Shall be lifted—nevermore!

Annabel Lee

It was many and many a year ago,
    In a kingdom by the sea,
That a maiden there lived whom you may know
    By the name of ANNABEL LEE;
And this maiden she lived with no other thought
    Than to love and be loved by me.

I was a child and *she* was a child,
    In this kingdom by the sea:
But we loved with a love that was more than love—
    I and my ANNABEL LEE;
With a love that the winged seraphs of heaven
    Coveted her and me.

And this was the reason that, long ago,
    In this kingdom by the sea,
A wind blew out of a cloud, chilling
    My beautiful ANNABEL LEE;
So that her high-born kinsman came
    And bore her away from me,
To shut her up in a sepulchre
    In this kingdom by the sea.

The angels, not half so happy in heaven,
    Went envying her and me—
Yes!—that was the reason (as all men know,
    In this kingdom by the sea)
That the wind came out of the cloud by night,
    Chilling and killing my ANNABEL LEE.

But our love it was stronger by far than the love
    Of those who were older than we—

Of many far wiser than we—
And neither the angels in heaven above,
    Nor the demons down under the sea,
Can ever dissever my soul from the soul
    Of the beautiful ANNABEL LEE.

For the moon never beams, without bringing me dreams
    Of the beautiful ANNABEL LEE;
And the stars never rise, but I feel the bright eyes
    Of the beautiful ANNABEL LEE;
And so, all the night-tide, I lie down by the side
Of my darling—my darling—my life and my bride,
    In the sepulchre there by the sea,
    In her tomb by the sounding sea.

To Helen

Helen, thy beauty is to me
    Like those Nicéan barks of yore,
That gently, o'er a perfumed sea,
    The weary, way-worn wanderer bore
    To his own native shore.

On desperate seas long wont to roam,
    Thy hyacinth hair, thy classic face,
Thy Naiad airs have brought me home
    To the glory that was Greece,
    And the grandeur that was Rome.

Lo! in yon brilliant window-niche
    How statue-like I see thee stand,
The agate lamp within thy hand!
    Ah, Psyche, from the regions which
    Are Holy-Land!

The Bells

I

Hear the sledges with the bells—
    Silver bells!
What a world of merriment their melody foretells!

How they tinkle, tinkle, tinkle,
In the icy air of night!
While the stars that oversprinkle
All the heavens, seem to twinkle
With a crystalline delight;
Keeping time, time, time,
In a sort of Runic rhyme,
To the tintinnabulation that so musically wells
From the bells, bells, bells, bells,
Bells, bells, bells—
From the jingling and tinkling of the bells.

II

Hear the mellow wedding bells—
Golden bells!
What a world of happiness their harmony foretells!
Through the balmy air of night
How they ring out their delight!—
From the molten-golden notes,
And all in tune,
What a liquid ditty floats
To the turtle-dove that listens, while she gloats
On the moon!
Oh, from out the sounding cells,
What a gush of euphony voluminously wells!
How it swells!
How it dwells
On the Future!—how it tells
Of the rapture that impels
To the swinging and the ringing
Of the bells, bells, bells—
Of the bells, bells, bells, bells,
Bells, bells, bells—
To the rhyming and the chiming of the bells!

III

Hear the loud alarum bells—
Brazen bells!
What a tale of terror, now their turbulency tells!
In the startled ear of night
How they scream out their affright!
Too much horrified to speak,

They can only shriek, shriek,
Out of tune,
In a clamorous appealing to the mercy of the fire,
In a mad expostulation with the deaf and frantic fire,
Leaping higher, higher, higher,
With a desperate desire,
And a resolute endeavour
Now—now to sit, or never,
By the side of the pale-faced moon.
Oh, the bells, bells, bells!
What a tale their terror tells
Of Despair!
How they clang, and clash, and roar!
What a horror they outpour
On the bosom of the palpitating air!
Yet the ear, it fully knows,
By the twanging,
And the clanging,
How the danger ebbs and flows;
Yet the ear distinctly tells,
In the jangling,
And the wrangling,
How the danger sinks and swells,
By the sinking or the swelling in the anger of the bells—
Of the bells—
Of the bells, bells, bells, bells,
Bells, bells, bells—
In the clamor and the clanging of the bells!

IV

Hear the tolling of the bells—
Iron bells!
What a word of solemn thought their monody compels!
In the silence of the night,
How we shiver with affright
At the melancholy menace of their tone!
For every sound that floats
From the rust within their throats
Is a groan.
And the people—ah, the people—
They that dwell up in the steeple,
All alone,
And who, tolling, tolling, tolling,

In that muffled monotone,
Feel a glory in so rolling
   On the human heart a stone—
They are neither man nor woman—
They are neither brute nor human—
    They are Ghouls:—
And their king it is who tolls:—
And he rolls, rolls, rolls,
    Rolls
A pæan from the bells!
And his merry bosom swells
With the pæan of the bells!
And he dances, and he yells;
  Keeping time, time, time,
  In a sort of Runic rhyme,
    To the pæan of the bells:—
    Of the bells:
  Keeping time, time, time
  In a sort of Runic rhyme,
    To the throbbing of the bells—
    Of the bells, bells, bells:—
  To the sobbing of the bells:—
Keeping time, time, time,
    As he knells, knells, knells,
  In a happy Runic rhyme,
    To the rolling of the bells—
    Of the bells, bells, bells:—
    To the tolling of the bells—
  Of the bells, bells, bells, bells,
    Bells, bells, bells—
To the moaning and the groaning of the bells.

ADELAIDE ANNE PROCTER
(1825–1864)

WHO TODAY can name the author of "The Lost Chord"? Adelaide Procter was born in London, the daughter of a famous father who wrote songs and plays under the pen name "Barry Cornwall." In 1853 she began submitting poems to Dickens' periodical *Household Words*, using the pseudonym "Mary Berwick" so that Dickens would not be influenced by his friendship with her father.

After Adelaide's death Dickens wrote a touching memoir for the *Atlantic Monthly* (December 1865) that later became the preface to the 1866 edition of Procter's *Legends and Lyrics*. In 1851 she converted to Roman Catholicism. She died of consumption in London at the age of thirty-nine.

Sir Arthur Sullivan set "The Lost Chord" to music. Enrico Caruso sang it often, and there is a famous recording of him singing it in broken English.

Freudians have had a field day with "The Lost Chord," seeing it as unconsciously symbolic of masturbation. There have been scores of parodies. In her *Parody Anthology* (1904) Carolyn Wells includes three amusing spoofs: "The Lost Voice," "The Lost Ape" and "The Lost Word." Here are their first stanzas:

> Seated at Church in the winter
> I was frozen in every limb;
> And the village choir shrieked wildly
> Over a noisy hymn.

> Seated one day on an organ,
> A monkey was ill at ease,
> When his fingers wandered idly,
> In search of the busy fleas.

> Seated one day at the typewriter,
> I was weary of a's and e's,
> And my fingers wandered wildly
> Over the consonant keys.

Jimmy Durante did a number called "I'm the Man Who Found the Lost Chord." A systematic procedure for finding the lost chord was given by E. N. Gilbert, a mathematician at Bell Labs, in his paper "Finding the Lost Chord" (*Journal of Irreproducible Results*, Vol. 24, No. 1, 1978; reprinted in *The Best of the Journal of Irreproducible Results*, 1983). Gilbert concludes, on the basis of an imagined experiment, that the most likely candidate for the lost chord is the chord of no notes, or silence.

The Lost Chord

Seated one day at the Organ,
I was weary and ill at ease,
And my fingers wandered idly
Over the noisy keys.

I do not know what I was playing,
Or what I was dreaming then;
But I struck one chord of music,
Like the sound of a great Amen.

It flooded the crimson twilight,
  Like the close of an Angel's Psalm,
And it lay on my fevered spirit
  With a touch of infinite calm.

It quieted pain and sorrow,
  Like love overcoming strife;
It seemed the harmonious echo
  From our discordant life.

It linked all perplexèd meanings
  Into one perfect peace,
And trembled away into silence
  As if it were loth to cease.

I have sought, but I seek it vainly,
  That one lost chord divine,
Which came from the soul of the Organ,
  And entered into mine.

It may be that Death's bright angel
  Will speak in that chord again,—
It may be that only in Heaven
  I shall hear that grand Amen.

JAMES WHITCOMB RILEY
(1849–1916)

INDIANA'S MOST famous poet, Riley began his career working for the Indianapolis *Daily Journal*. The four poems included here were all written for that
paper under the pseudonym "Benj. F. Johnson, of Boone." The same name
also appeared on Riley's first book, *The Old Swimmin'-Hole and 'Leven More
Poems* (1883). His voluminous output made him one of America's best-loved
and wealthiest versifiers.

The whimsical sentimentalism of Riley's poems—he liked to praise what he
called "the golden olden glory of the days gone by"—and their Hoosier dialect
offended many critics. Ambrose Bierce called Riley's verse a "ripple of a rill of
buttermilk falling into a pig-trough. His pathos is bathos; his sentiment
sediment." When a ninety-year-old Louis Untermeyer was interviewed by the
New York Times (September 30, 1975), he was asked what poets in his many
anthologies he would now omit. "James Whitcomb Riley," he replied. "Why,
why, why, why, oh God, why did I ever include him? I guess I was impressed
by all the good clean Midwestern corn."

"An Old Sweetheart of Mine" first appeared in the Indianapolis *Daily Journal* on March 2, 1877. A popular 1902 edition of the poem was illustrated by Howard Chandler Christy. "Little Orphant Annie" ran in the same paper on November 15, 1885. It was titled "The Elf Child," and the girl's name was "Little Orphant Allie." The poem was set to music by E. Appleton in 1892.

As a young man Riley annoyed the critics by publishing "Leonainie," a poem he claimed to be a newly discovered work by Edgar Allan Poe. The hoax got him fired from the newspaper for which he was working.

Shortly before Riley's death, "Riley Day" was declared by Indiana to honor the poet's birthday on October 7. It is still celebrated in the state. Riley's home on Lockerbie Street, Indianapolis, has been preserved and is open to the public. A children's hospital in Indianapolis is named for him. When Riley died, Edgar Guest wrote a poem about how happy the children in heaven would be when he arrived there.

The Old Swimmin'-Hole

Oh! the old swimmin'-hole! whare the crick so still and deep
Looked like a baby-river that was laying half asleep,
And the gurgle of the worter round the drift jest below
Sounded like the laugh of something we onc't ust to know
Before we could remember anything but the eyes
Of the angels lookin' out as we left Paradise;
But the merry days of youth is beyond our controle,
And it's hard to part ferever with the old swimmin'-hole.

Oh! the old swimmin'-hole! In the happy days of yore,
When I ust to lean above it on the old sickamore,
Oh! it showed me a face in its warm sunny tide
That gazed back at me so gay and glorified,
It made me love myself, as I leaped to caress
My shadder smilin' up at me with sich tenderness.
But them days is past and gone, and old Time's tuck his toll
From the old man come back to the old swimmin'-hole.

Oh! the old swimmin'-hole! In the long, lazy days
When the humdrum of school made so many run-a-ways,
How plesant was the jurney down the old dusty lane,
Whare the tracks of our bare feet was all printed so plane
You could tell by the dent of the heel and the sole
They was lots o' fun on hands at the old swimmin'-hole.
But the lost joys is past! Let your tears in sorrow roll
Like the rain that ust to dapple up the old swimmin'-hole.

Thare the bullrushes growed, and the cattails so tall,
And the sunshine and shadder fell over it all;
And it mottled the worter with amber and gold
Tel the glad lilies rocked in the ripples that rolled;
And the snake-feeder's four gauzy wings fluttered by
Like the ghost of a daisy dropped out of the sky,
Or a wownded apple-blossom in the breeze's controle
As it cut acrost some orchurd to'rds the old swimmin'-hole.

Oh! the old swimmin'-hole! When I last saw the place,
The scenes was all changed, like the change in my face;
The bridge of the railroad now crosses the spot
Whare the old divin'-log lays sunk and fergot.
And I stray down the banks whare the trees ust to be—
But never again will theyr shade shelter me!
And I wish in my sorrow I could strip to the soul,
And dive off in my grave like the old swimmin'-hole.

An Old Sweetheart of Mine

An old sweetheart of mine!—Is this her presence here with
    me,
Or but a vain creation of a lover's memory?
A fair, illusive vision that would vanish into air
Dared I even touch the silence with the whisper of a prayer?

Nay, let me then believe in all the blended false and true—
The semblance of the *old* love and the substance of the *new*,—
The *then* of changeless sunny days—the *now* of shower and
    shine—
But Love forever smiling—as that old sweetheart of mine.

This ever-restful sense of *home*, though shouts ring in the
    hall.—
The easy chair—the old book-shelves and prints along the
    wall;
The rare *Habanas* in their box, or gaunt church-warden-stem
That often wags, above the jar, derisively at them.

As one who cons at evening o'er an album, all alone,
And muses on the faces of the friends that he has known,

So I turn the leaves of Fancy, till, in shadowy design,
I find the smiling features of an old sweetheart of mine.

The lamplight seems to glimmer with a flicker of surprise,
As I turn it low—to rest me of the dazzle in my eyes,
And light my pipe in silence, save a sigh that seems to yoke
Its fate with my tobacco and to vanish with the smoke.

'Tis a *fragrant* retrospection,—for the loving thoughts that
     start
Into being are like perfume from the blossom of the heart;
And to dream the old dreams over is a luxury divine—
When my truant fancies wander with that old sweetheart of
     mine.

Though I hear beneath my study, like a fluttering of wings,
The voices of my children and the mother as she sings—
I feel no twinge of conscience to deny me any theme
When Care has cast her anchor in the harbor of a dream—

In fact, to speak in earnest, I believe it adds a charm
To spice the good a trifle with a little dust of harm,—
For I find an extra flavor in Memory's mellow wine
That makes me drink the deeper to that old sweetheart of
     mine.

O Childhood-days enchanted! O the magic of the Spring!—
With all green boughs to blossom white, and all bluebirds to
     sing!
When all the air, to toss and quaff, made life a jubilee
And changed the children's song and laugh to shrieks of
     ecstasy.

With eyes half closed in clouds that ooze from lips that taste,
     as well,
The peppermint and cinnamon, I hear the old School bell,
And from "Recess" romp in again from "Blackman's" broken
     line,
To smile, behind my "lesson," at that old sweetheart of mine.

A face of lily beauty, with a form of airy grace,
Floats out of my tobacco as the Genii from the vase;
And I thrill beneath the glances of a pair of azure eyes
As glowing as the summer and as tender as the skies.

I can see the pink sunbonnet and the little checkered dress
She wore when first I kissed her and she answered the caress

With the written declaration that, "as surely as the vine
Grew 'round the stump," she loved me—that old sweetheart
    of mine.

Again I made her presents, in a really helpless way,—
The big "Rhode Island Greening"—I was hungry, too, that
    day!—
But I followed her from Spelling, with her hand behind her—
    so—
And I slip the apple in it—and the Teacher doesn't know!

I give my *treasures* to her—all,—my pencil—blue-and-red;—
And, if little girls played marbles, *mine* should all be *hers*,
    instead!
But *she* gave me her *photograph*, and printed "Ever Thine"
Across the back—in blue-and-red—that old sweetheart of
    mine!

And again I feel the pressure of her slender little hand,
As we used to talk together of the future we had planned,—
When I should be a poet, and with nothing else to do
But write the tender verses that she set the music to . . .

When we should live together in a cozy little cot
Hid in a nest of roses, with a fairy garden-spot,
Where the vines were ever fruited, and the weather ever fine,
And the birds were ever singing for that old sweetheart of
    mine.

When I should be her lover forever and a day,
And she my faithful sweetheart till the golden hair was gray;
And we should be so happy that when either's lips were dumb
They would not smile in Heaven till the other's kiss had come.

But, ah! my dream is broken by a step upon the stair,
And the door is softly opened, and—my wife is standing
    there:
Yet with eagerness and rapture all my visions I resign,—
To greet the *living* presence of that old sweetheart of mine.

Little Orphant Annie

INSCRIBED
WITH ALL FAITH AND AFFECTION

To all the little children:—The happy ones; and sad ones;
The sober and the silent ones; the boisterous and glad ones;
The good ones—Yes, the good ones, too; and all the lovely bad ones.

Little Orphant Annie's come to our house to stay,
An' wash the cups an' saucers up, an' brush the crumbs away,
An' shoo the chickens off the porch, an' dust the hearth, an'
    sweep,
An' make the fire, an' bake the bread, an' earn her board-an'-
    keep;
An' all us other childern, when the supper-things is done,
We set arourd the kitchen fire an' has the mostest fun
A-list'nin' to the witch-tales 'at Annie tells about,
An' the Gobble-uns 'at gits you
        Ef you
          Don't
            Watch
              Out!

Wunst they wuz a little boy wouldn't say his prayers,—
An' when he went to bed at night, away up-stairs,
His Mammy heerd him holler, an' his Daddy heerd him bawl,
An' when they turn't the kivvers down, he wuzn't there at all!
An' they seeked him in the rafter-room, an' cubby-hole, an'
    press,
An' seeked him up the chimbly-fluc, an' ever'-wheres, I guess;
But all they ever found wuz thist his pants an' roundabout:—
An' the Gobble-uns 'll git you
        Ef you
          Don't
            Watch
              Out!

An' one time a little girl 'ud allus laugh an' grin,
An' make fun of ever' one, an' all her blood-an'-kin;
An' wunst, when they was "company," an' ole folks wuz
    there,
She mocked 'em an' shocked 'em, an' said she didn't care!
An' thist as she kicked her heels, an' turn't to run an' hide,
They wuz two great big Black Things a-standin' by her side,

An' they snatched her through the ceilin' 'fore she knowed
    what she's about!
An' the Gobble-uns 'll git you
        Ef you
           Don't
               Watch
                  Out!

An' little Orphant Annie says, when the blaze is blue,
An' the lamp-wick sputters, an' the wind goes *woo-oo!*
An' you hear the crickets quit, an' the moon is gray,
An' the lightnin'-bugs in dew is all squenched away,—
You better mind yer parunts, an' yer teachurs fond an' dear,
An' churish them 'at loves you, an' dry the orphant's tear,
An' he'p the pore an' needy ones 'at clusters all about,
Er the Gobble-uns 'll git you
        Ef you
           Don't
               Watch
                  Out!

When the Frost Is on the Punkin

When the frost is on the punkin and the fodder's in the shock,
And you hear the kyouck and gobble of the struttin' turkey-
    cock
And the clackin' of the guineys, and the cluckin' of the hens,
And the rooster's hallylooer as he tiptoes on the fence;
O, it's then the times a feller is a-feelin' at his best,
With the risin' sun to greet him from a night of peaceful rest,
As he leaves the house, bareheaded, and goes to feed the
    stock,
When the frost is on the punkin and the fodder's in the shock.

They's something kindo' harty-like about the atmusfere
When the heat of summer's over and the coolin' fall is here—
Of course we miss the flowers, and the blossoms on the trees,
And the mumble of the hummin'-birds and buzzin' of the
    bees;
But the air's so appetizin'; and the landscape through the
    haze

Of a crisp and sunny morning of the airly autumn days
Is a pictur' that no painter has the colorin' to mock—
When the frost is on the punkin and the fodder's in the shock.

The husky, rusty russel of the tossels of the corn,
And the raspin' of the tangled leaves, as golden as the morn;
The stubble in the furries—kindo' lonesome-like, but still
A-preachin' sermons to us of the barns they growed to fill;
The strawstack in the medder, and the reaper in the shed;
The hosses in theyr stalls below—the clover overhead!—
O, it sets my hart a-clickin' like the tickin' of a clock,
When the frost is on the punkin and the fodder's in the shock!

Then your apples all is gethered, and the ones a feller keeps
Is poured around the celler-floor in red and yeller heaps;
And your cider-makin' 's over, and your wimmern-folks is
　　　through
With their mince and apple-butter, and theyr souse and
　　　saussage, too!
I don't know how to tell it—but ef sich a thing could be
As the Angels wantin' boardin', and they'd call around on
　　　me—
I'd want to 'commodate 'em—all the whole-indurin' flock—
When the frost is on the punkin and the fodder's in the shock!

CARL SANDBURG
(1878–1967)

CARL SANDBURG's father was a Swedish immigrant who could not sign his name. Born in Galesburg, Illinois, young Carl rode boxcars as a hobo and worked at a variety of laboring jobs before he became a journalist and an organizer for democratic socialism. (He was secretary to Emil Seidel, Milwaukee's first socialist mayor.) Not until "Chicago" ran in *Poetry* magazine in 1914 did his career as a poet take off. This, his best-known poem, along with "Fog," are in his first book, *Chicago Poems* (1916). Ten years later Rebecca West edited his *Selected Poems*.

Sandburg's monumental six-volume biography of Lincoln won him a Pulitzer Prize in 1940, and a decade later his *Complete Poems* won him a second Pulitzer. He died on a large goat farm in Flat Rock, North Carolina, where he and his wife, a sister of photographer Edward Steichen, had settled.

Sandburg's rugged free verse, in the tradition of Walt Whitman, whom he revered, is both admired and scorned by today's critics. Is free verse, as Robert

Frost once said, like playing tennis without a net, or does it free the poet from the necessity of struggling to distort meanings in order to make the rhythms and rhymes work? "For myself," wrote the Chicago critic and poet Vincent Starrett, "I rate him [Sandburg] above Whitman, and read him with greater pleasure."

"Here is the difference between Dante, Milton, and me," Sandburg said to his friend Harry Golden. "They wrote about hell and never saw the place. I wrote about Chicago after looking the town over for years and years."

Chicago

Hog Butcher for the World,
Tool Maker, Stacker of Wheat,
Player with Railroads and the Nation's Freight Handler;
Stormy, husky, brawling,
City of the Big Shoulders:

They tell me you are wicked and I believe them, for I have
    seen your painted women under the gas lamps luring the
    farm boys.
And they tell me you are crooked and I answer: Yes, it is true
    I have seen the gunman kill and go free to kill again.
And they tell me you are brutal and my reply is: On the faces
    of the women and children I have seen the marks of
    wanton hunger.
And having answered so I turn once more to those who sneer
    at this my city, and I give them back the sneer and say
    to them:
Come and show me another city with lifted head singing so
    proud to be alive and coarse and strong and cunning.

Flinging magnetic curses amid the toil of piling job on job,
    here is a tall bold slugger set vivid against the little soft
    cities;
Fierce as a dog with tongue lapping for action, cunning as a
    savage pitted against the wilderness,
        Bareheaded,
        Shoveling,
        Wrecking,
        Planning,
        Building, breaking, rebuilding,

Under the smoke, dust all over his mouth, laughing with
   white teeth,
Under the terrible burden of destiny laughing as a young man
   laughs,
Laughing even as an ignorant fighter laughs who has never
   lost a battle,
Bragging and laughing that under his wrist is the pulse and
   under his ribs the heart of the people,
      Laughing!
Laughing the stormy, husky, brawling laughter of Youth, half-
   naked, sweating, proud to be Hog Butcher, Tool Maker,
   Stacker of Wheat, Player with the Railroads and Freight
   Handler to the Nation.

Fog

The fog comes
on little cat feet.
It sits looking
over harbor and city
on silent haunches
and then moves on.

JOHN GODFREY SAXE
(1816–1887)

A VERMONT-BORN-AND-EDUCATED lawyer and journalist, Saxe was editor of
the Burlington, Vermont, *Sentinel* from 1850 until 1856, an attorney general of
Vermont and an unsuccessful Democratic candidate for governor in 1859. In
1860 he moved to Albany, New York, where he edited the *Evening Journal*. He
was part of the Knickerbocker group that contributed to *Knickerbocker* magazine. His last years were spent in deep depression after the deaths of his wife
and five of his six children. He was also severely injured in a train accident.
Ironically, one of his most anthologized poems, "Railroad Rhyme," celebrates
the pleures and excitement of train travel.
   Saxe's books of humorous verse were popular in their day, but now only
"The Blind Men and the Elephant" is remembered.

The Blind Men and the Elephant

It was six men of Indostan
   To learning much inclined,
Who went to see the Elephant
   (Though all of them were blind),
That each by observation
   Might satisfy his mind.

The *First* approached the Elephant,
   And happening to fall
Against his broad and sturdy side,
   At once began to bawl:
"God bless me! but the Elephant
   Is very like a wall!"

The *Second*, feeling of the tusk,
   Cried, "Ho! what have we here
So very round and smooth and sharp?
   To me 'tis mighty clear
This wonder of an Elephant
   Is very like a spear!"

The *Third* approached the animal,
   And happening to take
The squirming trunk within his hands,
   Thus boldly up and spake:
"I see," quoth he, "the Elephant
   Is very like a snake!"

The *Fourth* reached out an eager hand,
   And felt about the knee.
"What most this wonderous beast is like
   Is mighty plain," quoth he;
"'Tis clear enough, the Elephant
   Is very like a tree!"

The *Fifth*, who chanced to touch the ear,
   Said: "E'en the blindest man
Can tell what this resembles most;
   Deny the fact who can,
This marvel of an Elephant
   Is very like a fan!"

The *Sixth* no sooner had begun
   About the beast to grope,

Than, seizing on the swinging tail
  That fell within his scope,
"I see," quoth he, "the Elephant
  Is very like a rope!"

And so these men of Indostan
  Disputed loud and long,
Each in his own opinion
  Exceeding stiff and strong,
Though each was partly in the right
  And all were in the wrong!

MORAL

So oft in theologic wars,
  The disputants, I ween,
Rail on in utter ignorance
  Of what each other mean,
*And prate about an Elephant
  Not one of them has seen!*

ALAN SEEGER
(1888–1916)

AFTER GRADUATING from Harvard, New York City-born Seeger moved to France where, at the outset of the First World War, he enlisted in the French Foreign Legion. He was killed by machine-gun fire at the Battle of the Somme.

"I Have a Rendezvous with Death" was printed in the *North American Review* (October 1916), and later in the posthumous *Poems of Alan Seeger* (1916). He was called the "Rupert Brooke of America," though only this single poem has remained popular. Millions of soldiers, and of course not only U.S. soldiers, must have felt the emotions expressed in this poem in the wars that have plagued humanity since it was written and will probably blast the earth for centuries to come.

I Have a Rendezvous with Death

I have a rendezvous with Death
At some disputed barricade,

When Spring comes back with rustling shade
And apple blossoms fill the air—
I have a rendezvous with Death
When Spring brings back blue days and fair.

It may be he shall take my hand,
And lead me into his dark land,
And close my eyes and quench my breath—
It may be I shall pass him still.
I have a rendezvous with Death
On some scarred slope of battered hill,
When Spring comes round again this year
And the first meadow flowers appear.

God knows 'twere better to be deep
Pillowed in silk and scented down,
Where Love throbs out in blissful sleep,
Pulse nigh to pulse, and breath to breath,
Where hushed awakenings are dear . . .
But I've a rendezvous with Death
At midnight in some flaming town,
When Spring trips north again this year;
And I to my pledged word am true,
I shall not fail that rendezvous.

ROBERT SERVICE
(1874–1958)

WHO COULD stop reading a ballad that begins: "A bunch of the boys were whooping it up"? "The Shooting of Dan McGrew" was far and away Service's most popular poem, with "The Cremation of Sam McGee" running a close second. Both poems are from his first verse collection, *The Spell of the Yukon* (1907), originally titled *Songs of a Sourdough*.

Born in England, raised in Glasgow, Service emigrated to Canada in 1894 and worked at all sorts of odd jobs up and down the Pacific coast and in Alaska. He was an ambulance driver for the Red Cross in the First World War, and a resident of France from 1912. He also wrote five novels and a two-volume autobiography.

Like Robert Burns, Service never considered himself a great poet. Dozens of his poems admit he is "only a rhymester," and tell of his preference for such verse as "Mary's Lamb," "Casey at the Bat" and the poems of Kipling and Burns, rather than the unintelligible *Cantos* of Ezra Pound. Service also admits to having once tried to write great poetry, but fame and fortune did not come to him until "The night I roasted Sam McGee / and perforated Dan":

> So what's the use to burn and bleed
> And strive for beauty's sake?
> No one your poetry will read,
> Your heart will only break.
> But set your song in vulgar pitch,
> If rhyme you will not rue,
> And make your heroine a bitch . . .
> Like *Lady Lou.*

"Spread misère," in the seventh stanza of "The Shooting of Dan McGrew," is a card game in which one spreads all one's cards face up and bets one will lose every trick. Dangerous Dan's choice of this game foreshadows his approaching demise.

The Shooting of Dan McGrew

A bunch of the boys were whooping it up in the Malamute
    saloon;
The kid that handles the music-box was hitting a jag-time
    tune;
Back of the bar, in a solo game, sat Dangerous Dan McGrew,
And watching his luck was his light-o'-love, the lady that's
    known as Lou.

When out of the night, which was fifty below, and into the din
    and the glare,
There stumbled a miner fresh from the creeks, dog-dirty, and
    loaded for bear.
He looked like a man with a foot in the grave and scarcely the
    strength of a louse,
Yet he tilted a poke of dust on the bar, and he called for
    drinks for the house.
There was none could place the stranger's face, though we
    searched ourselves for a clue;
But we drank his health, and the last to drink was Dangerous
    Dan McGrew.

There's men that somehow just grip your eyes, and hold them
    hard like a spell;

And such was he, and he looked to me like a man who had
     lived in hell;
With a face most hair, and the dreary stare of a dog whose
     day is done,
As he watered the green stuff in his glass, and the drops fell
     one by one.
Then I got to figgering who he was, and wondering what he'd
     do,
And I turned my head—and there watching him was the lady
     that's known as Lou.

His eyes went rubbering round the room, and he seemed in a
     kind of daze,
Till at last that old piano fell in the way of his wandering
     gaze.
The rag-time kid was having a drink; there was no one else on
     the stool,
So the stranger stumbles across the room, and flops down
     there like a fool.
In a buckskin shirt that was glazed with dirt he sat, and I saw
     him sway;
Then he clutched the keys with his talon hands—my God!
     but that man could play.

Were you ever out in the Great Alone, when the moon was
     awful clear,
And the icy mountains hemmed you in with a silence you
     could almost *hear;*
With only the howl of a timber wolf, and you camped there in
     the cold,
A half-dead thing in a stark, dead world, clean mad for the
     muck called gold;
While high overhead, green, yellow and red, the North Lights
     swept in bars?—
Then you've a hunch what the music meant . . . hunger and
     night and the stars.

And hunger not of the belly kind, that's banished with bacon
     and beans,
But the gnawing hunger of lonely men for a home and all that
     it means;
For a fireside far from the cares that are, four walls and a roof
     above;

But oh! so cramful of cosy joy, and crowned with a woman's
    love—
A woman dearer than all the world, and true as Heaven is
    true—
(God! how ghastly she looks through her rouge,—the lady
    that's known as Lou.)

Then on a sudden the music changed, so soft that you scarce
    could hear;
But you felt that your life had been looted clean of all that it
    once held dear;
That someone had stolen the woman you loved; that her love
    was a devil's lie;
That your guts were gone, and the best for you was to crawl
    away and die.
'Twas the crowning cry of a heart's despair, and it thrilled
    you through and through—
"I guess I'll make it a spread misère," said Dangerous Dan
    McGrew.

The music almost died away . . . then it burst like a pent-up
    flood;
And it seemed to say, "Repay, repay," and my eyes were
    blind with blood.
The thought came back of an ancient wrong, and it stung like
    a frozen lash,
And the lust awoke to kill, to kill . . . then the music stopped
    with a crash,
And the stranger turned, and his eyes they burned in a most
    peculiar way;
In a buckskin shirt that was glazed with dirt he sat, and I saw
    him sway;
Then his lips went in in a kind of grin, and he spoke, and his
    voice was calm,
And "Boys," says he, "you don't know me, and none of you
    care a damn;
But I want to state, and my words are straight, and I'll bet
    my poke they're true,
That one of you is a hound of hell . . . and that one is Dan
    McGrew."

Then I ducked my head, and the lights went out, and two
    guns blazed in the dark,

And a woman screamed, and the lights went up, and two men
  lay stiff and stark.
Pitched on his head, and pumped full of lead, was Dangerous
  Dan McGrew,
While the man from the creeks lay clutched to the breast of
  the lady that's known as Lou.

These are the simple facts of the case, and I guess I ought to
  know.
They say that the stranger was crazed with "hooch," and I'm
  not denying it's so.
I'm not so wise as the lawyer guys, but strictly between us
  two—
The woman that kissed him and—pinched his poke—was the
  lady that's known as Lou.

The Cremation of Sam McGee

There are strange things done in the midnight sun
  By the men who moil for gold;
The Arctic trails have their secret tales
  That would make your blood run cold;
The Northern Lights have seen queer sights,
  But the queerest they ever did see
Was that night on the marge of Lake Lebarge
  I cremated Sam McGee.

Now Sam McGee was from Tennessee, where the cotton
  blooms and blows.
Why he left home in the South to roam 'round the Pole, God
  only knows.
He was always cold, but the land of gold seemed to hold him
  like a spell;
Though he'd often say in his homely way that "he'd sooner
  live in hell."

On a Christmas Day we were mushing our way over the
  Dawson trail.
Talk of your cold! through the parka's fold it stabbed like a
  driven nail.
If our eyes we'd close, then the lashes froze till sometimes we
  couldn't see;

It wasn't much fun, but the only one to whimper was Sam
McGee.

And that very night, as we lay packed tight in our robes
beneath the snow,
And the dogs were fed, and the stars o'erhead were dancing
heel and toe,
He turned to me, and "Cap," says he, "I'll cash in this trip, I
guess;
And if I do, I'm asking that you won't refuse my last request."

Well, he seemed so low that I couldn't say no; then he says
with a sort of moan:
"It's the cursèd cold, and it's got right hold till I'm chilled
clean through to the bone.
Yet 'tain't being dead—it's my awful dread of the icy grave
that pains;
So I want you to swear that, foul or fair, you'll cremate my
last remains."

A pal's last need is a thing to heed, so I swore I would not
fail;
And we started on at the streak of the dawn; but God! he
looked ghastly pale.
He crouched on the sleigh, and he raved all day of his home
in Tennessee;
And before nightfall a corpse was all that was left of Sam
McGee.

There wasn't a breath in that land of death, and I hurried,
horror-driven,
With a corpse half hid that I couldn't get rid, because of a
promise given;
It was lashed to the sleigh, and it seemed to say: "You may
tax your brawn and brains,
But you promised true, and it's up to you to cremate those
last remains."

Now a promise made is a debt unpaid, and the trail has its
own stern code.
In the days to come, though my lips were dumb, in my heart
how I cursed that load.
In the long, long night, by the lone firelight, while the huskies,
round in a ring,

Howled out their woes to the homeless snows—O God! how I
    loathed the thing.

And every day that quiet clay seemed to heavy and heavier
    grow;
And on I went, though the dogs were spent and the grub was
    getting low;
The trail was bad, and I felt half mad, but I swore I would
    not give in;
And I'd often sing to the hateful thing, and it hearkened with
    a grin.

Till I came to the marge of Lake Lebarge, and a derelict there
    lay;
It was jammed in the ice, but I saw in a trice it was called the
    "Alice May."
And I looked at it, and I thought a bit, and I looked at my
    frozen chum;
Then "Here," said I, with a sudden cry, "is my cre-ma-tor-
    eum."

Some planks I tore from the cabin floor, and I lit the boiler
    fire;
Some coal I found that was lying around, and I heaped the
    fuel higher;
The flames just soared, and the furnace roared—such a blaze
    you seldom see;
And I burrowed a hole in the glowing coal, and I stuffed in
    Sam McGee.

Then I made a hike, for I didn't like to hear him sizzle so;
And the heavens scowled, and the huskies howled, and the
    wind began to blow.
It was icy cold, but the hot sweat rolled down my cheeks, and
    I don't know why;
And the greasy smoke in an inky cloak went streaking down
    the sky.

I do not know how long in the snow I wrestled with grisly
    fear;
But the stars came out and they danced about ere again I
    ventured near;
I was sick with dread, but I bravely said: "I'll just take a peep
    inside.

I guess he's cooked, and it's time I looked"; . . . then the door
I opened wide.

And there sat Sam, looking cool and calm, in the heart of the
furnace roar;
And he wore a smile you could see a mile, and he said: "Please
close that door.
It's fine in here, but I greatly fear you'll let in the cold and
storm—
Since I left Plumtree, down in Tennessee, it's the first time
I've been warm."

> *There are strange things done in the midnight sun*
> *By the men who moil for gold;*
> *The Arctic trails have their secret tales*
> *That would make your blood run cold;*
> *The Northern Lights have seen queer sights,*
> *But the queerest they ever did see*
> *Was that night on the marge of Lake Lebarge*
> *I cremated Sam McGee.*

PERCY BYSSHE SHELLEY
(1792–1822)

OF ALL great English poets, Shelley was the most radical politically, theologically and sexually. He was sent down from Oxford when he was nineteen for writing the pamphlet "The Necessity of Atheism" (actually, he was more of a pantheist). That same year he married the sixteen-year-old Harriet Westbrook, who drowned herself five years later after Shelley had abandoned her to elope with Mary Wollstonecraft Godwin. Mary became famous two years later by writing *Frankenstein*. Ironically, Shelley himself drowned at the age of twenty-nine when a boat he was in capsized during a storm off Leghorn. His friends Byron and Leigh Hunt were present on the beach when his fish-eaten body was cremated.

The most famous description of Shelley is by Matthew Arnold who calls him "a beautiful and ineffectual angel, beating in the void his luminous wings in vain." Shelley's poetry had an enormous influence on the young Bertrand Russell, who memorized many of the poet's lyrics. T. S. Eliot was one of the numerous critics who intensely disliked Shelley's poetry. Of all people, Eliot complained in an essay that he couldn't understand what Shelley meant by the "silver sphere" in the fifth stanza of "To a Skylark." Was Eliot so ignorant of astronomy that he did not know a full moon can hang like a silver sphere during early sunrise, to fade gradually as the sky brightens?

Shelley is caricatured as Scythrop (who can't decide which of two women he loves best) in Thomas Love Peacock's *Nightmare Abbey*, a book that also contains spoofs of Byron and Coleridge.

Mary Shelley gave the following description of how her husband came to write "To a Skylark":

> In the spring we spent a week or two near Leghorn, borrowing the house of some friends, who were absent on a journey to England. It was on a beautiful summer evening while wandering among the lanes, whose myrtle hedges were the bowers of the fireflies, that we heard the carolling of the skylark, which inspired one of the most beautiful of his poems.

The sonnet "Ozymandias" was first published by Shelley's friend Leigh Hunt in his periodical *The Examiner* (January 1818).

To a Skylark

Hail to thee, blithe Spirit!
  Bird thou never wert,
That from Heaven, or near it,
  Pourest thy full heart
In profuse strains of unpremeditated art.

Higher still and higher
  From the earth thou springest
Like a cloud of fire;
  The blue deep thou wingest,
And singing still dost soar, and soaring ever singest.

In the golden lightning
  Of the sunken sun,
O'er where clouds are bright'ning,
  Thou dost float and run;
Like an unbodied joy whose race is just begun.

The pale purple even
  Melts around thy flight;
Like a star of Heaven,
  In the broad daylight
Thou art unseen, but yet I hear thy shrill delight,

Keen as are the arrows
  Of that silver sphere,
Whose intense lamp narrows

In the white dawn clear
Until we hardly see—we feel that it is there.

All the earth and air
    With thy voice is loud,
As, when night is bare,
    From one lonely cloud
The moon rains out her beams, and Heaven is overflowed.

What thou art we know not;
    What is most like thee?
From rainbow clouds there flow not
    Drops so bright to see
As from thy presence showers a rain of melody.

Like a Poet hidden
    In the light of thought,
Singing hymns unbidden,
    Till the world is wrought
To sympathy with hopes and fears it heeded not:

Like a high-born maiden
    In a palace-tower,
Soothing her love-laden
    Soul in secret hour
With music sweet as love, which overflows her bower:

Like a glow-worm golden
    In a dell of dew,
Scattering unbeholden
    Its aëreal hue
Among the flowers and grass, which screen it from the view!

Like a rose embowered
    In its own green leaves,
By warm winds deflowered,
    Till the scent it gives
Makes faint with too much sweet those heavy-wingèd thieves:

Sound of vernal showers
    On the twinkling grass,
Rain-awakening flowers,
    All that ever was
Joyous, and clear, and fresh, thy music doth surpass:

Teach us, Sprite or Bird,
    What sweet thoughts are thine:

I have never heard
   Praise of love or wine
That panted forth a flood of rapture so divine.

Chorus Hymeneal,
   Or triumphal chant,
Matched with thine would be all
   But an empty vaunt,
A thing wherein we feel there is some hidden want.

What objects are the fountains
   Of thy happy strain?
What fields, or waves, or mountains?
   What shapes of sky or plain?
What love of thine own kind? what ignorance of pain?

With thy clear joyance
   Languor cannot be:
Shadow of annoyance
   Never came near thee:
Thou lovest—but ne'er knew love's sad satiety.

Waking or asleep,
   Thou of death must deem
Things more true and deep
   Than we mortals dream,
Or how could thy notes flow in such a crystal stream?

We look before and after,
   And pine for what is not:
Our sincerest laughter
   With some pain is fraught;
Our sweetest songs are those that tell of saddest thought.

Yet if we could scorn
   Hate, and pride, and fear;
If we were things born
   Not to shed a tear,
I know not how thy joy we ever should come near.

Better than all measures
   Of delightful sound,
Better than all treasures
   That in books are found,
Thy skill to poet were, thou scorner of the ground!

Teach me half the gladness
   That thy brain must know,
Such harmonious madness
   From my lips would flow
The world should listen then—as I am listening now.

Ozymandias

I met a traveller from an antique land
Who said: Two vast and trunkless legs of stone
Stand in the desert . . . Near them, on the sand,
Half sunk, a shattered visage lies, whose frown,
And wrinkled lip, and sneer of cold command,
Tell that its sculptor well those passions read
Which yet survive, stamped on these lifeless things,
The hand that mocked them, and the heart that fed:
And on the pedestal these words appear:
'My name is Ozymandias, king of kings:
Look on my works, ye Mighty, and despair!'
Nothing beside remains. Round the decay
Of that colossal wreck, boundless and bare
The lone and level sands stretch far away.

LANGDON SMITH
(1858–1908)

ALMOST NOTHING is known about Langdon Smith beyond a few sparse statements in a *Who Was Who in America* entry. He was born somewhere in Kentucky, and was a war correspondent in Cuba for the New York *Journal*. He later wrote feature stories and a sports column for the *Journal*. The entry says he wrote a novel, *On the Panhandle*, and a number of short stories. Smith may be the only author of a famous poem who never had another poem in print.

I am indebted to Janet Jurist for running down the first appearance of "Evolution." It was in the New York *Herald* (September 22, 1895). The ballad is illustrated with five drawings, and is set in quatrains. There is no by-line. Several years later Smith added seven new quatrains, and the expanded poem was printed in the New York *Morning Journal* in the middle of a page of want ads—the date remains unknown. When the ballad was published in *The Scrap Book* (April 1906) the lines were divided into stanzas of eight lines each except for the final stanza of four lines. If you number the quatrains from 1 through 27, those not in the first printing are quatrains 15, 16, 17, 18, 19, 25 and 26. *The Scrap Book* headed its reprinting: "A Rescued Poem. *The Scrap Book* resurrects from distressing obscurity a gem that might otherwise have been lost to posterity."

In 1909, a year after Smith's death, the Boston house of John W. Luce published a hardcover edition of "Evolution," illustrated by an unknown artist, and with an introduction by Lewis Allen Browne. There are also notes on the poem's geological terms, and a short essay on "Fifty Years of Evolution," perhaps also written by Browne. The poem is identical to *The Scrap Book* version.

Now for a little mystery. In 1927 Edwin Markham edited *The Book of Poetry*, a two-volume anthology. He included "Evolution," prefacing it with the statement: "Strange to say, this is the only poem of distinction that he [Smith] is known (to me) to have written." Strange also is the fact that four lines are added to the beginning of the final stanza:

> For we know that the clod, by the grace of God,
>   Will quicken with voice and breath;
> And we know that Love, with gentle hand,
>   Will beckon from death to death.

Are these four lines in the second newspaper printing of the ballad? Did Smith decide to drop them because he rightly considered them inferior, or were they cut by some editor for a reprinting?

No other poem about evolution has become as popular with geologists and the general public as Smith's. It is also about reincarnation, though if you are not sympathetic to that doctrine you can take it as a whimsical metaphor for the continuity of life. Whether Smith believed in reincarnation is not known.

I have added notes to indicate the major word changes presumably made by Smith for the second printing (my notes give the words of the first printing), and which in all cases are improvements. Delmonico's, referred to in the eleventh stanza of the poem, was a fashionable Manhattan restaurant in Smith's day until it went out of business in 1923. You can read its history in Lately Thomas' book *Delmonico's: A Century of Splendor* (1967).

Evolution

When you were a tadpole and I was a fish,
    In the Paleozoic time,
And side by side on the ebbing[1] tide
    We sprawled through the ooze and slime,
Or skittered with many a caudal flip
    Through the depths of the Cambrian fen,
My heart was rife with the joy of life,
    For I loved you even then.

Mindless we lived and mindless we loved,
    And mindless at last we died;
And deep in a rift of the Caradoc drift
    We slumbered side by side.
The world turned on in the lathe of time,
    The hot lands heaved amain,
Till we caught our breath from the womb of death,
    And crept into light again.

We were Amphibians, scaled and tailed,
    And drab as a dead man's hand;
We coiled at ease 'neath the dripping trees,
    Or trailed through the mud and sand,
Croaking and blind, with our three-clawed feet
    Writing a language dumb,
With never a spark in the empty dark
    To hint at a life to come.

Yet happy we lived, and happy we loved,
    And happy we died once more;
Our forms were rolled in the clinging mold
    Of a Neocomian shore.
The eons came, and the eons fled,
    And the sleep that wrapped[2] us fast
Was riven away in a newer day,
    And the night of death was past.

Then light and swift through the jungle trees
    We swung in our airy flights,
Or breathed in the balms of the fronded palms,
    In the hush of the moonless[3] nights.
And oh! what beautiful years were these,
    When our hearts clung each to each;
When life was filled, and our senses thrilled
    In the first faint dawn of speech.

Thus life by life, and love by love,
    We passed through the cycles strange,
And breath by breath, and death by death,
    We followed the chain of change.
Till there came a time in the law of life
    When over the nursing sod
The shadows broke, and the soul awoke
    In a strange, dim dream of God.

I was thewed like an Auroch bull,
    And tusked like the great Cave Bear;
And you, my sweet, from head to feet,
    Were gowned in your glorious hair.
Deep in the gloom of a fireless cave,
    When the night fell o'er the plain,
And the moon hung red o'er the river bed,
    We mumbled the bones of the slain.

I flaked a flint to a cutting edge,
    And shaped it with brutish craft;
I broke a shank from the woodland dank,
    And fitted it, head and haft.
Then I hid me close to the reedy tarn,
    Where the Mammoth came to drink;—
Through brawn and bone I drave the stone,
    And slew him upon the brink.

Loud I howled through the moonlit wastes,
    Loud answered our kith and kin;
From west to east to the crimson feast
    The clan came trooping in.
O'er joint and gristle and padded hoof,
    We fought, and clawed and tore,
And cheek by jowl, with many a growl,
    We talked the marvel o'er.

I carved that fight on a reindeer bone,
    With rude and hairy hand,
I pictured his fall on the cavern wall
    That men might understand.
For we lived by blood, and the right of might,
    Ere human laws were drawn,
And the Age of Sin did not begin
    Till our brutal[4] tusks were gone.

And that was a million years ago,
    In a time that no man knows;
Yet here to-night in the mellow light,
    We sit at Delmonico's;
Your eyes are deep as the Devon springs,
    Your hair is as dark as jet.
Your years are few, your life is new,
    Your soul untried, and yet—

Our trail is on the Kimmeridge clay,
  And the scarp of the Purbeck flags,
We have left our bones in the Bagshot stones,
  And deep in the Coraline crags;
Our love is old, our lives are old,
  And death shall come amain;
Should it come to-day, what man may say
  We shall not live[5] again?

God wrought our souls from the Tremadoc beds
  And furnished them wings to fly;
He sowed our spawn in the world's dim dawn,
  And I know that it shall not die.
Though cities have sprung above the graves
  Where the crook-boned men made war,
And the ox-wain creaks o'er the buried caves,
  Where the mummied mammoths are.

Then as we linger at luncheon here,
  O'er many a dainty dish,
Let us drink anew to the time when you
  Were a Tadpole and I was a Fish.

---

[1] Sluggish.
[2] Bound.
[3] Moonlit.
[4] Brutish.
[5] Meet.

ROBERT SOUTHEY
(1774–1843)

IN HIS day Southey was more famous than his brother-in-law Coleridge (for a time the two friends were married to the Fricker sisters). For thirty years as England's Poet Laureate, Southey produced enormous quantities of verse and prose, including a biography of John Wesley. Today, only "The Battle of Blenheim" and "The Inchcape Rock" survive in anthologies. Southey is best remembered for his story about a little girl and three bears, and for writing a poem that Lewis Carroll parodies in "Father William." Mr Feathernest, in Thomas Love Peacock's novel *Melincourt*, is a caricature of Southey.

One of Southey's most forgettable poems was about the entrance of King George III into heaven. Byron's "The Vision of Judgment" is a savage attack on this poem and on Southey:

He had written much blank verse, and blanker prose,
And more of both than any body knows.

In Byron's poem, when Southey turns up in heaven and starts to read his tribute to George, the angels stop their ears, devils flee back to hell, Michael gnashes his teeth and St. Peter uses his keys to knock Southey into a lake. The poet sinks to the bottom, "like his works," but rises like a cork, buoyed up by his "rottenness." Byron's long dedication in verse of *Don Juan* to Southey gave him another opportunity to bash the Poet Laureate.

The Battle of Blenheim was fought in Bavaria by England and France in 1704, one of many battles in the thirteen-year War of the Spanish Succession. England won a great victory, but who today can say what good came of it?

The Battle of Blenheim

It was a summer evening,
    Old Kaspar's work was done,
And he before his cottage door
    Was sitting in the sun,
And by him sported on the green
His little grandchild Wilhelmine.

She saw her brother Peterkin
    Roll something large and round,
Which he beside the rivulet
    In playing there had found;
He came to ask what he had found,
That was so large, and smooth, and round.

Old Kaspar took it from the boy,
    Who stood expectant by;
And then the old man shook his head,
    And with a natural sigh,
"'Tis some poor fellow's skull,' said he,
'Who fell in the great victory.

'I find them in the garden,
    For there's many here about;
And often when I go to plough,
    The ploughshare turns them out!
For many thousand men,' said he,
'Were slain in that great victory.'

'Now tell us what 't was all about,'
  Young Peterkin, he cries;
And little Wilhelmine looks up
  With wonder-waiting eyes;
'Now tell us all about the war,
And what they fought each other for.'

'It was the English,' Kaspar cried,
  'Who put the French to rout;
But what they fought each other for,
  I could not well make out;
But every body said,' quoth he,
'That 't was a famous victory.

'My father lived at Blenheim then,
  Yon little stream hard by;
They burnt his dwelling to the ground,
  And he was forced to fly;
So with his wife and child he fled,
Nor had he where to rest his head.

'With fire and sword the country round
  Was wasted far and wide,
And many a childing mother then,
  And new-born baby died;
But things like that, you know, must be
At every famous victory.

'They say it was a shocking sight
  After the field was won;
For many thousand bodies here
  Lay rotting in the sun;
But things like that, you know, must be
After a famous victory.

'Great praise the Duke of Marlbro' won,
  And our good Prince Eugene.'
'Why 't was a very wicked thing!'
  Said little Wilhelmine.
'Nay . . . nay . . . my little girl,' quoth he.
'It was a famous victory.

'And everybody praised the Duke
  Who this great fight did win.'
'But what good came of it at last?'

Quoth little Peterkin.
'Why that I cannot tell,' said he,
'But 't was a famous victory.'

ROBERT LOUIS STEVENSON
(1850–1894)

STEVENSON WAS born in Edinburgh. After marrying a California divorcee he had met in France, he moved restlessly from country to country, a tall, thin, olive-complexioned consumptive, always writing, always struggling to overcome his illness. Of his many essays, travel books, novels, short stories and plays, the best known of course are *Treasure Island* (1881) and *The Strange Case of Dr. Jekyll and Mr. Hyde* (1886). A long friendship with William Henley ended in a sad, irreconcilable quarrel.

"Requiem" (from the Latin word for "rest") is the name of a Catholic mass for the dead. Any hymn for the dead is now called a requiem. Stevenson wrote his own requiem when he was desperately ill and blind. He died at the age of forty-four, in Vailima, on the Western Samoan island of Upolu. He was buried under the "wide and starry sky" at the top of a nearby mountain. His "Requiem" is carved on a stone that marks his grave.

Stevenson's *A Child's Garden of Verses* (1885), from which "Bed in Summer" and "Happy Thought" are taken, is one of the best loved of all poetry books for children. As I write, a dozen different editions, most of them illustrated, are in print. "Happy Thought" was written when Stevenson was so near death that it moved Chesterton to write: "To read of such a thing is like hearing a corpse speak suddenly of birds and sunshine. It is the sublimest testimony to creation that the Creator himself could ask; the testimony of one who had lost all."

The first edition of *A Child's Garden of Verses*—it is the rarest of all Stevenson books—was titled *Penny Whistles*. It contains forty-eight poems, nine of which are not included in the second edition, which contains seventy-four. Several of the reprinted poems are heavily revised. Stevenson was fond of playing the penny whistle, an inexpensive tin flute something like a flageolet that was widely sold at the time.

Many well-known poets, including Bliss Carman and James Whitcomb Riley, wrote verse tributes to Stevenson after his death. A poem by B. Paul Neuman begins with this striking stanza:

> Long, hatchet face, black hair, and haunting gaze,
>   That follows, as you move about the room,
> Ah! that is he who trod the darkening ways,
>   And plucked the flowers upon the edge of doom.

Here is how Stevenson's one-time friend Henley described him in the sonnet "Apparition," written six years before Stevenson died:

Thin-legged, thin-chested, slight unspeakably,
Neat-footed and weak-fingered: in his face—
Lean, large-boned, curved of beak, and touched with race,
Bold-lipped, rich-tinted, mutable as the sea,
The brown eyes radiant with vivacity—
There shines a brilliant and romantic grace,
A spirit intense and rare, with trace on trace
Of passion, impudence, and energy.
Valiant in velvet, light in ragged luck,
Most vain, most generous, sternly critical,
Buffoon and poet, lover and sensualist:
A deal of Ariel, just a streak of Puck,
Much Antony, of Hamlet most of all,
And something of the Shorter-Catechist.

Requiem

Under the wide and starry sky
   Dig the grave and let me lie:
Glad did I live and gladly die,
   And I laid me down with a will.

This be the verse you grave for me:
Here he lies where he long'd to be;
Home is the sailor, home from sea,
   And the hunter home from the hill.

Bed in Summer

In winter I get up at night
And dress by yellow candle-light.
In summer, quite the other way,
I have to go to bed by day.

I have to go to bed and see
The birds still hopping on the tree,
Or hear the grown-up people's feet
Still going past me in the street.

And does it not seem hard to you,
When all the sky is clear and blue,
And I should like so much to play,
To have to go to bed by day?

Happy Thought

The world is so full of a number of things,
I'm sure we should all be as happy as kings.

JANE TAYLOR
(1783–1824)

JANE AND her year-older sister, Ann, were prolific writers of verse for children in England, but only the first four lines of Jane's "The Star" are remembered today. Their first book, *Original Poems for Infant Minds* (1804), was followed by *Rhymes for the Nursery* (1806), which included "The Star." Robert Browning called their verse "the most perfect things of this kind in the English language." John Keats, Robert Southey and Sir Walter Scott also expressed admiration for their poems.

After Ann married and had children (she raised eight), Jane remained single and began publishing books of her own, including the novel *Display: A Tale for Young People* (1815), which attacked conspicuous waste by the rich. She became more famous than her sister; so much so that mugs were sold with her picture on them.

Pious Christian sentiment pervades the verse of both sisters. Ann's best-known poem, "My Mother," ends with this grim quatrain:

> For God who lives above the skies,
> Would look with vengeance in his eyes,
> If I should ever dare despise
> My Mother.

William Cullen Bryant, in his mammoth *Family Library of Poetry and Song*, chose two poems by Jane. One of them, "The Philosopher," appears in numerous pre-1900 anthologies. It is about a philosopher who invents some magic scales capable of weighing the relative worth of any two things. Successive stanzas tell how it finds that the prayer of the penitent thief at the Crucifixion outweighs all the wit of Voltaire, how the widow's mite outweighs a row of almshouses, a plough weighs more than ten chariots, a nail more than a sword, a bee more than a lord and lady, a potato more than a diamond, and so on, until the last stanza in which the soul of a beggar proves to have more worth than the entire physical earth.

Children today no longer wonder what a star is. As Armand T. Ringer has put it:

> Twinkle, twinkle, little star,
> I know *exactly* what you are.
> You're just a sun. How do I know?
> My science teacher told me so.

"The Star" was set to the music of the French melody "Ah! Vous Dirai-Je, Maman." The poem's best-known parody is in *Alice in Wonderland* when the Mad Hatter sings:

> Twinkle, twinkle, little bat!
> How I wonder what you're at!
> Up above the world you fly,
> Like a tea-tray in the sky.

The Star

Twinkle, twinkle, little star,
How I wonder what you are
Up above the world so high,
Like a diamond in the sky.
Twinkle, twinkle, little star,
How I wonder what you are.

When the blazing sun is gone,
When he nothing shines upon,
Then you show your little light,
Twinkle, twinkle, all the night.
Twinkle, twinkle, little star,
How I wonder what you are.

Then the traveller in the dark
Thanks you for your tiny spark,
He could not see where to go
If you did not twinkle so.
Twinkle, twinkle, little star,
How I wonder what you are.

In the dark blue sky you keep,
While you through my curtains peep,
And you never shut your eye
Till the sun is in the sky.
Twinkle, twinkle, little star,
How I wonder what you are.

ALFRED, LORD TENNYSON
(1809–1892)

TENNYSON, WHO followed Wordsworth as England's Poet Laureate, was the most renowned and admired poet of the Victorian era. Queen Victoria herself said she treasured Tennyson's *In Memoriam* next to the Bible. The poem was an elegy on the death of Tennyson's best friend, Arthur Hallam, a young poet who was engaged to Tennyson's sister when he died suddenly. Prime Minister William Gladstone made Tennyson a baron. (James Joyce calls him Alfred, Lawn Tennyson in *Ulysses*.) He was buried in Westminster Abbey.

Tennyson's stature has rapidly declined since 1900, mainly in reaction to his Victorian ideals of religion and intense nationalism. He is usually praised for his melodic skills, but chastised for a dearth of ideas. Poe thought him "the noblest poet who ever lived." T. S. Eliot called him a "great poet" with "the finest ear of any English poet since Milton." To George Bernard Shaw he had the brain "of a third rate village policeman." Here is W. H. Auden's surprising description in his introduction to a selection of Tennyson poems:

> He had a large, loose-limbed body, a swarthy complexion, a high, narrow forehead, and huge bricklayer's hands; in youth he looked like a gypsy; in age like a dirty old monk; he had the finest ear, perhaps, of any English poet; he was also undoubtedly the stupidest; there was little about melancholia that he didn't know; there was little else that he did.

"The Charge of the Light Brigade" was first printed in *The Examiner* (December 9, 1854). Tennyson had read in the *Times* a description of the battle that contained the phrase "some one had blundered." The phrase determined the poem's meter. The "some one" was James Brudenell, Seventh Earl of Cardigan, for whom the cardigan jacket is named. Acting on what he mistakenly assumed were higher orders, Brudenell sent his six hundred cavalrymen against twelve thousand Russians. Half the brigade was slaughtered. This took place in 1854 in the Crimean War's Battle of Balaklava. Russia was trying to take Turkey, and England and France were doing their best to prevent it. Should soldiers who blindly follow orders they know are almost certain to get them killed be praised for their patriotism or criticized for their stupidity? The answer usually depends on whether the troops are on your side or the enemy's.

Overbearing and quarrelsome, Lord Cardigan was one of England's most hated officers. It was his wealth, not military skill, that advanced his career. At a time when he commanded a regiment of three hundred and fifty men he made seven hundred arrests and held one hundred and five court-martials. He fought a duel with one of his own officers. As Isaac Asimov tells it in *Familiar Poems Annotated*, Lord Cardigan left the battlefield slightly wounded, to be honored as a hero back in England where he died at the age of seventy.

"Crossing the Bar" was written when Tennyson was eighty-one. He asked his son to place it at the end of all editions of his works. "'Break, Break, Break'" was another tribute to Arthur Hallam.

The Charge of the Light Brigade

I

Half a league, half a league,
Half a league onward,
All in the valley of Death
   Rode the six hundred.
'Forward the Light Brigade!
Charge for the guns!' he said.
Into the valley of Death
   Rode the six hundred.

II

'Forward the Light Brigade!'
Was there a man dismay'd?
Not tho' the soldier knew
   Some one had blunder'd.
Theirs not to make reply,
Theirs not to reason why,
Theirs but to do and die.
Into the valley of Death
   Rode the six hundred.

III

Cannon to right of them,
Cannon to left of them,
Cannon in front of them
   Volley'd and thunder'd;
Storm'd at with shot and shell,
Boldly they rode and well,
Into the jaws of Death,
Into the mouth of hell
   Rode the six hundred.

IV

Flash'd all their sabres bare,
Flash'd as they turn'd in air

Sabring the gunners there,
Charging an army, while
   All the world wonder'd.
Plunged in the battery-smoke
Right thro' the line they broke;
Cossack and Russian
Reel'd from the sabre-stroke
   Shatter'd and sunder'd.
Then they rode back, but not,
   Not the six hundred.

V

Cannon to right of them,
Cannon to left of them,
Cannon behind them
   Volley'd and thunder'd;
Storm'd at with shot and shell,
While horse and hero fell,
They that had fought so well
Came thro' the jaws of Death,
Back from the mouth of hell,
All that was left of them,
   Left of six hundred.

VI

When can their glory fade?
O the wild charge they made!
   All the world wonder'd.
Honor the charge they made!
Honor the Light Brigade,
   Noble six hundred!

Crossing the Bar

Sunset and evening star,
   And one clear call for me!
And may there be no moaning of the bar,
   When I put out to sea,

But such a tide as moving seems asleep,
   Too full for sound and foam,

When that which drew from out the boundless deep
  Turns again home.

Twilight and evening bell,
  And after that the dark!
And may there be no sadness of farewell,
  When I embark;

For tho' from out our bourne of Time and Place
  The flood may bear me far,
I hope to see my Pilot face to face
  When I have crost the bar.

'Break, Break, Break'

Break, break, break,
  On thy cold gray stones, O Sea!
And I would that my tongue could utter
  The thoughts that arise in me.

O, well for the fisherman's boy,
  That he shouts with his sister at play!
O, well for the sailor lad,
  That he sings in his boat on the bay!

And the stately ships go on
  To their haven under the hill;
But O for the touch of a vanish'd hand,
  And the sound of a voice that is still!

Break, break, break,
  At the foot of thy crags, O Sea!
But the tender grace of a day that is dead
  Will never come back to me.

'Flower in the Crannied Wall'

Flower in the crannied wall,
I pluck you out of the crannies,
I hold you here, root and all, in my hand,

Little flower—but *if* I could understand
What you are, root and all, and all in all,
I should know what God and man is.

ERNEST LAWRENCE THAYER
(1863–1940)

No GREATER poem about baseball has ever been written than Thayer's "Casey at the Bat." Indeed, the Mighty Casey has become as lasting a part of our nation's mythology as Santa Claus.

The son of a wealthy Massachusetts owner of a woolen mill, Thayer majored in philosophy at Harvard and edited the University's *Harvard Lampoon*. William Randolph Hearst was the magazine's business manager. When Hearst took over the San Francisco *Examiner*, he invited his friend Thayer to write a humor column under the by-line of "Phin." It was in that column, on Sunday June 3, 1888, that "Casey" first appeared. It was reprinted anonymously all over the land, and for many years no one knew who had written it, including the actor William De Wolf Hopper, who spread Casey's fame by reciting the poem as an encore. Wallace Beery played Casey in a 1927 remake of an earlier film version of the poem.

Thayer wrote some dozen other humorous poems, but only "Casey" became immortal. Sportswriter Grantland Rice wrote the best of many sequels, and in my *Annotated Casey at the Bat* (1967) I gathered all the sequels and parodies I could find. In recent decades many illustrated editions of the poem have been published as books for children, but adults continue to be Casey's most loyal fans.

Thayer later tried to polish his lines, but without noticeable improvement. The version here is the original. "Johnnie," in the fourth stanza, is a printer's error for "Jimmy." The word "the" before "men" in the previous line of the same stanza so destroys the meter that it was probably another printer's error to insert it. Thayer removed it from his revised version. Many later printings substitute "they" for "the men." In the third stanza, "lulu" is slang for something extraordinary, here used derisively, and "cake" was current slang for a dandy. The second stanza's second line is from Alexander Pope's *Essay on Man*: "Hope springs eternal in the human breast."

Casey at the Bat

The outlook wasn't brilliant for the Mudville nine that day;
The score stood four to two with but one inning more to play.

And then when Cooney died at first, and Barrows did the
    same,
A sickly silence fell upon the patrons of the game.

A straggling few got up to go in deep despair. The rest
Clung to that hope which springs eternal in the human breast;
They thought if only Casey could but get a whack at that—
We'd put up even money now with Casey at the bat.

But Flynn preceded Casey, as did also Jimmy Blake,
And the former was a lulu and the latter was a cake;
So upon that stricken multitude grim melancholy sat,
For there seemed but little chance of Casey's getting to the
    bat.

But Flynn let drive a single, to the wonderment of all,
And Blake, the much despis-ed, tore the cover off the ball;
And when the dust had lifted, and the men saw what had
    occurred,
There was Johnnie safe at second and Flynn a-hugging third.

Then from 5,000 throats and more there rose a lusty yell;
It rumbled through the valley, it rattled in the dell;
It knocked upon the mountain and recoiled upon the flat,
For Casey, mighty Casey, was advancing to the bat.

There was ease in Casey's manner as he stepped into his
    place;
There was pride in Casey's bearing and a smile on Casey's
    face.
And when, responding to the cheers, he lightly doffed his hat,
No stranger in the crowd could doubt 'twas Casey at the bat.

Ten thousand eyes were on him as he rubbed his hands with
    dirt;
Five thousand tongues applauded when he wiped them on his
    shirt.
Then while the writhing pitcher ground the ball into his hip,
Defiance gleamed in Casey's eye, a sneer curled Casey's lip.

And now the leather-covered sphere came hurtling through
    the air,
And Casey stood a-watching it in haughty grandeur there.
Close by the sturdy batsman the ball unheeded sped—
"That ain't my style," said Casey. "Strike one," the umpire
    said.

From the benches, black with people, there went up a muffled
    roar,
Like the beating of the storm-waves on a stern and distant
    shore.
"Kill him! Kill the umpire!" shouted some one on the stand;
And it's likely they'd have killed him had not Casey raised his
    hand.

With a smile of Christian charity great Casey's visage shone;
He stilled the rising tumult; he bade the game go on;
He signaled to the pitcher, and once more the spheroid flew;
But Casey still ignored it, and the umpire said, "Strike two."

"Fraud!" cried the maddened thousands, and echo answered
    fraud;
But one scornful look from Casey and the audience was awed.
They saw his face grow stern and cold, they saw his muscles
    strain,
And they knew that Casey wouldn't let that ball go by again.

The sneer is gone from Casey's lip, his teeth are clenched in
    hate;
He pounds with cruel violence his bat upon the plate.
And now the pitcher holds the ball, and now he lets it go,
And now the air is shattered by the force of Casey's blow.

Oh, somewhere in this favored land the sun is shining bright;
The band is playing somewhere, and somewhere hearts are
    light,
And somewhere men are laughing, and somewhere children
    shout;
But there is no joy in Mudville—mighty Casey has struck
    out.

ROSE HARTWICK THORPE
(1850–1939)

Mrs. Thorpe was born in Mishawaka, Indiana, and died in San Diego,
California. She wrote several novels and a raft of popular verse, but is
remembered only for the wild, sentimental ballad "Curfew Must Not Ring
Tonight." She wrote it when she was seventeen, basing it on the story "Love
and Loyalty," which she had read in *Peterson's Magazine* (October 1865), and

which she took to be an account of an actual event. The poem is said to have first been printed in an autumn 1870 issue of the Detroit *Commercial Advertiser,* but the exact date seems not to be known.

Early printings of the poem differ markedly from one another. I have followed the version in an illustrated hardcover edition of the poem published in 1882 by the Boston house of Lee and Shepard. The final stanza of this version, usually omitted, is included here.

Curfew Must Not Ring Tonight

England's sun was slowly setting
O'er the hill-tops far away,
Filling all the land with beauty
At the close of one sad day;
And its last rays kissed the forehead
Of a man and maiden fair—
He with steps so slow and weary;
She with sunny, floating hair;
He with bowed head, sad and thoughtful;
She with lips so cold and white,
Struggled to keep back the murmur,
"Curfew must not ring tonight."

"Sexton," Bessie's white lips faltered,
Pointing to the prison old,
With its walls so tall and gloomy
Moss-grown walls dark, damp, and cold—
"I've a lover in that prison,
Doomed this very night to die,
At the ringing of the curfew,
And no earthly help is nigh.
Cromwell will not come till sunset";
And her lips grew strangely white,
As she spoke in husky whispers,
"Curfew must not ring tonight."

"Bessie," calmly spoke the sexton
(Every word pierced her young heart
Like a gleaming death-winged arrow,
Like a deadly poisoned dart),
"Long, long years I've rung the curfew
From that gloomy, shadowed tower;

Every evening, just at sunset,
It has told the twilight hour.
I have done my duty ever,
Tried to do it just and right:
Now I'm old, I will not miss it.
Curfew bell must ring tonight!"

Wild her eyes and pale her features,
Stern and white her thoughtful brow,
And within her heart's deep center,
Bessie made a solemn vow.
She had listened while the judges
Read, without a tear or sigh,
"At the ringing of the curfew
Basil Underwood *must die*."
And her breath came fast and faster,
And her eyes grew large and bright;
One low murmur, faintly spoken,
"Curfew *must not* ring tonight!"

She with quick step bounded forward,
Sprang within the old church door,
Left the old man coming slowly,
Paths he'd trod so oft before.
Not one moment paused the maiden,
But with cheek and brow aglow,
Staggered up the gloomy tower,
Where the bell swung to and fro;
Then she climbed the slimy ladder,
On which fell no ray of light,
Upward still, her pale lips saying,
"Curfew *shall not* ring tonight!"

She has reached the topmost ladder:
O'er her hangs the great dark bell,
Awful is the gloom beneath her,
Like the pathway down to Hell.
See! the ponderous tongue is swinging;
'Tis the hour of curfew now,
And the sight has chilled her bosom,
Stopped her breath, and paled her brow.
Shall she let it ring? No, never!
Her eyes flash with sudden light,

As she springs and grasps it firmly—
"Curfew *shall not* ring tonight."

Out she swung, far out, the city
Seemed a speck of light below;
There twixt heaven and earth suspended,
As the bell swung to and fro;
And the sexton at the bell rope,
Old and deaf, heard not the bell,
Sadly thought the twilight curfew
Rang young Basil's funeral knell.
Still the maiden clinging firmly,
Quivering lip and fair face white,
Still her frightened heart's wild beating—
"Curfew shall not ring tonight!"

It was o'er—the bell ceased swaying,
And the maiden stepped once more
Firmly on the damp old ladder,
Where for hundred years before
Human foot had not been planted.
The brave deed that she had done
Should be told long ages after.
As the rays of setting sun
Light the sky with golden beauty,
Aged sires with heads of white,
Tell the children why the curfew
Did not ring that one sad night.

O'er the distant hills came Cromwell.
Bessie sees him, and her brow,
Lately white with sickening terror,
Has no anxious traces now.
At his feet she tells her story,
Shows her hands all bruised and torn;
And her sweet young face, still haggard,
With the anguish it had worn
Touched his heart with sudden pity,
Lit his eyes with misty light.
"Go, your lover lives!" cried Cromwell;
"Curfew shall not ring tonight."

Wide they flung the massive portals,
Led the prisoner forth to die,
All his bright young life before him.

'Neath the darkening English sky,
Bessie came, with flying footsteps,
Eyes aglow with love-light sweet;
Kneeling on the turf beside him,
Laid his pardon at his feet.
In his brave strong arms he clasped her,
Kissed the face upturned and white,
Whispered, "Darling, you have saved me,
Curfew will not ring tonight."

WALT WHITMAN
(1819–1892)

BORN ON Long Island and brought up in Brooklyn, Whitman began his career working as a journalist for some ten different papers in New York, including a brief stint as editor of the Brooklyn *Daily Eagle*. During the Civil War he was a voluntary army nurse. The privately printed first edition of *Leaves of Grass* (1855) contained only twelve poems. An enlarged second edition, published in 1856 by the famous phrenological house of Fowler and Wells, included a chart of Whitman's cranium that proved what a fine fellow he was. Convinced that phrenology was an exact science, Whitman puzzled his early critics by lacing his verse with such phrenological terms as "adhesiveness" and "amativeness." Initially, the only critical praise for his book was to be found in reviews he himself had written anonymously.

Whitman was one of those poets who arouse either admiration or revulsion. After Emerson in a letter greeted Whitman "at the beginning of a great career," Whitman annoyed Emerson by stamping the sentence on the spine of his book's next printing.

Among Whitman's admirers were such contemporary American writers as Longfellow, Thoreau, Lowell, Howells and Holmes, and later such authors as Thomas Wolfe, Saul Bellow and Carl Sandburg. John Burroughs became a personal friend of Whitman and wrote the first biography of the poet, a book embarrassing in its unstinted, passionate praise. "In Whitman," he wrote, "we see the first appearance in literature of the genuinely democratic spirit on anything like an ample scale."

On the other hand, Whittier tossed *Leaves of Grass* into the fireplace, and D. H. Lawrence couldn't abide Whitman's "privacy leaking in a sort of dribble, oozing into the universe." George Santayana thought that what Whitman called his "barbaric yawp" was just that. So many parodies of Whitman's "O wow!" free verse were written that in 1923 Henry S. Saunders compiled an entire book of them, *Parodies on Walt Whitman*, with a preface by Christopher Morley.

In his early years Whitman, who was gay, dressed like a dandy, but when he became famous for his earthy verse, writing about how much he loved the smell of his armpits, he grew a beard and affected the clothes of a laborer. He thought of himself as a great poet of American democracy and the common people, but only the literary elite took to him. To convince everybody of his manliness, he professed to have six or more illegitimate children, but there is no evidence he ever slept with a woman. Some of his love poems that mention a "woman" had the word "man" in the original manuscript. There was a famous meeting with Oscar Wilde, who lavished praise on the "Good Gray Poet." Whitman spoke freely of his sexual preferences, and Wilde later wrote to a friend: "The kiss of Walt Whitman is still on my lips."

Whitman spent the last two decades of his life in Camden, New Jersey. A cult grew up around him, and there was even a monthly magazine in Philadelphia, *The Conservator*, devoted to his pantheism and boundless optimism. Like the flower children of the 1960s, Whitman claimed to love everybody and everything—especially himself.

"Song of Myself" and "Song of the Open Road" are Whitman's best-known long poems. "O Captain! My Captain!" a tribute to the assassinated Lincoln for having steered our Ship of State safely through the Civil War's fearful seas, is one of Whitman's rare poems with conventional rhyme and meter. Although his most popular work, Whitman himself became ashamed of its banality. It was first published in *When Lilacs Last in the Dooryard Bloom'd* (1865), a book of verses about Lincoln, and considerably revised when it was included in *Leaves of Grass*.

Every now and then a poet writes about how science dulls our sense of nature's beauty. Whitman's lyric "When I Heard the Learn'd Astronomer," from *By the Roadside* (1865), is a familiar example. Of course science does no such thing. As Isaac Asimov points out in an essay on science and beauty, even the most elementary understanding of astronomy should enhance the awe one feels in gazing at the starry heavens.

O Captain! My Captain!

O Captain! my Captain! our fearful trip is done,
The ship has weather'd every rack, the prize we sought is
     won,
The port is near, the bells I hear, the people all exulting,
While follow eyes the steady keel, the vessel grim and daring;
          But O heart! heart! heart!
          O the bleeding drops of red,
               Where on the deck my Captain lies,
               Fallen cold and dead.

O Captain! my Captain! rise up and hear the bells;
Rise up—for you the flag is flung—for you the bugle trills,

For you bouquets and ribbon'd wreaths—for you the shores
    a-crowding,
For you they call, the swaying mass, their eager faces turning;
        Here Captain! dear father!
           The arm beneath your head!
             It is some dream that on the deck,
               You've fallen cold and dead.

My Captain does not answer, his lips are pale and still,
My father does not feel my arm, he has no pulse nor will,
The ship is anchor'd safe and sound, its voyage closed and
    done,
From fearful trip the victor ship comes in with object won:
        Exult O shores, and ring O bells!
          But I with mournful tread,
             Walk the deck my Captain lies,
             Fallen cold and dead.

When I Heard the Learn'd Astronomer

When I heard the learn'd astronomer;
When the proofs, the figures, were ranged in columns before
    me;
When I was shown the charts and the diagrams, to add,
    divide, and measure them;
When I, sitting, heard the astronomer, where he lectured with
    much applause in the lecture-room,
How soon, unaccountable, I became tired and sick;
Till rising and gliding out, I wander'd off by myself,
In the mystical moist night-air, and from time to time,
Look'd up in perfect silence at the stars.

JOHN GREENLEAF WHITTIER
(1807–1892)

WHITTIER WAS a saintly Quaker, an ardent abolitionist, a lifelong bachelor
and one of New England's most popular nature poets. He had no formal

education, but early in life, entranced by the verse of Robert Burns, he decided to become a poet. In addition to his large output of verse, and one novel about the Salem witches, he also edited a variety of newspapers in Massachusetts, some of them dedicated to antislavery. It was said that Whittier hated the South more than he loved the North.

"The Barefoot Boy" first appeared in *The Little Pilgrim* (January 1855). "Maud Muller" first ran in *The National Era* (December 28, 1854).

"Maud Muller" is the most famous of all poems on the theme—later handled so effectively in John Galsworthy's famous story "The Apple Tree"— of the cultured man who falls in love with a rustic lass he cannot marry. The most amusing parody is Bret Harte's "Mrs. Maud Jenkins." It tells how the judge decides to marry Maud, only to become dismayed a few years later to find her growing "broad and red and stout," bored by his learned conversation, and giving him children that look like the men who rake hay on her father's farm. As for those "sad words of tongue or pen," Harte concludes:

> More sad are these we daily see:
> "It is, but hadn't ought to be."

Here is how Whittier described his inspiration for the poem:

> The poem had no real foundation in fact, though a hint of it may have been found in recalling an incident, trivial in itself, of a journey on the picturesque Maine seaboard with my sister some years before it was written. We had stopped to rest our tired horse under the shade of an apple-tree, and refresh him with water from a little brook which rippled through the stone wall across the road. A very beautiful young girl in scantest summer attire was at work in the hayfield, and as we talked with her we noticed that she strove to hide her bare feet by raking hay over them, blushing as she did so, through the tan of her cheek and neck.

When General Benjamin Franklin Butler, a great Civil War hero, sought the Republican nomination for governor of Massachusetts in 1871, the Boston *Post* exclaimed:

> Of all sad words of tongue or pen,
> The saddest are these, we may have Ben!

"Kate Ketchem," a long parody by Phoebe Cary, puts the moral this way:

> Of all hard things to bear and grin,
> The hardest is knowing you're taken in.

The Barefoot Boy

Blessings on thee, little man,
Barefoot boy, with cheek of tan!
With thy turned-up pantaloons,

And thy merry whistled tunes;
With thy red lip, redder still
Kissed by strawberries on the hill;
With the sunshine on thy face,
Through thy torn brim's jaunty grace;
From my heart I give thee joy,—
I was once a barefoot boy!
Prince thou art,—the grown-up man
Only is republican.
Let the million-dollared ride!
Barefoot, trudging at his side,
Thou hast more than he can buy
In the reach of ear and eye,—
Outward sunshine, inward joy:
Blessings on thee, barefoot boy!

Oh for boyhood's painless play,
Sleep that wakes in laughing day,
Health that mocks the doctor's rules,
Knowledge never learned of schools,
Of the wild bee's morning chase,
Of the wild-flower's time and place,
Flight of fowl and habitude
Of the tenants of the wood;
How the tortoise bears his shell,
How the woodchuck digs his cell,
And the ground-mole sinks his well;
How the robin feeds her young,
How the oriole's nest is hung;
Where the whitest lilies blow,
Where the freshest berries grow,
Where the ground-nut trails its vine,
Where the wood-grape's clusters shine;
Of the black wasp's cunning way,
Mason of his walls of clay,
And the architectural plans
Of gray hornet artisans!
For, eschewing books and tasks,
Nature answers all he asks;
Hand in hand with her he walks,
Face to face with her he talks,
Part and parcel of her joy,—
Blessings on the barefoot boy!

Oh for boyhood's time of June,
Crowding years in one brief moon,
When all things I heard or saw,
Me, their master, waited for.
I was rich in flowers and trees,
Humming-birds and honey-bees;
For my sport the squirrel played,
Plied the snouted mole his spade;
For my taste the blackberry cone
Purpled over hedge and stone;
Laughed the brook for my delight
Through the day and through the night,
Whispering at the garden wall,
Talked with me from fall to fall;
Mine the sand-rimmed pickerel pond,
Mine the walnut slopes beyond,
Mine, on bending orchard trees,
Apples of Hesperides!
Still as my horizon grew,
Larger grew my riches too;
All the world I saw or knew
Seemed a complex Chinese toy,
Fashioned for a barefoot boy!

Oh for festal dainties spread,
Like my bowl of milk and bread;
Pewter spoon and bowl of wood,
On the door-stone, gray and rude!
O'er me, like a regal tent,
Cloudy-ribbed, the sunset bent,
Purple-curtained, fringed with gold,
Looped in many a wind-swung fold;
While for music came the play
Of the pied frogs' orchestra;
And, to light the noisy choir,
Lit the fly his lamp of fire.
I was monarch: pomp and joy
Waited on the barefoot boy!

Cheerily, then, my little man,
Live and laugh, as boyhood can!
Though the flinty slopes be hard,
Stubble-speared the new-mown sward,
Every morn shall lead thee through

Fresh baptisms of the dew;
Every evening from thy feet
Shall the cool wind kiss the heat:
All too soon these feet must hide
In the prison cells of pride,
Lose the freedom of the sod,
Like a colt's for work be shod,
Made to tread the mills of toil,
Up and down in ceaseless moil:
Happy if their track be found
Never on forbidden ground;
Happy if they sink not in
Quick and treacherous sands of sin.
Ah! that thou couldst know thy joy,
Ere it passes, barefoot boy!

Maud Muller

Maud Muller on a summer's day
Raked the meadow sweet with hay.

Beneath her torn hat glowed the wealth
Of simple beauty and rustic health.

Singing, she wrought, and her merry glee
The mock-bird echoed from his tree.

But when she glanced to the far-off town,
White from its hill-slope looking down,

The sweet song died, and a vague unrest
And a nameless longing filled her breast,—

A wish that she hardly dared to own,
For something better than she had known.

The Judge rode slowly down the lane,
Smoothing his horse's chestnut mane.

He drew his bridle in the shade
Of the apple-trees, to greet the maid,

And asked a draught from the spring that flowed
Through the meadow across the road.

She stooped where the cool spring bubbled up,
And filled for him her small tin cup,

And blushed as she gave it, looking down
On her feet so bare, and her tattered gown.

"Thanks!" said the Judge; "a sweeter draught
From a fairer hand was never quaffed."

He spoke of the grass and flowers and trees,
Of the singing birds and the humming bees;

Then talked of the haying, and wondered whether
The cloud in the west would bring foul weather.

And Maud forgot her brier-torn gown,
And her graceful ankles bare and brown;

And listened, while a pleased surprise
Looked from her long-lashed hazel eyes.

At last, like one who for delay
Seeks a vain excuse, he rode away.

Maud Muller looked and sighed: "Ah me!
That I the Judge's bride might be!

"He would dress me up in silks so fine,
And praise and toast me at his wine.

"My father should wear a broadcloth coat:
My brother should sail a painted boat.

"I'd dress my mother so grand and gay,
And the baby should have a new toy each day.

"And I'd feed the hungry and clothe the poor,
And all should bless me who left our door."

The Judge looked back as he climbed the hill,
And saw Maud Muller standing still.

"A form more fair, a face more sweet,
Ne'er hath it been my lot to meet.

"And her modest answer and graceful air
Show her wise and good as she is fair.

"Would she were mine, and I to-day,
Like her, a harvester of hay;

"No doubtful balance of rights and wrongs,
Nor weary lawyers with endless tongues,

"But low of cattle and song of birds,
And health and quiet and loving words."

But he thought of his sisters, proud and cold,
And his mother, vain of her rank and gold.

So, closing his heart, the Judge rode on,
And Maud was left in the field alone.

But the lawyers smiled that afternoon,
When he hummed in court an old love-tune;

And the young girl mused beside the well
Till the rain on the unraked clover fell.

He wedded a wife of richest dower,
Who lived for fashion, as he for power.

Yet oft, in his marble hearth's bright glow,
He watched a picture come and go;

And sweet Maud Muller's hazel eyes
Looked out in their innocent surprise.

Oft, when the wine in his glass was red,
He longed for the wayside well instead;

And closed his eyes on his garnished rooms
To dream of meadows and clover-blooms.

And the proud man sighed, with a secret pain,
"Ah, that I were free again!

"Free as when I rode that day,
Where the barefoot maiden raked her hay."

She wedded a man unlearned and poor,
And many children played round her door.

But care and sorrow, and childbirth pain,
Left their traces on heart and brain.

And oft, when the summer sun shone hot
On the new-mown hay in the meadow lot,

And she heard the little spring brook fall
Over the roadside, through the wall,

In the shade of the apple-tree again
She saw a rider draw his rein;

And, gazing down with timid grace,
She felt his pleased eyes read her face.

Sometimes her narrow kitchen walls
Stretched away into stately halls;

The weary wheel to a spinnet turned,
The tallow candle an astral burned,

And for him who sat by the chimney lug,
Dozing and grumbling o'er pipe and mug,

A manly form at her side she saw,
And joy was duty and love was law.

Then she took up her burden of life again,
Saying only, "It might have been."

Alas for maiden, alas for Judge,
For rich repiner and household drudge!

God pity them both! and pity us all,
Who vainly the dreams of youth recall.

For of all sad words of tongue or pen,
The saddest are these: "It might have been!"

Ah, well! for us all some sweet hope lies
Deeply buried from human eyes;

And, in the hereafter, angels may
Roll the stone from its grave away!

ELLA WHEELER WILCOX
(1850–1919)

MRS. WILCOX, hailing from a farm in Johnstown Center, Wisconsin, has been called the nation's female Edgar Guest. She produced almost forty books of sentimental, moralizing verse, much of it close to doggerel. Her first book of poems, *Drops of Water* (1872), was devoted to attacks on alcoholic drinking. It was *Poems of Passion* (1883), however, that propelled her into enormous popularity. The book was roundly condemned as shameless eroticism, shocking everybody with such torrid lines as: "Here is my body, bruise it if you will."

In later years her verse reflected a passion for reincarnation, spiritualism and all things occult. She wrote books defending what was then called "New Thought," and contributed sensational articles to Hearst's Sunday newspapers on such topics as how to photograph thoughts (the New York *American*, January 3, 1909).

Of her huge output, I judge the two poems chosen here to be the best known today. "Solitude," from *Poems of Passion*, appeared first in the New York *Sun* (February 21, 1883). "The Winds of Fate" ran in the San Francisco *Examiner* (October 31, 1905), and probably in other Hearst papers, before it appeared in *Poems of Optimism*.

A Checkered Life (1885), a book by the peculiar Irish-born Colonel John Alexander Joyce (1840–1915), included "Solitude," identical with Mrs Wilcox's poem except for a transposition of the last two stanzas. Ten years later, in his second autobiography, *Jewels of Memory*, Joyce described how he came to write the poem in 1863 when he was with a Kentucky regiment. Mrs Wilcox was, of course, indignant. She offered five thousand dollars to anyone who could produce a published copy of the poem prior to its 1883 newspaper appearance. No such copy turned up, but the colonel never ceased to claim authorship. "He is only an insect," Mrs Wilcox wrote, "and yet his persistent buzz and sting can produce great discomfort."

Burton E. Stevenson, who devotes a chapter to all this in his *Famous Single Poems*, reprints a paragraph from the colonel's *A Checkered Life*, in which he admits to having been confined for several months in the Eastern Kentucky Lunatic Asylum, in Lexington, because of his "mania" for perpetual motion.

Although the colonel published biographies of Poe, Goldsmith, Burns and Lincoln, as well as other worthless works of prose and verse, few took seriously his claim to have written "Solitude." The controversy might have died quickly had not Eugene Field, as a running joke, kept devoting newspaper columns to defending Mrs. Wilcox against the colonel. Ella was not amused.

Solitude

Laugh, and the world laughs with you;
    Weep, and you weep alone.
For the sad old earth must borrow its mirth,
    But has trouble enough of its own.
Sing, and the hills will answer;
    Sigh, it is lost on the air.
The echoes bound to a joyful sound,
    But shrink from voicing care.

Rejoice, and men will seek you;
    Grieve, and they turn and go.
They want full measure of all your pleasure,
    But they do not need your woe.

Be glad, and your friends are many;
    Be sad, and you lose them all.
There are none to decline your nectared wine,
    But alone you must drink life's gall.

Feast, and your halls are crowded;
    Fast, and the world goes by.
Succeed and give, and it helps you live,
    But no man can help you die.
There is room in the halls of pleasure
    For a long and lordly train,
But one by one we must all file on
    Through the narrow aisles of pain.

The Winds of Fate

One ship drives east and another drives west
    With the selfsame winds that blow.
        'Tis the set of the sails
        And not the gales
    Which tells us the way to go.

Like the winds of the sea are the ways of fate,
    As we voyage along through life:
        'Tis the set of a soul
        That decides its goal,
    And not the calm or the strife.

SAMUEL WOODWORTH
(1784–1842)

WOODWORTH's "The Old Oaken Bucket"—originally titled "The Bucket"—
may be the most popular poem ever written by an American. The author,
born in Scituate, Massachusetts, was a self-educated printer, journalist and
playwright. After an unsuccessful effort to launch a weekly literary journal in
New Haven, he settled in New York City, where he printed and edited a
variety of short-lived periodicals. These included *Woodworth's Literary Casket*, a

children's magazine called *The Fly* and the *New York Mirror*, a weekly devoted to art and literature, founded with his friend George Pope Morris of "Woodman, Spare That Tree!" fame. A devout Swedenborgian, Woodworth published two magazines devoted to that then thriving religious cult.

In spare moments Woodworth turned out hundreds of sentimental poems—many about his memories of a happy childhood—which he published under the pseudonym "Selim." He also wrote a novel, *The Champions of Freedom*, about the War of 1812, and half a dozen plays and comic operas.

George Young, in *The New England Magazine*, told how "The Old Oaken Bucket" came to be written. It seems that Woodworth was in Mallory's saloon in Manhattan when he remarked to Mallory that his liquor was the best drink he had ever tasted. "No," said Mallory, it was far surpassed by "the draught of pure spring water we used to drink from the old oaken bucket that hung in the well." Woodworth tearfully agreed, had another swig, then hurried back to his print shop and wrote the poem in half an hour.

"The Old Oaken Bucket" was reprinted over and over again in newspapers, magazines, school readers, anthologies and in illustrated books containing only that one poem. Currier & Ives honored the bucket with two colored lithographs. It was set to music in 1843 by George Kiallmark, who based the tune on an old English-Irish melody.

Dozens of parodies have been perpetrated. One J. C. Bayles revised it "from a sanitary point of view" in a poem that ends:

> And now, far removed from the scenes I'm describing,
>   The story of warning to others I tell,
> As memory reverts to my youthful imbibing
>   And I gag at the thought of that horrible well,
> And the old oaken bucket, the fungus-grown bucket—
>   In fact, the slop bucket—that hung in the well.

Playwright Robert Sherwood produced a political spoof, "The Old Hokum Buncombe." Another takeoff tells of the "poor little kittens we drowned at the well," and there is a song recalling "the old family toothbrush that hung by the sink." Still another parody is about how dad "kicked the bucket that hung in the well," lost his balance, toppled in and was drowned. Recently Armand T. Ringer has praised "the bold-spoken lass who hung out at the well." Woodworth himself wrote what was almost a parody. Titled "The Needle," it has the same lilting rhythm as "The Old Oaken Bucket," each stanza ending: "The bright little needle—the swift flying needle, / The needle directed by beauty and art."

"The Old Oaken Bucket" is in Woodworth's *Poems, Odes, Songs, and Other Metrical Effusions* (1818), but probably appeared somewhere earlier. Although in most printings the last word of the last stanza's fifth line is "habitation," early printings have the awkward word "situation." I do not know if the change was made by Woodworth or by someone else.

Although few today can name the poem's author, Woodworth has not been totally neglected by literary savants. A 1936 PhD thesis at the University of Chicago by Kendall Taft is on Woodworth. Bellamy Partridge's novel *Old Oaken Bucket* (1949) centers around a garden club's discovery of Woodworth's original home.

The Old Oaken Bucket

How dear to this heart are the scenes of my childhood,
    When fond recollection presents them to view!
The orchard, the meadow, the deep-tangled wild-wood,
    And every loved spot which my infancy knew!
The wide-spreading pond, and the mill that stood by it,
    The bridge, and the rock where the cataract fell,
The cot of my father, the dairy-house nigh it,
    And e'en the rude bucket that hung in the well—
The old oaken bucket, the iron-bound bucket,
The moss-covered bucket which hung in the well.

That moss-covered vessel I hailed as a treasure,
    For often at noon, when returned from the field,
I found it the source of an exquisite pleasure,
    The purest and sweetest that nature can yield.
How ardent I seized it with hands that were glowing,
    And quick to the white-pebbled bottom it fell;
Then soon, with the emblem of truth overflowing,
    And dripping with coolness, it rose from the well—
The old oaken bucket, the iron-bound bucket,
The moss-covered bucket arose from the well.

How sweet from the green mossy brim to receive it,
    As poised on the curb it inclined to my lips!
Not a full blushing goblet would tempt me to leave it,
    The brightest that beauty or revelry sips.
And now, far removed from the loved habitation,
    The tear of regret will intrusively swell,
As fancy reverts to my father's plantation,
    And sighs for the bucket that hangs in the well—
The old oaken bucket, the iron-bound bucket,
The moss-covered bucket that hangs in the well!

WILLIAM WORDSWORTH
(1770–1850)

FOLLOWING A Cambridge University education, Wordsworth enjoyed a year in France where he met and fell in love with Annette Vallon. The fact that they had an illegitimate daughter, Caroline, did not come to light until more than half a century after Wordsworth's death. She is the "child," by the way, in Wordsworth's fine sonnet "'It Is a Beauteous Evening, Calm and Free.'"

Wordsworth's enthusiasm for the French Revolution cooled after the Reign of Terror. In later years he grew politically conservative, and replaced his youthful pantheism with a return to traditional Church of England theology.

These conservative turns angered many contemporary poets who cared little for Wordsworth's poetry to begin with. Byron thought him "crazed beyond all hope." Shelley said he "had as much imagination as a pint-pot." Emerson called him a "bell with a wooden tongue." In the unkindest cut of all, Browning wrote "The Lost Leader," a poem that begins: "Just for a handful of silver he left us, / Just for a riband to stick on his coat." Parodists called him "Wordswords" and "Worstworst."

Was it Wordsworth's piety that turned off Bertrand Russell? Here is a paragraph from the last volume of the latter's autobiography:

> In particular, my great hate is Wordsworth. I have to admit the excellence of some of his work—to admire and love it, in fact—but much of it is too dull, too pompous and silly to be borne. Unfortunately, I have a knack of remembering bad verse with ease, so I can puzzle almost anyone who upholds Wordsworth.

On the other hand, Wordsworth was highly praised by equally great writers. Matthew Arnold ranked him, after Shakespeare and Milton, as England's third finest poet. Coleridge considered him "the first and greatest philosophical poet," and "one who strides so far before you that he dwindles in the distance." For a time, Wordsworth and Coleridge were great friends. They began the Romantic movement in English poetry by jointly writing *Lyrical Ballads* (1798), though at the time critics disliked the book. In 1843 Wordsworth followed one of the dislikers, Robert Southey, as Poet Laureate.

Critics are still trying to puzzle out the exact psychological relationship between Wordsworth and his younger sister Dorothy. Dorothy kept house for her brother, even after his marriage, until her health failed. The two adored one another, and some critics have even wondered about a semi-incestuous relationship close to romantic love. Dorothy's letters, journals and a few poems suggest that had she not been overwhelmed by her brother, and living at a time when women were not supposed to have careers, she might herself have become a great poet. Describing the scene depicted by her brother in "'I Wandered Lonely as a Cloud,'" Dorothy wrote in her journal:

> When we were in the woods beyond Gowbarrow Park we saw a few daffodils close to the water-side. We fancied that the sea had floated the seeds ashore, and that the little colony had so sprung up. But as we went along there were more, and yet more; and, at last, under the boughs of the trees, we saw there was a long belt of them along the shore, about the breadth of a country turnpike road. I never saw daffodils so beautiful. They grew among the mossy stones, about and above them; some rested their heads on these stones as on a pillow for weariness; and the rest tossed, and reeled, and danced, and seemed as if they verily laughed with the wind that blew upon them over the lake. They looked so gay, ever glancing, ever changing. The wind blew directly over the lake to them. There was here and there a

little knot, and a few stragglers higher up; but they were so few as not to disturb the simplicity, unity, and life of that one busy highway.

Dorothy added that what her brother considered the poem's two best lines—"They flash upon that inward eye / Which is the bliss of solitude"—were written by his wife, Mary.

Dozens of poems in Wordsworth's large body of verse can qualify as famous. From among his many superb sonnets I have selected the three I think best known. The poem "Composed upon Westminster Bridge, Sept. 3, 1802" was inspired by a view from the roof of a coach as Wordsworth and Dorothy were crossing the Thames on their way to France. Here is how she paints the scene:

> We mounted the Dover coach at Charing Cross. It was a beautiful morning. The city, St. Paul's, with the river, and a multitude of little boats made a most beautiful sight as we crossed Westminster Bridge. The houses were not overhung by their cloud of smoke, and they spread out endlessly, yet the sun shone so brightly, with such a fierce light, that there was something like the purity of one of Nature's own grand spectacles.

The last line of "'The World Is Too Much with Us; Late and Soon'" echoes the line "Triton blowing loud his wreathed horn," in Edmund Spenser's poem "Colin Clout's Come Home Again."

The sonnet "'It Is a Beauteous Evening, Calm and Free,'" is one of several written in 1802 during a month's visit by Wordsworth and his sister to Calais.

Wordsworth and Coleridge are both caricatured in Thomas Love Peacock's novel *Melincourt*: Coleridge as "Mr. Mystic" and Wordsworth as "Mr. Paperstamp." The name "Paperstamp" derives from the fact that for a time Wordsworth was the official distributor of stamps for Westmorland, a county in the Lake District.

'I Wandered Lonely as a Cloud'

I wandered lonely as a cloud
That floats on high o'er vales and hills,
When all at once I saw a crowd,
A host, of golden daffodils;
Beside the lake, beneath the trees,
Fluttering and dancing in the breeze.

Continuous as the stars that shine
And twinkle on the milky way,
They stretched in never-ending line
Along the margin of a bay:
Ten thousand saw I at a glance,
Tossing their heads in sprightly dance.

The waves beside them danced; but they
Out-did the sparkling waves in glee:
A poet could not but be gay,
In such a jocund company:
I gazed—and gazed—but little thought
What wealth the show to me had brought:

For oft, when on my couch I lie
In vacant or in pensive mood,
They flash upon that inward eye
Which is the bliss of solitude;
And then my heart with pleasure fills,
And dances with the daffodils.

Composed upon Westminster Bridge, Sept. 3, 1802

Earth has not anything to show more fair:
Dull would he be of soul who could pass by
A sight so touching in its majesty:
This City now doth, like a garment, wear
The beauty of the morning; silent, bare,
Ships, towers, domes, theatres, and temples lie
Open unto the fields, and to the sky;
All bright and glittering in the smokeless air.
Never did sun more beautifully steep
In his first splendour, valley, rock, or hill;
Ne'er saw I, never felt, a calm so deep!
The river glideth at his own sweet will:
Dear God! the very houses seem asleep;
And all that mighty heart is lying still!

'The World Is Too Much with Us; Late and Soon'

The world is too much with us; late and soon,
Getting and spending, we lay waste our powers:
Little we see in Nature that is ours;

We have given our hearts away, a sordid boon!
The Sea that bares her bosom to the moon;
The winds that will be howling at all hours,
And are up-gathered now like sleeping flowers;
For this, for everything, we are out of tune;
It moves us not.—Great God! I'd rather be
A Pagan suckled in a creed outworn;
So might I, standing on this pleasant lea,
Have glimpses that would make me less forlorn;
Have sight of Proteus rising from the sea;
Or hear old Triton blow his wreathèd horn.

'It Is a Beauteous Evening, Calm and Free'

It is a beauteous evening, calm and free,
The holy time is quiet as a Nun
Breathless with adoration; the broad sun
Is sinking down in its tranquillity;
The gentleness of heaven broods o'er the Sea:
Listen! the mighty Being is awake,
And doth with his eternal motion make
A sound like thunder—everlastingly.
Dear Child! dear Girl! that walkest with me here,
If thou appear untouched by solemn thought,
Thy nature is not therefore less divine:
Thou liest in Abraham's bosom all the year;
And worship'st at the Temple's inner shrine,
God being with thee when we know it not.

ALPHABETICAL LIST
OF TITLES

ALPHABETICAL LIST
OF FIRST LINES

A CATALOG OF SELECTED
DOVER BOOKS
IN ALL FIELDS OF INTEREST

A CATALOG OF SELECTED DOVER
BOOKS IN ALL FIELDS OF INTEREST

CONCERNING THE SPIRITUAL IN ART, Wassily Kandinsky. Pioneering work by father of abstract art. Thoughts on color theory, nature of art. Analysis of earlier masters. 12 illustrations. 80pp. of text. 5⅜ x 8½. 23411-8 Pa. $3.95

ANIMALS: 1,419 Copyright-Free Illustrations of Mammals, Birds, Fish, Insects, etc., Jim Harter (ed.). Clear wood engravings present, in extremely lifelike poses, over 1,000 species of animals. One of the most extensive pictorial sourcebooks of its kind. Captions. Index. 284pp. 9 x 12. 23766-4 Pa. $12.95

CELTIC ART: The Methods of Construction, George Bain. Simple geometric techniques for making Celtic interlacements, spirals, Kells-type initials, animals, humans, etc. Over 500 illustrations. 160pp. 9 x 12. (USO) 22923-8 Pa. $9.95

AN ATLAS OF ANATOMY FOR ARTISTS, Fritz Schider. Most thorough reference work on art anatomy in the world. Hundreds of illustrations, including selections from works by Vesalius, Leonardo, Goya, Ingres, Michelangelo, others. 593 illustrations. 192pp. 7⅛ x 10¼. 20241-0 Pa. $9 95

CELTIC HAND STROKE-BY-STROKE (Irish Half-Uncial from "The Book of Kells"): An Arthur Baker Calligraphy Manual, Arthur Baker. Complete guide to creating each letter of the alphabet in distinctive Celtic manner. Covers hand position, strokes, pens, inks, paper, more. Illustrated. 48pp. 8¼ x 11. 24336-2 Pa. $3.95

EASY ORIGAMI, John Montroll. Charming collection of 32 projects (hat, cup, pelican, piano, swan, many more) specially designed for the novice origami hobbyist. Clearly illustrated easy-to-follow instructions insure that even beginning papercrafters will achieve successful results. 48pp. 8¼ x 11. 27298-2 Pa. $2.95

THE COMPLETE BOOK OF BIRDHOUSE CONSTRUCTION FOR WOODWORKERS, Scott D. Campbell. Detailed instructions, illustrations, tables. Also data on bird habitat and instinct patterns. Bibliography. 3 tables. 63 illustrations in 15 figures. 48pp. 5¼ x 8½. 24407-5 Pa. $2.50

BLOOMINGDALE'S ILLUSTRATED 1886 CATALOG: Fashions, Dry Goods and Housewares, Bloomingdale Brothers. Famed merchants' extremely rare catalog depicting about 1,700 products: clothing, housewares, firearms, dry goods, jewelry, more. Invaluable for dating, identifying vintage items. Also, copyright-free graphics for artists, designers. Co-published with Henry Ford Museum & Greenfield Village. 160pp. 8¼ x 11. 25780-0 Pa. $9.95

HISTORIC COSTUME IN PICTURES, Braun & Schneider. Over 1,450 costumed figures in clearly detailed engravings—from dawn of civilization to end of 19th century. Captions. Many folk costumes. 256pp. 8⅜ x 11¾. 23150-X Pa. $12.95

STICKLEY CRAFTSMAN FURNITURE CATALOGS, Gustav Stickley and L. & J. G. Stickley. Beautiful, functional furniture in two authentic catalogs from 1910. 594 illustrations, including 277 photos, show settles, rockers, armchairs, reclining chairs, bookcases, desks, tables. 183pp. 6½ x 9¼. 23838-5 Pa. $9.95

AMERICAN LOCOMOTIVES IN HISTORIC PHOTOGRAPHS: 1858 to 1949, Ron Ziel (ed.). A rare collection of 126 meticulously detailed official photographs, called "builder portraits," of American locomotives that majestically chronicle the rise of steam locomotive power in America. Introduction. Detailed captions. xi + 129pp. 9 x 12. 27393-8 Pa. $12.95

AMERICA'S LIGHTHOUSES: An Illustrated History, Francis Ross Holland, Jr. Delightfully written, profusely illustrated fact-filled survey of over 200 American lighthouses since 1716. History, anecdotes, technological advances, more. 240pp. 8 x 10¾. 25576-X Pa. $12.95

TOWARDS A NEW ARCHITECTURE, Le Corbusier. Pioneering manifesto by founder of "International School." Technical and aesthetic theories, views of industry, economics, relation of form to function, "mass-production split" and much more. Profusely illustrated. 320pp. 6⅛ x 9¼. (USO) 25023-7 Pa. $9.95

HOW THE OTHER HALF LIVES, Jacob Riis. Famous journalistic record, exposing poverty and degradation of New York slums around 1900, by major social reformer. 100 striking and influential photographs. 233pp. 10 x 7⅞. 22012-5 Pa. $10.95

FRUIT KEY AND TWIG KEY TO TREES AND SHRUBS, William M. Harlow. One of the handiest and most widely used identification aids. Fruit key covers 120 deciduous and evergreen species; twig key 160 deciduous species. Easily used. Over 300 photographs. 126pp. 5⅜ x 8½. 20511-8 Pa. $3.95

COMMON BIRD SONGS, Dr. Donald J. Borror. Songs of 60 most common U.S. birds: robins, sparrows, cardinals, bluejays, finches, more–arranged in order of increasing complexity. Up to 9 variations of songs of each species. Cassette and manual 99911-4 $8.95

ORCHIDS AS HOUSE PLANTS, Rebecca Tyson Northen. Grow cattleyas and many other kinds of orchids–in a window, in a case, or under artificial light. 63 illustrations. 148pp. 5⅜ x 8½. 23261-1 Pa. $4.95

MONSTER MAZES, Dave Phillips. Masterful mazes at four levels of difficulty. Avoid deadly perils and evil creatures to find magical treasures. Solutions for all 32 exciting illustrated puzzles. 48pp. 8¼ x 11. 26005-4 Pa. $2.95

MOZART'S DON GIOVANNI (DOVER OPERA LIBRETTO SERIES), Wolfgang Amadeus Mozart. Introduced and translated by Ellen H. Bleiler. Standard Italian libretto, with complete English translation. Convenient and thoroughly portable–an ideal companion for reading along with a recording or the performance itself. Introduction. List of characters. Plot summary. 121pp. 5¼ x 8½. 24944-1 Pa. $2.95

TECHNICAL MANUAL AND DICTIONARY OF CLASSICAL BALLET, Gail Grant. Defines, explains, comments on steps, movements, poses and concepts. 15-page pictorial section. Basic book for student, viewer. 127pp. 5⅜ x 8½. 21843-0 Pa. $4.95

BRASS INSTRUMENTS: Their History and Development, Anthony Baines. Authoritative, updated survey of the evolution of trumpets, trombones, bugles, cornets, French horns, tubas and other brass wind instruments. Over 140 illustrations and 48 music examples. Corrected and updated by author. New preface. Bibliography. 320pp. 5⅜ x 8½. 27574-4 Pa. $9.95

HOLLYWOOD GLAMOR PORTRAITS, John Kobal (ed.). 145 photos from 1926-49. Harlow, Gable, Bogart, Bacall; 94 stars in all. Full background on photographers, technical aspects. 160pp. 8⅜ x 11¼. 23352-9 Pa. $11.95

MAX AND MORITZ, Wilhelm Busch. Great humor classic in both German and English. Also 10 other works: "Cat and Mouse," "Plisch and Plumm," etc. 216pp. 5⅜ x 8½. 20181-3 Pa. $6.95

THE RAVEN AND OTHER FAVORITE POEMS, Edgar Allan Poe. Over 40 of the author's most memorable poems: "The Bells," "Ulalume," "Israfel," "To Helen," "The Conqueror Worm," "Eldorado," "Annabel Lee," many more. Alphabetic lists of titles and first lines. 64pp. 5$^{3}/_{16}$ x 8¼. 26685-0 Pa. $1.00

PERSONAL MEMOIRS OF U. S. GRANT, Ulysses Simpson Grant. Intelligent, deeply moving firsthand account of Civil War campaigns, considered by many the finest military memoirs ever written. Includes letters, historic photographs, maps and more. 528pp. 6⅛ x 9¼. 28587-1 Pa. $11.95

AMULETS AND SUPERSTITIONS, E. A. Wallis Budge. Comprehensive discourse on origin, powers of amulets in many ancient cultures: Arab, Persian Babylonian, Assyrian, Egyptian, Gnostic, Hebrew, Phoenician, Syriac, etc. Covers cross, swastika, crucifix, seals, rings, stones, etc. 584pp. 5⅜ x 8½. 23573-4 Pa. $12.95

RUSSIAN STORIES/PYCCKNE PACCKA3bl: A Dual-Language Book, edited by Gleb Struve. Twelve tales by such masters as Chekhov, Tolstoy, Dostoevsky, Pushkin, others. Excellent word-for-word English translations on facing pages, plus teaching and study aids, Russian/English vocabulary, biographical/critical introductions, more. 416pp. 5⅜ x 8½. 26244-8 Pa. $8.95

PHILADELPHIA THEN AND NOW: 60 Sites Photographed in the Past and Present, Kenneth Finkel and Susan Oyama. Rare photographs of City Hall, Logan Square, Independence Hall, Betsy Ross House, other landmarks juxtaposed with contemporary views. Captures changing face of historic city. Introduction. Captions. 128pp. 8¼ x 11. 25790-8 Pa. $9.95

AIA ARCHITECTURAL GUIDE TO NASSAU AND SUFFOLK COUNTIES, LONG ISLAND, The American Institute of Architects, Long Island Chapter, and the Society for the Preservation of Long Island Antiquities. Comprehensive, well-researched and generously illustrated volume brings to life over three centuries of Long Island's great architectural heritage. More than 240 photographs with authoritative, extensively detailed captions. 176pp. 8¼ x 11. 26946-9 Pa. $14.95

NORTH AMERICAN INDIAN LIFE: Customs and Traditions of 23 Tribes, Elsie Clews Parsons (ed.). 27 fictionalized essays by noted anthropologists examine religion, customs, government, additional facets of life among the Winnebago, Crow, Zuni, Eskimo, other tribes. 480pp. 6⅛ x 9¼. 27377-6 Pa. $10.95

FRANK LLOYD WRIGHT'S HOLLYHOCK HOUSE, Donald Hoffmann. Lavishly illustrated, carefully documented study of one of Wright's most controversial residential designs. Over 120 photographs, floor plans, elevations, etc. Detailed perceptive text by noted Wright scholar. Index. 128pp. 9¼ x 10¾. 27133-1 Pa. $11.95

THE MALE AND FEMALE FIGURE IN MOTION: 60 Classic Photographic Sequences, Eadweard Muybridge. 60 true-action photographs of men and women walking, running, climbing, bending, turning, etc., reproduced from rare 19th-century masterpiece. vi + 121pp. 9 x 12. 24745-7 Pa. $10.95

1001 QUESTIONS ANSWERED ABOUT THE SEASHORE, N. J. Berrill and Jacquelyn Berrill. Queries answered about dolphins, sea snails, sponges, starfish, fishes, shore birds, many others. Covers appearance, breeding, growth, feeding, much more. 305pp. 5¼ x 8¼. 23366-9 Pa. $8.95

GUIDE TO OWL WATCHING IN NORTH AMERICA, Donald S. Heintzelman. Superb guide offers complete data and descriptions of 19 species: barn owl, screech owl, snowy owl, many more. Expert coverage of owl-watching equipment, conservation, migrations and invasions, etc. Guide to observing sites. 84 illustrations. xiii + 193pp. 5⅜ x 8½. 27344-X Pa. $8.95

MEDICINAL AND OTHER USES OF NORTH AMERICAN PLANTS: A Historical Survey with Special Reference to the Eastern Indian Tribes, Charlotte Erichsen-Brown. Chronological historical citations document 500 years of usage of plants, trees, shrubs native to eastern Canada, northeastern U.S. Also complete identifying information. 343 illustrations. 544pp. 6½ x 9¼. 25951-X Pa. $12.95

STORYBOOK MAZES, Dave Phillips. 23 stories and mazes on two-page spreads: Wizard of Oz, Treasure Island, Robin Hood, etc. Solutions. 64pp. 8¼ x 11. 23628-5 Pa. $2.95

NEGRO FOLK MUSIC, U.S.A., Harold Courlander. Noted folklorist's scholarly yet readable analysis of rich and varied musical tradition. Includes authentic versions of over 40 folk songs. Valuable bibliography and discography. xi + 324pp. 5⅜ x 8½. 27350-4 Pa. $7.95

MOVIE-STAR PORTRAITS OF THE FORTIES, John Kobal (ed.). 163 glamor, studio photos of 106 stars of the 1940s: Rita Hayworth, Ava Gardner, Marlon Brando, Clark Gable, many more. 176pp. 8⅜ x 11¼. 23546-7 Pa. $12.95

BENCHLEY LOST AND FOUND, Robert Benchley. Finest humor from early 30s, about pet peeves, child psychologists, post office and others. Mostly unavailable elsewhere. 73 illustrations by Peter Arno and others. 183pp. 5⅜ x 8½. 22410-4 Pa. $6.95

YEKL and THE IMPORTED BRIDEGROOM AND OTHER STORIES OF YIDDISH NEW YORK, Abraham Cahan. Film Hester Street based on Yekl (1896). Novel, other stories among first about Jewish immigrants on N.Y.'s East Side. 240pp. 5⅜ x 8½. 22427-9 Pa. $6.95

SELECTED POEMS, Walt Whitman. Generous sampling from *Leaves of Grass*. Twenty-four poems include "I Hear America Singing," "Song of the Open Road," "I Sing the Body Electric," "When Lilacs Last in the Dooryard Bloom'd," "O Captain! My Captain!"–all reprinted from an authoritative edition. Lists of titles and first lines. 128pp. 5³⁄₁₆ x 8¼. 26878-0 Pa. $1.00

THE BEST TALES OF HOFFMANN, E. T. A. Hoffmann. 10 of Hoffmann's most important stories: "Nutcracker and the King of Mice," "The Golden Flowerpot," etc. 458pp. 5⅜ x 8½. 21793-0 Pa. $9.95

FROM FETISH TO GOD IN ANCIENT EGYPT, E. A. Wallis Budge. Rich detailed survey of Egyptian conception of "God" and gods, magic, cult of animals, Osiris, more. Also, superb English translations of hymns and legends. 240 illustrations. 545pp. 5⅜ x 8½. 25803-3 Pa. $11.95

FRENCH STORIES/CONTES FRANÇAIS: A Dual-Language Book, Wallace Fowlie. Ten stories by French masters, Voltaire to Camus: "Micromegas" by Voltaire; "The Atheist's Mass" by Balzac; "Minuet" by de Maupassant; "The Guest" by Camus, six more. Excellent English translations on facing pages. Also French-English vocabulary list, exercises, more. 352pp. 5⅜ x 8½. 26443-2 Pa. $8.95

CHICAGO AT THE TURN OF THE CENTURY IN PHOTOGRAPHS: 122 Historic Views from the Collections of the Chicago Historical Society, Larry A. Viskochil. Rare large-format prints offer detailed views of City Hall, State Street, the Loop, Hull House, Union Station, many other landmarks, circa 1904-1913. Introduction. Captions. Maps. 144pp. 9⅜ x 12¼. 24656-6 Pa. $12.95

OLD BROOKLYN IN EARLY PHOTOGRAPHS, 1865-1929, William Lee Younger. Luna Park, Gravesend race track, construction of Grand Army Plaza, moving of Hotel Brighton, etc. 157 previously unpublished photographs. 165pp. 8⅞ x 11¾. 23587-4 Pa. $13.95

THE MYTHS OF THE NORTH AMERICAN INDIANS, Lewis Spence. Rich anthology of the myths and legends of the Algonquins, Iroquois, Pawnees and Sioux, prefaced by an extensive historical and ethnological commentary. 36 illustrations. 480pp. 5⅜ x 8½. 25967-6 Pa. $8.95

AN ENCYCLOPEDIA OF BATTLES: Accounts of Over 1,560 Battles from 1479 B.C. to the Present, David Eggenberger. Essential details of every major battle in recorded history from the first battle of Megiddo in 1479 B.C. to Grenada in 1984. List of Battle Maps. New Appendix covering the years 1967-1984. Index. 99 illustrations. 544pp. 6½ x 9¼. 24913-1 Pa. $14.95

SAILING ALONE AROUND THE WORLD, Captain Joshua Slocum. First man to sail around the world, alone, in small boat. One of great feats of seamanship told in delightful manner. 67 illustrations. 294pp. 5⅜ x 8½. 20326-3 Pa. $5.95

ANARCHISM AND OTHER ESSAYS, Emma Goldman. Powerful, penetrating, prophetic essays on direct action, role of minorities, prison reform, puritan hypocrisy, violence, etc. 271pp. 5⅜ x 8½. 22484-8 Pa. $6.95

MYTHS OF THE HINDUS AND BUDDHISTS, Ananda K. Coomaraswamy and Sister Nivedita. Great stories of the epics; deeds of Krishna, Shiva, taken from puranas, Vedas, folk tales; etc. 32 illustrations. 400pp. 5⅜ x 8½. 21759-0 Pa. $10.95

BEYOND PSYCHOLOGY, Otto Rank. Fear of death, desire of immortality, nature of sexuality, social organization, creativity, according to Rankian system. 291pp. 5⅜ x 8½. 20485-5 Pa. $8.95

A THEOLOGICO-POLITICAL TREATISE, Benedict Spinoza. Also contains unfinished Political Treatise. Great classic on religious liberty, theory of government on common consent. R. Elwes translation. Total of 421pp. 5⅜ x 8½. 20249-6 Pa. $9.95

MY BONDAGE AND MY FREEDOM, Frederick Douglass. Born a slave, Douglass became outspoken force in antislavery movement. The best of Douglass' autobiographies. Graphic description of slave life. 464pp. 5⅜ x 8½. 22457-0 Pa. $8.95

FOLLOWING THE EQUATOR: A Journey Around the World, Mark Twain. Fascinating humorous account of 1897 voyage to Hawaii, Australia, India, New Zealand, etc. Ironic, bemused reports on peoples, customs, climate, flora and fauna, politics, much more. 197 illustrations. 720pp. 5⅜ x 8½.   26113-1 Pa. $15.95

THE PEOPLE CALLED SHAKERS, Edward D. Andrews. Definitive study of Shakers: origins, beliefs, practices, dances, social organization, furniture and crafts, etc. 33 illustrations. 351pp. 5⅜ x 8½.   21081-2 Pa. $8.95

THE MYTHS OF GREECE AND ROME, H. A. Guerber. A classic of mythology, generously illustrated, long prized for its simple, graphic, accurate retelling of the principal myths of Greece and Rome, and for its commentary on their origins and significance. With 64 illustrations by Michelangelo, Raphael, Titian, Rubens, Canova, Bernini and others. 480pp. 5⅜ x 8½.   27584-1 Pa. $9.95

PSYCHOLOGY OF MUSIC, Carl E. Seashore. Classic work discusses music as a medium from psychological viewpoint. Clear treatment of physical acoustics, auditory apparatus, sound perception, development of musical skills, nature of musical feeling, host of other topics. 88 figures. 408pp. 5⅜ x 8½.   21851-1 Pa. $10.95

THE PHILOSOPHY OF HISTORY, Georg W. Hegel. Great classic of Western thought develops concept that history is not chance but rational process, the evolution of freedom. 457pp. 5⅜ x 8½.   20112-0 Pa. $9.95

THE BOOK OF TEA, Kakuzo Okakura. Minor classic of the Orient: entertaining, charming explanation, interpretation of traditional Japanese culture in terms of tea ceremony. 94pp. 5⅜ x 8½.   20070-1 Pa. $3.95

LIFE IN ANCIENT EGYPT, Adolf Erman. Fullest, most thorough, detailed older account with much not in more recent books, domestic life, religion, magic, medicine, commerce, much more. Many illustrations reproduce tomb paintings, carvings, hieroglyphs, etc. 597pp. 5⅜ x 8½.   22632-8 Pa. $11.95

SUNDIALS, Their Theory and Construction, Albert Waugh. Far and away the best, most thorough coverage of ideas, mathematics concerned, types, construction, adjusting anywhere. Simple, nontechnical treatment allows even children to build several of these dials. Over 100 illustrations. 230pp. 5⅜ x 8½. 22947-5 Pa. $7.95

DYNAMICS OF FLUIDS IN POROUS MEDIA, Jacob Bear. For advanced students of ground water hydrology, soil mechanics and physics, drainage and irrigation engineering, and more. 335 illustrations. Exercises, with answers. 784pp. 6⅛ x 9¼.
65675-6 Pa. $19.95

SONGS OF EXPERIENCE: Facsimile Reproduction with 26 Plates in Full Color, William Blake. 26 full-color plates from a rare 1826 edition. Includes "The Tyger," "London," "Holy Thursday," and other poems. Printed text of poems. 48pp. 5¼ x 7.
24636-1 Pa. $4.95

OLD-TIME VIGNETTES IN FULL COLOR, Carol Belanger Grafton (ed.). Over 390 charming, often sentimental illustrations, selected from archives of Victorian graphics–pretty women posing, children playing, food, flowers, kittens and puppies, smiling cherubs, birds and butterflies, much more. All copyright-free. 48pp. 9¼ x 12¼.
27269-9 Pa. $5.95

PERSPECTIVE FOR ARTISTS, Rex Vicat Cole. Depth, perspective of sky and sea, shadows, much more, not usually covered. 391 diagrams, 81 reproductions of drawings and paintings. 279pp. 5⅜ x 8½. 22487-2 Pa. $6.95

DRAWING THE LIVING FIGURE, Joseph Sheppard. Innovative approach to artistic anatomy focuses on specifics of surface anatomy, rather than muscles and bones. Over 170 drawings of live models in front, back and side views, and in widely varying poses. Accompanying diagrams. 177 illustrations. Introduction. Index. 144pp. 8⅜ x11¼. 26723-7 Pa. $8.95

GOTHIC AND OLD ENGLISH ALPHABETS: 100 Complete Fonts, Dan X. Solo. Add power, elegance to posters, signs, other graphics with 100 stunning copyright-free alphabets: Blackstone, Dolbey, Germania, 97 more–including many lower-case, numerals, punctuation marks. 104pp. 8⅛ x 11. 24695-7 Pa. $8.95

HOW TO DO BEADWORK, Mary White. Fundamental book on craft from simple projects to five-bead chains and woven works. 106 illustrations. 142pp. 5⅜ x 8. 20697-1 Pa. $4.95

THE BOOK OF WOOD CARVING, Charles Marshall Sayers. Finest book for beginners discusses fundamentals and offers 34 designs. "Absolutely first rate . . . well thought out and well executed."–E. J. Tangerman. 118pp. 7¾ x 10⅝. 23654-4 Pa. $6.95

ILLUSTRATED CATALOG OF CIVIL WAR MILITARY GOODS: Union Army Weapons, Insignia, Uniform Accessories, and Other Equipment, Schuyler, Hartley, and Graham. Rare, profusely illustrated 1846 catalog includes Union Army uniform and dress regulations, arms and ammunition, coats, insignia, flags, swords, rifles, etc. 226 illustrations. 160pp. 9 x 12. 24939-5 Pa. $10.95

WOMEN'S FASHIONS OF THE EARLY 1900s: An Unabridged Republication of "New York Fashions, 1909," National Cloak & Suit Co. Rare catalog of mail-order fashions documents women's and children's clothing styles shortly after the turn of the century. Captions offer full descriptions, prices. Invaluable resource for fashion, costume historians. Approximately 725 illustrations. 128pp. 8⅜ x 11¼. 27276-1 Pa. $11.95

THE 1912 AND 1915 GUSTAV STICKLEY FURNITURE CATALOGS, Gustav Stickley. With over 200 detailed illustrations and descriptions, these two catalogs are essential reading and reference materials and identification guides for Stickley furniture. Captions cite materials, dimensions and prices. 112pp. 6½ x 9¼. 26676-1 Pa. $9.95

EARLY AMERICAN LOCOMOTIVES, John H. White, Jr. Finest locomotive engravings from early 19th century: historical (1804–74), main-line (after 1870), special, foreign, etc. 147 plates. 142pp. 11⅜ x 8¼. 22772-3 Pa. $10.95

THE TALL SHIPS OF TODAY IN PHOTOGRAPHS, Frank O. Braynard. Lavishly illustrated tribute to nearly 100 majestic contemporary sailing vessels: Amerigo Vespucci, Clearwater, Constitution, Eagle, Mayflower, Sea Cloud, Victory, many more. Authoritative captions provide statistics, background on each ship. 190 black-and-white photographs and illustrations. Introduction. 128pp. 8⅞ x 11¾. 27163-3 Pa. $13.95

EARLY NINETEENTH-CENTURY CRAFTS AND TRADES, Peter Stockham (ed.). Extremely rare 1807 volume describes to youngsters the crafts and trades of the day: brickmaker, weaver, dressmaker, bookbinder, ropemaker, saddler, many more. Quaint prose, charming illustrations for each craft. 20 black-and-white line illustrations. 192pp. 4⅝ x 6.   27293-1 Pa. $4.95

VICTORIAN FASHIONS AND COSTUMES FROM HARPER'S BAZAR, 1867–1898, Stella Blum (ed.). Day costumes, evening wear, sports clothes, shoes, hats, other accessories in over 1,000 detailed engravings. 320pp. 9⅜ x 12¼.
22990-4 Pa. $14.95

GUSTAV STICKLEY, THE CRAFTSMAN, Mary Ann Smith. Superb study surveys broad scope of Stickley's achievement, especially in architecture. Design philosophy, rise and fall of the Craftsman empire, descriptions and floor plans for many Craftsman houses, more. 86 black-and-white halftones. 31 line illustrations. Introduction 208pp. 6½ x 9¼.   27210-9 Pa. $9.95

THE LONG ISLAND RAIL ROAD IN EARLY PHOTOGRAPHS, Ron Ziel. Over 220 rare photos, informative text document origin (1844) and development of rail service on Long Island. Vintage views of early trains, locomotives, stations, passengers, crews, much more. Captions. 8⅞ x 11¾.   26301-0 Pa. $13.95

THE BOOK OF OLD SHIPS: From Egyptian Galleys to Clipper Ships, Henry B. Culver. Superb, authoritative history of sailing vessels, with 80 magnificent line illustrations. Galley, bark, caravel, longship, whaler, many more. Detailed, informative text on each vessel by noted naval historian. Introduction. 256pp. 5⅜ x 8½.
27332-6 Pa. $7.95

TEN BOOKS ON ARCHITECTURE, Vitruvius. The most important book ever written on architecture. Early Roman aesthetics, technology, classical orders, site selection, all other aspects. Morgan translation. 331pp. 5⅜ x 8½. 20645-9 Pa. $8.95

THE HUMAN FIGURE IN MOTION, Eadweard Muybridge. More than 4,500 stopped-action photos, in action series, showing undraped men, women, children jumping, lying down, throwing, sitting, wrestling, carrying, etc. 390pp. 7⅞ x 10⅝.
20204-6 Clothbd. $25.95

TREES OF THE EASTERN AND CENTRAL UNITED STATES AND CANADA, William M. Harlow. Best one-volume guide to 140 trees. Full descriptions, woodlore, range, etc. Over 600 illustrations. Handy size. 288pp. 4½ x 6⅜.
20395-6 Pa. $5.95

SONGS OF WESTERN BIRDS, Dr. Donald J. Borror. Complete song and call repertoire of 60 western species, including flycatchers, juncoes, cactus wrens, many more–includes fully illustrated booklet.   Cassette and manual 99913-0 $8.95

GROWING AND USING HERBS AND SPICES, Milo Miloradovich. Versatile handbook provides all the information needed for cultivation and use of all the herbs and spices available in North America. 4 illustrations. Index. Glossary. 236pp. 5⅜ x 8½.
25058-X Pa. $6.95

BIG BOOK OF MAZES AND LABYRINTHS, Walter Shepherd. 50 mazes and labyrinths in all–classical, solid, ripple, and more–in one great volume. Perfect inexpensive puzzler for clever youngsters. Full solutions. 112pp. 8⅛ x 11.
22951-3 Pa. $4.95

CATALOG OF DOVER BOOKS

PIANO TUNING, J. Cree Fischer. Clearest, best book for beginner, amateur. Simple repairs, raising dropped notes, tuning by easy method of flattened fifths. No previous skills needed. 4 illustrations. 201pp. 5⅜ x 8½. 23267-0 Pa. $6.95

A SOURCE BOOK IN THEATRICAL HISTORY, A. M. Nagler. Contemporary observers on acting, directing, make-up, costuming, stage props, machinery, scene design, from Ancient Greece to Chekhov. 611pp. 5⅜ x 8½. 20515-0 Pa. $12.95

THE COMPLETE NONSENSE OF EDWARD LEAR, Edward Lear. All nonsense limericks, zany alphabets, Owl and Pussycat, songs, nonsense botany, etc., illustrated by Lear. Total of 320pp. 5⅜ x 8½. (USO) 20167-8 Pa. $6.95

VICTORIAN PARLOUR POETRY: An Annotated Anthology, Michael R. Turner. 117 gems by Longfellow, Tennyson, Browning, many lesser-known poets. "The Village Blacksmith," "Curfew Must Not Ring Tonight," "Only a Baby Small," dozens more, often difficult to find elsewhere. Index of poets, titles, first lines. xxiii + 325pp. 5⅝ x 8¼. 27044-0 Pa. $8.95

DUBLINERS, James Joyce. Fifteen stories offer vivid, tightly focused observations of the lives of Dublin's poorer classes. At least one, "The Dead," is considered a masterpiece. Reprinted complete and unabridged from standard edition. 160pp. 5$\frac{3}{16}$ x 8¼. 26870-5 Pa. $1.00

THE HAUNTED MONASTERY and THE CHINESE MAZE MURDERS, Robert van Gulik. Two full novels by van Gulik, set in 7th-century China, continue adventures of Judge Dee and his companions. An evil Taoist monastery, seemingly supernatural events; overgrown topiary maze hides strange crimes. 27 illustrations. 328pp. 5⅜ x 8½. 23502-5 Pa. $8.95

THE BOOK OF THE SACRED MAGIC OF ABRAMELIN THE MAGE, translated by S. MacGregor Mathers. Medieval manuscript of ceremonial magic. Basic document in Aleister Crowley, Golden Dawn groups. 268pp. 5⅜ x 8½. 23211-5 Pa. $8.95

NEW RUSSIAN-ENGLISH AND ENGLISH-RUSSIAN DICTIONARY, M. A. O'Brien. This is a remarkably handy Russian dictionary, containing a surprising amount of information, including over 70,000 entries. 366pp. 4½ x 6⅛. 20208-9 Pa. $9.95

HISTORIC HOMES OF THE AMERICAN PRESIDENTS, Second, Revised Edition, Irvin Haas. A traveler's guide to American Presidential homes, most open to the public, depicting and describing homes occupied by every American President from George Washington to George Bush. With visiting hours, admission charges, travel routes. 175 photographs. Index. 160pp. 8¼ x 11. 26751-2 Pa. $11.95

NEW YORK IN THE FORTIES, Andreas Feininger. 162 brilliant photographs by the well-known photographer, formerly with *Life* magazine. Commuters, shoppers, Times Square at night, much else from city at its peak. Captions by John von Hartz. 181pp. 9¼ x 10¾. 23585-8 Pa. $12.95

INDIAN SIGN LANGUAGE, William Tomkins. Over 525 signs developed by Sioux and other tribes. Written instructions and diagrams. Also 290 pictographs. 111pp. 6⅛ x 9¼. 22029-X Pa. $3.95

ANATOMY: A Complete Guide for Artists, Joseph Sheppard. A master of figure drawing shows artists how to render human anatomy convincingly. Over 460 illustrations. 224pp. 8⅜ x 11¼. 27279-6 Pa. $10.95

MEDIEVAL CALLIGRAPHY: Its History and Technique, Marc Drogin. Spirited history, comprehensive instruction manual covers 13 styles (ca. 4th century thru 15th). Excellent photographs; directions for duplicating medieval techniques with modern tools. 224pp. 8⅜ x 11¼. 26142-5 Pa. $11.95

DRIED FLOWERS: How to Prepare Them, Sarah Whitlock and Martha Rankin. Complete instructions on how to use silica gel, meal and borax, perlite aggregate, sand and borax, glycerine and water to create attractive permanent flower arrangements. 12 illustrations. 32pp. 5⅜ x 8½. 21802-3 Pa. $1.00

EASY-TO-MAKE BIRD FEEDERS FOR WOODWORKERS, Scott D. Campbell. Detailed, simple-to-use guide for designing, constructing, caring for and using feeders. Text, illustrations for 12 classic and contemporary designs. 96pp. 5⅜ x 8½. 25847-5 Pa. $2.95

SCOTTISH WONDER TALES FROM MYTH AND LEGEND, Donald A. Mackenzie. 16 lively tales tell of giants rumbling down mountainsides, of a magic wand that turns stone pillars into warriors, of gods and goddesses, evil hags, powerful forces and more. 240pp. 5⅜ x 8½. 29677-6 Pa. $6.95

THE HISTORY OF UNDERCLOTHES, C. Willett Cunnington and Phyllis Cunnington. Fascinating, well-documented survey covering six centuries of English undergarments, enhanced with over 100 illustrations: 12th-century laced-up bodice, footed long drawers (1795), 19th-century bustles, 19th-century corsets for men, Victorian "bust improvers," much more. 272pp. 5⅜ x 8¼. 27124-2 Pa. $9.95

ARTS AND CRAFTS FURNITURE: The Complete Brooks Catalog of 1912, Brooks Manufacturing Co. Photos and detailed descriptions of more than 150 now very collectible furniture designs from the Arts and Crafts movement depict davenports, settees, buffets, desks, tables, chairs, bedsteads, dressers and more, all built of solid, quarter-sawed oak. Invaluable for students and enthusiasts of antiques, Americana and the decorative arts. 80pp. 6½ x 9¼. 27471-3 Pa. $7.95

HOW WE INVENTED THE AIRPLANE: An Illustrated History, Orville Wright. Fascinating firsthand account covers early experiments, construction of planes and motors, first flights, much more. Introduction and commentary by Fred C. Kelly. 76 photographs. 96pp. 8¼ x 11. 25662-6 Pa. $8.95

THE ARTS OF THE SAILOR: Knotting, Splicing and Ropework, Hervey Garrett Smith. Indispensable shipboard reference covers tools, basic knots and useful hitches; handsewing and canvas work, more. Over 100 illustrations. Delightful reading for sea lovers. 256pp. 5⅜ x 8½. 26440-8 Pa. $7.95

FRANK LLOYD WRIGHT'S FALLINGWATER: The House and Its History, Second, Revised Edition, Donald Hoffmann. A total revision—both in text and illustrations—of the standard document on Fallingwater, the boldest, most personal architectural statement of Wright's mature years, updated with valuable new material from the recently opened Frank Lloyd Wright Archives. "Fascinating"—*The New York Times*. 116 illustrations. 128pp. 9¼ x 10¾. 27430-6 Pa. $11.95

AUTOBIOGRAPHY: The Story of My Experiments with Truth, Mohandas K. Gandhi. Boyhood, legal studies, purification, the growth of the Satyagraha (nonviolent protest) movement. Critical, inspiring work of the man responsible for the freedom of India. 480pp. 5⅜ x 8½. (USO) 24593-4 Pa. $8.95

CELTIC MYTHS AND LEGENDS, T. W. Rolleston. Masterful retelling of Irish and Welsh stories and tales. Cuchulain, King Arthur, Deirdre, the Grail, many more. First paperback edition. 58 full-page illustrations. 512pp. 5⅜ x 8½. 26507-2 Pa. $9.95

THE PRINCIPLES OF PSYCHOLOGY, William James. Famous long course complete, unabridged. Stream of thought, time perception, memory, experimental methods; great work decades ahead of its time. 94 figures. 1,391pp. 5⅜ x 8½. 2-vol. set.
Vol. I: 20381-6 Pa. $12.95
Vol. II: 20382-4 Pa. $12.95

THE WORLD AS WILL AND REPRESENTATION, Arthur Schopenhauer. Definitive English translation of Schopenhauer's life work, correcting more than 1,000 errors, omissions in earlier translations. Translated by E. F. J. Payne. Total of 1,269pp. 5⅜ x 8½. 2-vol. set. Vol. 1: 21761-2 Pa. $11.95
Vol. 2: 21762-0 Pa. $11.95

MAGIC AND MYSTERY IN TIBET, Madame Alexandra David-Neel. Experiences among lamas, magicians, sages, sorcerers, Bonpa wizards. A true psychic discovery. 32 illustrations. 321pp. 5⅜ x 8½. (USO) 22682-4 Pa. $8.95

THE EGYPTIAN BOOK OF THE DEAD, E. A. Wallis Budge. Complete reproduction of Ani's papyrus, finest ever found. Full hieroglyphic text, interlinear transliteration, word-for-word translation, smooth translation. 533pp. 6½ x 9¼.
21866-X Pa. $10.95

MATHEMATICS FOR THE NONMATHEMATICIAN, Morris Kline. Detailed, college-level treatment of mathematics in cultural and historical context, with numerous exercises. Recommended Reading Lists. Tables. Numerous figures. 641pp. 5⅜ x 8½.
24823-2 Pa. $11.95

THEORY OF WING SECTIONS: Including a Summary of Airfoil Data, Ira H. Abbott and A. E. von Doenhoff. Concise compilation of subsonic aerodynamic characteristics of NACA wing sections, plus description of theory. 350pp. of tables. 693pp. 5⅜ x 8½. 60586-8 Pa. $14.95

THE RIME OF THE ANCIENT MARINER, Gustave Doré, S. T. Coleridge. Doré's finest work; 34 plates capture moods, subtleties of poem. Flawless full-size reproductions printed on facing pages with authoritative text of poem. "Beautiful. Simply beautiful."–*Publisher's Weekly*. 77pp. 9¼ x 12. 22305-1 Pa. $6.95

NORTH AMERICAN INDIAN DESIGNS FOR ARTISTS AND CRAFTSPEOPLE, Eva Wilson. Over 360 authentic copyright-free designs adapted from Navajo blankets, Hopi pottery, Sioux buffalo hides, more. Geometrics, symbolic figures, plant and animal motifs, etc. 128pp. 8⅜ x 11. (EUK) 25341-4 Pa. $8.95

SCULPTURE: Principles and Practice, Louis Slobodkin. Step-by-step approach to clay, plaster, metals, stone; classical and modern. 253 drawings, photos. 255pp. 8⅛ x 11.
22960-2 Pa. $10.95

CATALOG OF DOVER BOOKS

PHOTOGRAPHIC SKETCHBOOK OF THE CIVIL WAR, Alexander Gardner. 100 photos taken on field during the Civil War. Famous shots of Manassas Harper's Ferry, Lincoln, Richmond, slave pens, etc. 244pp. 10⅞ x 8¼. 22731-6 Pa. $9.95

FIVE ACRES AND INDEPENDENCE, Maurice G. Kains. Great back-to-the-land classic explains basics of self-sufficient farming. The one book to get. 95 illustrations. 397pp. 5⅜ x 8½. 20974-1 Pa. $7.95

SONGS OF EASTERN BIRDS, Dr. Donald J. Borror. Songs and calls of 60 species most common to eastern U.S.: warblers, woodpeckers, flycatchers, thrushes, larks, many more in high-quality recording. Cassette and manual 99912-2 $8.95

A MODERN HERBAL, Margaret Grieve. Much the fullest, most exact, most useful compilation of herbal material. Gigantic alphabetical encyclopedia, from aconite to zedoary, gives botanical information, medical properties, folklore, economic uses, much else. Indispensable to serious reader. 161 illustrations. 888pp. 6½ x 9¼. 2-vol. set. (USO) Vol. I: 22798-7 Pa. $9.95
Vol. II: 22799-5 Pa. $9.95

HIDDEN TREASURE MAZE BOOK, Dave Phillips. Solve 34 challenging mazes accompanied by heroic tales of adventure. Evil dragons, people-eating plants, blood-thirsty giants, many more dangerous adversaries lurk at every twist and turn. 34 mazes, stories, solutions. 48pp. 8¼ x 11. 24566-7 Pa. $2.95

LETTERS OF W. A. MOZART, Wolfgang A. Mozart. Remarkable letters show bawdy wit, humor, imagination, musical insights, contemporary musical world; includes some letters from Leopold Mozart. 276pp. 5⅜ x 8½. 22859-2 Pa. $7.95

BASIC PRINCIPLES OF CLASSICAL BALLET, Agrippina Vaganova. Great Russian theoretician, teacher explains methods for teaching classical ballet. 118 illustrations. 175pp. 5⅜ x 8½. 22036-2 Pa. $5.95

THE JUMPING FROG, Mark Twain. Revenge edition. The original story of The Celebrated Jumping Frog of Calaveras County, a hapless French translation, and Twain's hilarious "retranslation" from the French. 12 illustrations. 66pp. 5⅜ x 8½. 22686-7 Pa. $3.95

BEST REMEMBERED POEMS, Martin Gardner (ed.). The 126 poems in this superb collection of 19th- and 20th-century British and American verse range from Shelley's "To a Skylark" to the impassioned "Renascence" of Edna St. Vincent Millay and to Edward Lear's whimsical "The Owl and the Pussycat." 224pp. 5⅜ x 8½. 27165-X Pa. $4.95

COMPLETE SONNETS, William Shakespeare. Over 150 exquisite poems deal with love, friendship, the tyranny of time, beauty's evanescence, death and other themes in language of remarkable power, precision and beauty. Glossary of archaic terms. 80pp. 5³⁄₁₆ x 8¼. 26686-9 Pa. $1.00

BODIES IN A BOOKSHOP, R. T. Campbell. Challenging mystery of blackmail and murder with ingenious plot and superbly drawn characters. In the best tradition of British suspense fiction. 192pp. 5⅜ x 8½. 24720-1 Pa. $6.95

THE WIT AND HUMOR OF OSCAR WILDE, Alvin Redman (ed.). More than 1,000 ripostes, paradoxes, wisecracks: Work is the curse of the drinking classes; I can resist everything except temptation; etc. 258pp. 5⅜ x 8½. 20602-5 Pa. $5.95

SHAKESPEARE LEXICON AND QUOTATION DICTIONARY, Alexander Schmidt. Full definitions, locations, shades of meaning in every word in plays and poems. More than 50,000 exact quotations. 1,485pp. 6½ x 9¼. 2-vol. set.
Vol. 1: 22726-X Pa. $16.95
Vol. 2: 22727-8 Pa. $16.95

SELECTED POEMS, Emily Dickinson. Over 100 best-known, best-loved poems by one of America's foremost poets, reprinted from authoritative early editions. No comparable edition at this price. Index of first lines. 64pp. 5³⁄₁₆ x 8¼. 26466-1 Pa. $1.00

CELEBRATED CASES OF JUDGE DEE (DEE GOONG AN), translated by Robert van Gulik. Authentic 18th-century Chinese detective novel; Dee and associates solve three interlocked cases. Led to van Gulik's own stories with same characters. Extensive introduction. 9 illustrations. 237pp. 5⅜ x 8½. 23337-5 Pa. $6.95

THE MALLEUS MALEFICARUM OF KRAMER AND SPRENGER, translated by Montague Summers. Full text of most important witchhunter's "bible," used by both Catholics and Protestants. 278pp. 6⅝ x 10. 22802-9 Pa. $12.95

SPANISH STORIES/CUENTOS ESPAÑOLES: A Dual-Language Book, Angel Flores (ed.). Unique format offers 13 great stories in Spanish by Cervantes, Borges, others. Faithful English translations on facing pages. 352pp. 5⅜ x 8½. 25399-6 Pa. $8.95

THE CHICAGO WORLD'S FAIR OF 1893: A Photographic Record, Stanley Appelbaum (ed.). 128 rare photos show 200 buildings, Beaux-Arts architecture, Midway, original Ferris Wheel, Edison's kinetoscope, more. Architectural emphasis; full text. 116pp. 8¼ x 11. 23990-X Pa. $9.95

OLD QUEENS, N.Y., IN EARLY PHOTOGRAPHS, Vincent F. Seyfried and William Asadorian. Over 160 rare photographs of Maspeth, Jamaica, Jackson Heights, and other areas. Vintage views of DeWitt Clinton mansion, 1939 World's Fair and more. Captions. 192pp. 8⅞ x 11. 26358-4 Pa. $12.95

CAPTURED BY THE INDIANS: 15 Firsthand Accounts, 1750-1870, Frederick Drimmer. Astounding true historical accounts of grisly torture, bloody conflicts, relentless pursuits, miraculous escapes and more, by people who lived to tell the tale. 384pp. 5⅜ x 8½. 24901-8 Pa. $8.95

THE WORLD'S GREAT SPEECHES, Lewis Copeland and Lawrence W. Lamm (eds.). Vast collection of 278 speeches of Greeks to 1970. Powerful and effective models; unique look at history. 842pp. 5⅜ x 8½. 20468-5 Pa. $14.95

THE BOOK OF THE SWORD, Sir Richard F. Burton. Great Victorian scholar/adventurer's eloquent, erudite history of the "queen of weapons"—from prehistory to early Roman Empire. Evolution and development of early swords, variations (sabre, broadsword, cutlass, scimitar, etc.), much more. 336pp. 6⅛ x 9¼. 25434-8 Pa. $9.95

THE INFLUENCE OF SEA POWER UPON HISTORY, 1660–1783, A. T. Mahan. Influential classic of naval history and tactics still used as text in war colleges. First paperback edition. 4 maps. 24 battle plans. 640pp. 5⅜ x 8½. 25509-3 Pa. $12.95

THE STORY OF THE TITANIC AS TOLD BY ITS SURVIVORS, Jack Winocour (ed.). What it was really like. Panic, despair, shocking inefficiency, and a little heroism. More thrilling than any fictional account. 26 illustrations. 320pp. 5⅜ x 8½. 20610-6 Pa. $8.95

FAIRY AND FOLK TALES OF THE IRISH PEASANTRY, William Butler Yeats (ed.). Treasury of 64 tales from the twilight world of Celtic myth and legend: "The Soul Cages," "The Kildare Pooka," "King O'Toole and his Goose," many more. Introduction and Notes by W. B. Yeats. 352pp. 5⅜ x 8½. 26941-8 Pa. $8.95

BUDDHIST MAHAYANA TEXTS, E. B. Cowell and Others (eds.). Superb, accurate translations of basic documents in Mahayana Buddhism, highly important in history of religions. The Buddha-karita of Asvaghosha, Larger Sukhavativyuha, more. 448pp. 5⅜ x 8½. 25552-2 Pa. $9.95

ONE TWO THREE . . . INFINITY: Facts and Speculations of Science, George Gamow. Great physicist's fascinating, readable overview of contemporary science: number theory, relativity, fourth dimension, entropy, genes, atomic structure, much more. 128 illustrations. Index. 352pp. 5⅜ x 8½. 25664-2 Pa. $8.95

ENGINEERING IN HISTORY, Richard Shelton Kirby, et al. Broad, nontechnical survey of history's major technological advances: birth of Greek science, industrial revolution, electricity and applied science, 20th-century automation, much more. 181 illustrations. ". . . excellent . . ."–Isis. Bibliography. vii + 530pp. 5⅜ x 8¼. 26412-2 Pa. $14.95

DALÍ ON MODERN ART: The Cuckolds of Antiquated Modern Art, Salvador Dalí. Influential painter skewers modern art and its practitioners. Outrageous evaluations of Picasso, Cézanne, Turner, more. 15 renderings of paintings discussed. 44 calligraphic decorations by Dalí. 96pp. 5⅜ x 8½. (USO) 29220-7 Pa. $4.95

ANTIQUE PLAYING CARDS: A Pictorial History, Henry René D'Allemagne. Over 900 elaborate, decorative images from rare playing cards (14th–20th centuries): Bacchus, death, dancing dogs, hunting scenes, royal coats of arms, players cheating, much more. 96pp. 9¼ x 12¼. 29265-7 Pa. $11.95

MAKING FURNITURE MASTERPIECES: 30 Projects with Measured Drawings, Franklin H. Gottshall. Step-by-step instructions, illustrations for constructing handsome, useful pieces, among them a Sheraton desk, Chippendale chair, Spanish desk, Queen Anne table and a William and Mary dressing mirror. 224pp. 8⅛ x 11¼. 29338-6 Pa. $13.95

THE FOSSIL BOOK: A Record of Prehistoric Life, Patricia V. Rich et al. Profusely illustrated definitive guide covers everything from single-celled organisms and dinosaurs to birds and mammals and the interplay between climate and man. Over 1,500 illustrations. 760pp. 7½ x 10⅛. 29371-8 Pa. $29.95

Prices subject to change without notice.

Available at your book dealer or write for free catalog to Dept. GI, Dover Publications, Inc., 31 East 2nd St., Mineola, N.Y. 11501. Dover publishes more than 500 books each year on science, elementary and advanced mathematics, biology, music, art, literary history, social sciences and other areas.